AF541778

India's Pathways to Success

Pune International Centre (PIC) has distinguished itself through its publications, and this comprehensive volume is no exception. The present flows from the past, and the future flows from the present. While the future is always uncertain, this book teases out past and present trends to project the future—growth, digital economy, urbanization, mobility, environment, S&T, trade and employment. Tucked into these chapters is a reform agenda and template for the future.

—Bibek Debroy, Chairman,
Economic Advisory Council to the Prime Minister of India

A highly recommended read for policymakers as well as corporate and civil service, including foreign service practitioners, engaged in promotion of trade and economic collaboration, with technology as the key transformative factor for progress.

—Ronen Sen,
Former Indian Ambassador to the United States

India's Pathways *to* Success

Winning in the
NEXT DECADE

Edited by
Ganesh Natarajan
and Ejaz Ghani

Thought and Writing Partners

Raghunath Mashelkar, Vijay Kelkar, Harsha Vardhana Singh, Ravi Pandit, Uma Ganesh, Ajay Shah, Abhay Vaidya, Pradeep Apte, Aravind Chinchure, Kaustubh Pathak, Shilpa Phadke, Manoj Soman

RUPA

Published by
Rupa Publications India Pvt. Ltd 2023
7/16, Ansari Road, Daryaganj
New Delhi 110002

Sales centres:
Prayagraj Bengaluru Chennai
Hyderabad Jaipur Kathmandu
Kolkata Mumbai

P-ISBN: 978-93-5520-979-5
E-ISBN: 978-93-5520-981-8

Second impression 2023

10 9 8 7 6 5 4 3 2

Printed in India

To the young people of India, their efforts to strengthen India's vibrant democracy and make her a strong, resilient, compassionate and prosperous nation.

CONTENTS

FOREWORD

It is a huge privilege to be invited to write the foreword to this eminent tome on India's last 75 years, the challenges, the opportunities and the exciting future that can come our way if we follow the policy prescriptions laid out so lucidly by various authors in the book. What is even more exciting is to be associated with Ganesh Natarajan and Ramesh (Raghunath) Mashelkar, two notable fountainheads of enthusiasm and positivism, and generators of great ideas. Both these authors have been my friends for over 30 years now. When I feel despondent and down, I call Ramesh. I feel better after listening to his pep talk full of positivism, his dream, hope and resolve. I first interacted with Dr Vijay Kelkar when he gave a scintillating lecture on his PhD thesis at Berkeley to the faculty at IIM-A about 50 years ago. Vijay is a shining light of intellect in our country. I have remained his admirer ever since that day. I have learnt much from Dr Ajay Shah on economic policy from the much-acclaimed book by Vijay and Ajay. Uma Ganesh is as smart, energetic and enthusiastic as her husband, Ganesh Natarajan. I have known Ravi Pandit as a first-rate entrepreneur. He is full of stunning ideas. The other authors have inspired me by their scholarly work in this book.

Ganesh and Ejaz give a good account of the admirable progress our country has achieved since Independence. I largely agree with them. This book also covers almost every gamut of causal factors that can realize the dream of our nation in agriculture, manufacturing, services, digitalization and communications, international trade, transport and roadways, women's emancipation, education, healthcare, poverty alleviation, and even social capital. I wish our universities make this book recommended reading for every entrant before they start their collegiate education, just as it happens in the United States. It will give our young minds a raison d'être for their three to four years of mental gymnastics, devotion and hard work. It will also turn them into enlightened and determined citizens full of enthusiasm to achieve the plausibly impossible for our nation. The narrations in the book are buttressed by abundant data to make the arguments of the authors solid. I hope our politicians and policy-planners will read this book, analyse it objectively, accept the good ideas in it and adopt them for creating a highly successful India@100, deserving the plaudits of every nation and every culture in the world. This book is necessary for India's betterment. Without these prescriptions, the probability of our success in our quest for India's betterment and for wiping the tears of the poorest of the poor child (as the founders of our republic desired) will be low.

However, these prescriptions alone are not sufficient. They form a grand and impressive superstructure that will bring joy, satisfaction and pride to our citizens. But the real sufficiency comes from the most important causal variable for the success of a nation—*culture*. Culture is the strong foundation on which the superstructure of aspirations, dreams and hopes, and their conversion to reality rests. India has made good progress, but we still have unemployment, poverty and ill health rising in absolute numbers even though, as a percentage, it is decreasing. That is where culture becomes critical in helping us execute the various policy options suggested by the authors. Such on-time, under-the-budget and quality execution of policy options requires a culture full of honesty, meritocracy, devotion, alacrity, discipline, good work ethic and efficiency. While the book does not focus on culture, Vijay and Ajay have covered some aspects of the role of culture in their excellent article on social capital.

I will dwell a little here on this important causal variable for economic growth and betterment of our beloved country. What is culture? Culture is what our aspirations are; what our value system is; what importance we place on competence for a given job or responsibility; how honest we are in dealing with public assets; how we conduct ourselves in public; what our work ethic is; how disciplined we are; what our desire and effort for excellence is; how tolerant we are in dealing with people who have differing views; whether we believe in leadership by example; how we treat strangers; how we conduct our debates and disagreements without being disagreeable; how we strengthen and uphold the rights of others to disagree with us; how we strengthen our public institutions; whether we are open to learn from cultures that have progressed faster and better than us; what value and respect we give to our intellectuals and to our competent and meritorious citizens; how we leverage such people in our politics, policy formation, execution of these policies and in governance; why we take more time for decisions and execution of such decisions than most other cultures and how we can overcome this lacuna; how we accept others' view of us and improve rather than gloating about how great we were once upon a time and rejecting any suggestions offered by them for our improvement; our conviction in the four freedoms as propounded by President Roosevelt—*freedom of speech, freedom of faith, freedom from fear and freedom from want*; how disciplined, hardworking, honest and committed we are; how we put the interest of our public institutions, our communities and our nation ahead of our personal interest in the short and medium term so that the quality of life of our children and grandchildren will be better than what it has been for us; how we adapt our education system for our education to provide problem-solving tools rather than tools for rote learning and passing mere examinations; what brings us joy and what makes us sad; and how we rise above the strangling hold of religion, creed and caste that has been the bane of our nation; and many other such attributes. I can go on and on in describing what culture is. Let me stop here.

My indoctrination to the role of culture as an important causal variable in economic growth and prosperity of our country took place more than 50 years ago. This event happened due to three seminal reasons. The first reason was a very influential teacher of mine in my engineering college. He had spent over four years doing his PhD in engineering in a highly developed country in the late fifties and early sixties. During his free time, he studied and contrasted the culture of that developed country with the culture of developing countries in South Asia and Africa. The second reason was my reading of Frantz Fanon's books—*Peau noire, masques blancs* (*Black Skin, White Masks*) and *Les damnés de la terre* (*The Wretched of the Earth*) in French, discussing these books with some outstanding sociology scholars at the Sorbonne, Paris, and contemplating on the future of my beloved country during the early seventies. The third and, perhaps, the most impactful reason was reading and contemplating on Max Weber's book, *The Protestant Ethic and the Spirit of Capitalism*. This book primarily looks at why Anglo-Germanic nations advanced better during the nineteenth century than the Latin countries. The book also speaks about the role of culture, aspiration, austerity, speed of action, honesty, hard work and several other variables.

I can understand why most of us are hesitant to comment on our culture. That discussion is tough, unpleasant, controversial and, perhaps, contrary to the culture that we have adopted since Independence. But just as medicines are bitter and surgical operations are painful, it is important that we do not desist from such discussions any longer. We have tasted economic success since liberalization for the last 30 years. This is the time to gird our loins and resolve to complete the task of transforming our country to a developed country that our founders sacrificed their lives for. It is very important for us to remember that an urgent panacea for our economic growth and better prosperity for our nation lies only in our retaining every good aspect of our culture while embracing the good aspects of culture of those nations that have progressed faster than us.

Of all the leaders of India, it is undebatable to say that Mahatma Gandhi was an apostle for the role of culture in the emancipation of our country. He understood and practised the most important attribute of the desired culture—*leadership by example*. He travelled throughout the country by third class like ordinary citizens, shunned luxury, opposed security for himself, ate simple food like poor Indians, interacted enthusiastically with people who thronged railway stations and learnt about the challenges and difficulties of the poor to overcome their poverty. To make sure that he was not bumped off by his opponents, his associates had to use several people disguised as ordinary train passengers in plain clothes to travel with the Mahatma and keep him safe. An apocryphal story is that his compatriot known for humour, Sarojini Naidu, is supposed to have remarked that *it took a fortune to keep the old man in poverty*! I must say that that fortune was well spent, since here was the world's first person to lead by example. He taught us some important, indelible lessons that should live till eternity.

Why did I raise the Mahatma's example? The reason is the Mahatma, by and large, represented the culture that I have talked about above. Like all human beings, he too had his frailties. But overall, I am not sure the world has seen another leader like him. Our urgent task is to pay our respect to Mahatma Gandhi and his team of extraordinary individuals who fought for our independence. The best way to do it is not through speeches and slogans but by embracing a culture and a mindset that the Mahatma and his team members embodied. The success of the wonderful policy prescriptions that these deep-thinking authors have articulated in this most engaging book rests on this cultural foundation. The formidable challenge for every Indian is to embrace the culture that I have spoken about. If we did, then we too can successfully accelerate the eradication of the scourge of unemployment, poverty, malnutrition, ill health and homelessness, and bring better hope for the poorest child in the most distant village of the country.

It was my privilege to read this book, learn from it, to resolve to work towards overcoming my weaknesses and to work hard with discipline and honesty to add my miniscule effort to strengthen our country. I am positive that the readers of this book too will be inspired to do so. That is the objective of the book. I wish the authors and the readers the best in succeeding in this objective.

Narayana Murthy
11 October 2022
Founder, Infosys

INTRODUCTION

INDIA—CURRENT REALITIES AND GROWTH IMPERATIVES

India is today at a crossroads. We have overcome a period of economic decline aggravated by Covid-19 and smartly bounced back to perform better than the global best in economic growth in the last fiscal year. While cynics may point to a low base on which this growth has been reported, there is a mood of positivism in the air, and if one looks beyond the hype created by political forces, there are still many strong foundations that have been laid, some excellent initiatives have borne fruit, and there is reason to say 'Yes, we can.'

'India at 75' is a milestone that has been reached, and it is time to look back and look forward. Looking back, one can remember the first Indian prime minister, Pandit Jawaharlal Nehru, exhorting India to move towards a 'tryst with destiny' from the ramparts of the Red Fort. Looking forward to the end of this decade, one wonders: what is the destiny we should be aspiring to reach? Do we want to be a manufacturing powerhouse to rival China? Can we stay content with services and be the 'Information Superpower' of the world? Or should we look beyond the obvious and find new opportunities in agriculture, healthcare and other segments, and become the world's best user of technology to create best-in-class global industries? And, most importantly, can a new wave of research and innovation be unleashed? Will we build urban and rural habitats where high-quality education and skills are available to create sustainable livelihood through employment and entrepreneurship for all?

As a collateral benefit of strategy success, can we look at being a $5 trillion GDP economy in the foreseeable future? Will the trillion-dollar digital opportunity get addressed in all its aspects to power the traditional economy as well as create new opportunities for all in a truly inclusive environment? Can we create jobs for the millions of youth who seek to be well employed or successful entrepreneurs in the India of the future? Can we ensure that women participate gainfully in every field of human endeavour in the country, and we are able to grow in a harmonious climate of love and inclusion that helps us overcome all the traditional divisions of class, caste and community, and sees all of us proud Indians carrying our country to the most desirable destination of being a happy place to live, grow and dream? And, will this all be in an environment of equal opportunities in a thriving democracy without fear or favour?

And, in the process, will we extend the excellent work already initiated to create better physical infrastructure through roads and airports in the country to homogenous digital infrastructure enabling access to every Indian in every smart city, town and village of the country? Will urban mobility be transformed, and autonomous, connected, electric and shared mobility become the norm across the country? And, will we focus on all the sustainable development goals, thwart the inexorable effects of climate change and build a country every citizen and every Indian abroad will be truly proud of?

There are many questions indeed, and in this book, we have sought to find some answers and many directions for the next 10 years to set our country on a truly positive path to success.

THE STORY SO FAR

India has been, in many ways, a tale of lost opportunities while remaining a robust and open democracy that is a pride and joy for all Indians. Our history, of course, records a period of glory when India represented around 30 per cent of the world's GDP a thousand years ago.[1] We were battered by many invaders and looters, and decades of external rule, and in the years up to 1947, we did not grow at all. In the first 30 or so years post Independence, we could only record a 'Hindu rate of growth' of 3 to 3.5 per cent, while the world grew a percentage point greater than us.[2]

While this book has no intention of taking sides in a political slugfest, there is no denying the fact that the early decades post Independence, with the government helmed by Pandit Nehru and his successors, saw India adopt a socialistic model of growth with a large public sector, a somewhat overdone role of the government and the unwillingness to encourage private capital investments at scale in the country. The Soviet model adopted by the leaders of that era did not do enough to address the problems of a country, with a majority in substantial poverty, or to enable people to move from an attitude of servility towards our former British masters, practise fearless entrepreneurship and encourage wholehearted participation of women in the economy.

In the years following liberalization, India grew at a fast clip, which was a result of some wisdom and the opening up of the economy to extensive participation by both Indian and global businesses. And in the last 20 years, growth rates have been far from optimal. We have still not been able to provide all Indians with the essentials of 'roti, kapda, makan (food, clothing and shelter)', and in more recent times, 'bijli and bandwidth (electricity and internet)',[3] which are so essential for the digital economy to really take off, add revenues and ensure population success the way we have seen in Bengaluru, Chennai, Hyderabad, Pune and a few other cities. This, in spite of recent initiatives like the JAM trinity—Jan Dhan, Aadhaar and Mobility—which enables bank accounts for all and direct transfer of money to happen country-wide, and Ayushman Bharat with the mission of healthcare for all, which has been made even more urgent in the Covid-19 era. Decent education, skills for livelihoods and a better future for the coming generations are what any society must offer to its people, and we are just beginning to get there.

The nature of our growth, too, has been somewhat skewed. Due to our inability or unwillingness to invest strongly in labour-oriented manufacturing, we have let China show many decades of growth, over 9 per cent, and become the veritable 'factory of the world'. Even nimble neighbours like Bangladesh have stolen a march over India in building their textile and clothing industry to global supply levels. Because of this, our GDP composition shows less than 25 per cent from industry and less than 20 per cent from agriculture, with the larger percentage coming from services, including the government.[4] With a large percentage of working-age people employed in agriculture with low levels of productivity and incomes, the comparison is stark. China has a fairly small percentage of its population dependent on agriculture, with many farm workers moving to better jobs in manufacturing, and China's farm productivity, too, is double that of India's.

Job creation, on the other hand, has been weak. Every year, tens of millions of people come of working age, and most of them need jobs.[5] Less than 10 million jobs are being created every year. A good job can be said to pay at least ₹30,000 per month, but those are limited to government employees and IT employees, with more and more employment now in the informal sector.

While this is the general bleak situation in India, the city of Bengaluru stands out as an exception. Anecdotally, in the rampaging tech industry in India, it boasts a dominant share in IT services and a major share of the $300 billion value start-up ecosystem. Of the much-vaunted hundred-plus unicorns in India (entrepreneurial firms with a valuation of over a billion dollars), a significant number are in Bengaluru. Does this city represent what the country itself can become in the future? Maybe, but it will need some effort! As we write this, millions of youth, many quite well-educated, are searching for jobs, and the numbers will only grow larger.

The devastation wreaked by Covid-19 is also showing up in development parameters across the country, particularly in rural India. The National Family Health Survey (NFHS-5) for the period 2019–21 points out sanitation, clean fuel and health as issues that continue to be major inhibitors for millions of families, particularly in the poorer states of India where the population continues to grow in spite of the total fertility rate of India falling slightly below the replacement rate of the population for the first time. For a country with soaring ambitions, it is sad that 24.9 per 1,000 children die at birth, 35.2 during infancy and 41.9 within the first five years, and many children in rural India and urban slums are stunted (35.5) and suffer nutritional deficiencies (32.1).[6]

On the education front, too, matters are far from satisfactory. There is widespread belief among educators and parents that 'learning loss' has been very high in the last two years. Economic issues have caused a large number of families in rural India to shift their children from private schools to government schools, which are ill-equipped in terms of capacity and capability to cater to these pressures. One NGO, Educate Girls, which works with rural girl children in Rajasthan, Madhya Pradesh and Uttar Pradesh, has seen children moving out of school at a significant rate. Access to digital materials for many children has been too weak to compensate for the learning loss due to schools being closed for as long as 73 weeks against a global average of 35 weeks.[7] For a country that needs to create a constant flow of talent for local and global opportunities, the weaknesses in child healthcare, education and youth skills apparatus are areas of significant concern that must be addressed in this decade.

At a macro level, there are some green shoots. The population is stabilizing, with birth rates coming down and lower replacement levels of children. An ageing population means the next 10 years will be extremely critical for India, and geriatric care needs to be a key focus area. The ageing of a country's population is an inevitable consequence of the post-demographic transition period. The size and share of the elderly population in India will grow significantly in the future, reaching nearly 316 million by 2050.[8] The rise in share of elderly people will raise issues of retirement age and pensions.

If the trends continue, the effects of a higher old-age dependency ratio will be more than counteracted by a lower youth dependency ratio. This increase will be further augmented by greater participation of women in the labour force due to smaller family sizes. The effect of this rise will be that India should be able to produce more, not less, goods and services, and accelerate the pace of growth.

THROUGH THE ECONOMIC LENS

India entered a technical recession in October 2020, already coming out of many quarters of tepid growth, then buffeted by Covid-19. Sadly, the weak recovery that began after that was again damaged by the second wave of Covid-19 in mid-2021. When it seemed that the economy would rival the stock market and ride to a much-hoped-for V-shaped recovery, the reappearance of the Covid-19 clouds in the form of the Omicron variant again threatened to be a dampener to the recovery as 2021 came to a close. While the GDP may yet come back to the pre-Covid-19 levels sometime in FY 2022–23, and the trends in the first half are good, the big concern is the continuing weak demand and the number of people who are unemployed or underemployed in the country—not a healthy beginning for future growth and prosperity.

The K-shaped recovery that was forecast by the less optimistic economists (one could argue in economics that a pessimist is a well-informed optimist) had become a reality at the end of FY 2021–22 with some sectors, which were already well-funded and hence able to withstand the impact of Covid-19, showing smart recovery. Banking and financial services are a case in point, where both the large banks and the top-end non-banking financial companies (NBFCs) continue to show impressive growth in deposits and credit, although the mark-to-market provisions in a volatile stock market have led to some softness in reported profits in the first quarter of the fiscal year. However, other sectors are struggling. Hospitality and aviation have limped back post the Covid-19 crisis. But, with inflation beginning to bite, retail growth is also likely to remain sluggish, at least in the near term. The recovery has also not been even, with a market preference for scale players. The natural outcome of this is that larger and financially stronger firms are taking market share from weaker and smaller competitors, and are also competing for the lion's share of future opportunity areas—not a healthy sign for a robust small and medium-sized enterprises (SME) sector, which is essential for a resilient economy with a firm foundation.

As we describe in the various chapters of this book, policy decisions, growth strategies and tactical shifts in key industry segments, such as agriculture, manufacturing and services, and quick capitalization of opportunities in information and communications technology (ICT), and mobility can change the gears of the economic engine. In the medium term, investments in better-quality education and skills, and carefully targeted research and innovation can still move India to higher levels of economic growth across both the developed and developing countries of the world. However, speed breakers that need to be watched out for are inflation, which persists at high levels, caused in part by the rise in crude oil prices and supply chain bottlenecks, a slump in private consumption due to job and income losses, and reluctance of most categories of people to spend. The twin demons of poverty and economic inequality are also a cause, with many individuals and families dipping down to poverty levels in the last two years.

In the seventy-fifth year of India's independence and the FY

2022–23, India has to first overcome impacts of Omicron and build a Covid-19-independent growth agenda, assuming that people will learn to live with the virus for the next few years without suffering knee-jerk actions on the part of city and state administrations. Much will be expected from successive Union Budgets and economic policies of the government to tackle inflation and unemployment. These policies also need to resist the temptation of taking policy actions with an eye on multiple state elections rather than the overall good of the people. The monetary policy of foreign governments, particularly in the Unites States (US) and Europe, will have a bearing on our own actions, and we need to be watchful and flexible in our decision-making till the economic ship safely navigates out of the present stormy waters.

There are many challenges. At the same time, there are many opportunities, including the robust rise and status of the information technology (IT) and engineering services industry and the demographic dividend that will be an advantage we continue to enjoy for a couple more decades. These and other inherent advantages must be exploited as both an opportunity and an imperative to secure the future of India and all Indians.

TORCHES FOR NEW PATHWAYS

India has come through many challenges in the 75 years since Independence. We take an optimist's view and use a lens of success to view that past, examine the present and identify torches that can shine a light on the darkness of the unknown and identify robust pathways to the future.

How does one define what India can be in 2030? Certainly the short-term goal of being a $5 trillion economy will have been well surpassed. Through a robust growth model centered around not automation but use of human capital, we would have put over a hundred million jobseekers to work. Our infrastructure—

physical, digital and social—will have been put in place to rival the developed world and we will have been at a 10 per cent or more growth vector that can be sustained through the next 17 years. That will take 'India at 100', in 2047, to a level of a $40 billion GDP and create a robust sense of optimism to tell the world 'India's time has come'.[9]

What are these torches that are lit by the successes of the past and burn even brighter for the future? The first, obviously, is the demographic dividend as the country brings every child and youth, from rural to urban India, into the fold of education, skills, and digital and financial literacy, and finds them opportunities to realize their dreams of a sustainable livelihood through employment or entrepreneurship. The second is the diffusion of technology into every aspect of life and work. The success of the IT and engineering service sector in India, and the creation of a world-class $200 billion industry has had the collateral benefit of creating millions of well-qualified technology practitioners who have in the past built products for global tech corporations and developed solutions to power 70 per cent and more of the largest corporations in the world. Their brains can now be deployed for the creation of global best-in-class products in India and platforms that will enable a truly digital India to emerge as a world-beater in multiple industry segments. India's rural and urban environments, with a high quality of living in both, will be the third torch for development as the rich–poor divide gets less sharp and most citizens begin to enjoy the quality of life and livelihoods they so richly deserve. And the final torch, which could be the most important of all, is that we would see this development happen in an environment of a robust democracy, which has survived through seven decades of economic ups and downs in our country.

The barely interrupted rise in the stock market is evidence of the global investor confidence in the India story. In December 2021, Goldman Sachs said, 'Based on our refreshed estimates, we expect India's equity market cap could increase significantly over the next 2–3 years and cross US$5tn by 2024. Relative to other markets, the estimates suggest India will likely surpass the UK and the Middle East to become the 5th largest market in the next two years.'[10] What we need to be on the watch for is a sharp increase in the digital divide as Covid-19-battered communities struggle to revive, while the rich businesses in developed parts of the country continue to show robust recovery.

India needs to balance the growth between the urban and rural parts of the country, and reduce the gap between what is popularly called 'India' vs 'Bharat'. Wise investment in a new model of urbanization, where not just the select hundred-plus smart cities but at least 2,000 of the 7,000 and more urban towns in the country can be energized with reasonable physical, digital and social infrastructure, and adequate opportunities for livelihoods through low-cost manufacturing and micro entrepreneurship. This will take the pressure off large cities and also enable large numbers of people to move from agriculture to well-paying jobs. This was the model China adopted during its decades of manufacturing and investment-led growth till a level of prosperity was reached where the focus could shift from the urban setting to the rural and from investment to consumption. In turn, this will create a rethink on agriculture produce, with productivity imperatives and automation influencing the choice of crops in small farms throughout the country.

As we take stock of the present state of our nation, Covid-19 and its aftermath have necessitated a significant rethinking on multiple fronts. Trade in manufactured goods has been sluggish globally, being outpaced by trade in services. As we still struggle with weak investments by large corporations and sluggish demand, some steps have been taken and more will have to be strategically taken, not only to move beyond the present sluggishness in growth but to build a platform where a higher near-double-digit growth can be achieved, and, more importantly, sustained, for at least two decades to really lift India from its status of being a perpetually 'developing' nation.

TOWARDS A BETTER FUTURE

By 2030, India's urban population will increase to more than 600 million people,[11] more than twice the size of the US. The size of India's urban demographic dividend, with millions joining the labour force every year, is potentially huge. India's economic growth and job growth are strongly linked with urbanization. As the urbanization process continues, connectivity, proximity and diversity will accelerate knowledge diffusion, spark further innovation and enhance productivity and employment growth.

Urbanization promotes both entrepreneurship and growth. We find strong evidence of this in countries such as Japan and Korea, where a city-centric labour force and proximity to customers has led to greater economic success. Job growth is linked more with city diversification than city specialization, and there is also a secular growth of opportunities in all key sectors in urban locations.

The government needs to focus not just on the megacities but secondary cities as new drivers of growth. It needs to leverage land assets, and modify financial regulations and incentives to increase investors' risk appetite. As mentioned earlier, if this can happen in 2,000-plus new towns, the future growth of the economy can be truly broad-based. This will need visionary strategy from the central government, an energized Ministry of Urban Affairs and a substantial expansion of the Smart Cities Mission to impact multiple areas of development and governance.

India's middle class can reach a billion people by 2030.[12] India has young demographics compared to China, Europe and the US. India's youth bulge and demographic dividend will boost the country's growth through many channels: it increases the ability to invest more in physical and human infrastructure, and less on pensions (in Organisation for Economic Co-operation and Development [OECD] countries, a third of government expenditure is assigned to pensions). Working age also happens to cover the prime period in life for savings. The fate of the middle class and that of the Indian economy are in lockstep: rising incomes will fuel consumption, which will drive demand and productivity, leading to more employment and a further rise in incomes.

In the global knowledge economy, a global talent race has already started for high-skilled workers. A very large percentage of software engineers in Silicon Valley are foreign-born.[13] Since the end of the Second World War, trade and capital flows have been further liberalized. It is now the turn of global migration. Demographics and wages will play a key role in global migration trends. In India, the population below 30 is many times more than those who are over 65 years old; in Western Europe, that ratio is near equal. Average earnings in high-income countries are 70 times higher than in India.[14] Demographics and wage differentials have become a strong impetus for global migration.

Most multinational corporations now insist that high-potential executives gain global experience. Some of the global economy's most familiar players—including Google, Microsoft, Coca-Cola, McDonald's, Pepsi and Pfizer—have immigrant CEOs. Global mobility of the workforce is a given, and although Covid-19 and earlier protectionist moves by countries have sought to thwart human mobility, we will eventually inevitably become a global village and will all be competing and collaborating globally. India must take the lead in building human capabilities that will enable all Indians to find their true tryst with destiny in a changing world.

India has the potential to create an era of truly rapid growth by meeting the twin challenges that face us—closing the infrastructure financing gap and changing the composition of financing. Changing the composition of capital flow has the potential to increase the efficiency and sustainability of public finance and infrastructure projects. While commercial banks will continue to be an important source of infrastructure finance, capital markets will play a bigger role in the future, given the increased demand for long-term sources of finance for infrastructure projects. Bond markets, especially local currency bond markets, will be critical to filling the infrastructure investment gap.

India, today, has a GDP which is 70 per cent dependent on consumption and only 30 per cent on investments.[15] We need to create investible assets that will encourage domestic and foreign capital and reverse these proportions. Maximizing finance for development, from billions to trillions, will be achieved by combining resources—international and domestic, public and private, corporate and philanthropic.

India needs a new digital/economic/social contract to scale up investments in digital infrastructure, change the data landscape to promote the use and reuse of digital data, foster trust that data will not be misused in harmful ways, reduce the digital divide and promote digital freedom.

What will happen if policymakers do nothing? The most likely major effect will be that young working-age people will be unemployed or underemployed. Large numbers of unemployed workers can lead to increased internal conflict. In addition, unemployed young people will effectively increase the share of the population that is dependent on workers, slowing economic growth. And the economic insecurity of the elderly can increase because there will be fewer productively employed workers to generate the wealth on which both governments and families rely to support the elderly.

India will face many challenges in the future. Correcting poor rural productivity, providing jobs for those who need them, and increasing the availability and quality of education, skills, healthcare and the digital, physical and social infrastructure will be imperatives for inclusive success. Ensuring a form of government as well as state and national leadership that cares for all, does not differentiate between classes, castes or communities, and truly works towards the benefit of all citizens will determine the quality of our vision and the robustness of the actions we take to ensure we succeed. Corruption at all levels—transactional, payment and policy level—needs to be nipped in the bud. The justice system must be revamped with legal recourse available easily and in a timely fashion—for all. An environment must be created where every citizen participates and is able to succeed in the creation and enjoyment of the fruits of sustainable livelihoods. Entrepreneurship must bloom and tens of millions of new job creators have to emerge in every corner of the country, creating opportunities and wealth-creation potential for all. This, indeed, will be our new tryst with destiny by 2030.

There are so many aspects of growth and success that we, as a nation, can and must aspire for that it would be futile for any tome to attempt to be all-encompassing in its research and coverage. This book is intended to cover some broad themes that could well be pillars for a new India to be built, and the mission that will unfold will be the articulation of imperatives and opportunities in each of these areas.

- **Economic realities and imperatives**: Where are our strengths and weaknesses? Where have we slipped? Where have we opened up or can create opportunities that can catalyse our growth?
- **The three pillars of economic growth**: The three pillars are agriculture, manufacturing and services. We have seen low productivity and sometimes poor choices made in agriculture, inadequate use of skilled labour or strategic automation in manufacturing and a rather fortuitous focus on IT and related areas, including fintech, which has led to many other citizen-focussed services. Can we address these and correct the processes and improve outcomes?
- **The trillion-dollar digital India**: How much of it is the

extension of one global success story that we have already created through IT and business process management (BPM) services and how much will be enabled by technology and create products and platforms that can transform India and the world? Will the new focus on chips, microprocessors and hardware unlock more wealth from the core layers of ICT that hold so much possibility for GDP growth and employment?

- **The future of mobility and natural resource rejuvenation**: While our cities turn green, can we embrace wholeheartedly new methods of mobility that shuns polluting vehicles and enables mobility for all with minimum climate impact? Can we also develop a circular economy with a focus on conservation of natural resources and sustainable growth?
- **Building new capabilities**: The imperative to increase funding and focus on research, innovation and high-quality education to make Indians a tour de force for the new global civilization. What must we do to develop the much-needed edge that will fuel science and technology innovations in this country?
- **Women's participation in economic growth**: Starting from the necessity to keep every girl child in school till she can choose her life options to providing the education, skills and mindset to encourage women to participate in every field, this is a social as well as economic imperative for the country.
- **Livelihoods and social harmony**: After facing the twin challenges of jobs growth, lagging economic growth, and automation and AI threatening present and future employment, can we now create ample employment and entrepreneurship opportunities for our people? Can inclusive growth be achieved in an environment of harmony between classes, castes and communities?
- **Policy interventions and dialogues needed for India's**

growth: Can we identify specific areas where policies must be altered or put in place?

- **Building trust and an environment of harmony and collaboration to ensure growth and success:** Can we ensure that the benefits of economic progress are shared amongst all sections of society and there is no strife between classes or communities?
- **Development imperatives**: Can we formulate pathways for the next eight years to ensure that when we arrive at 2030 we are a truly transformed country?

Your authors and the dozen and more domain experts, who have been key contributors, have truly enjoyed putting these ideas together in this book. We hope you will enjoy the read.

1

GROWTH PILLARS OF THE ECONOMY—AGRICULTURE, INDUSTRY AND SERVICES

Pradeep Apte, Ganesh Natarajan, Ejaz Ghani and Aravind Chinchure

The growth story of India has largely been one of an agriculture-based economy, and the country has been somewhat slow to embrace manufacturing and capture the service industry, particularly technology services. Like India, China is one of the fastest-growing economies in the world. But the two nations have followed very different growth paths. China has been a formidable exporter of manufactured goods, while India has acquired a global reputation for exporting services. India went straight from agriculture into services, leapfrogging the manufacturing sector. India's growth pattern resembles that of the US. This raises big questions. Can services sustain output and job growth? Should India allow itself to be a laggard in manufacturing? And, is there any hope at all for being a high-productivity player in global agriculture?

In this chapter, we will address the progress and the future opportunities in each of these key pillars of economic growth. To start on a positive note, the research paper and subsequent book produced by the Pune International Centre (PIC) in 2021[1] clearly pointed out that the Indian economy has demonstrated stellar growth from 1991 to 2019—$275 billion to $2.9 trillion GDP, $18 to $330 billion exports, though imports have also accelerated from $24 to $514 billion, foreign exchanges from less than a billion to $425 billion, and the most heartening data, that population below the poverty line has dipped from 45 to 22 per cent.[2] In 2019, an Electronic National Agriculture Market research study, eNAM Report 2019, mentions that India was ranked globally ninth by market capitalization and fifth in nominal GDP, on course to become the third-largest economy in the world by 2030.

AGRICULTURE—POLICY AND PROSPECTS

During the last seven decades, Indian agriculture and, consequently, policies in agriculture have undergone several transformations and changes. In the initial 18 years post Independence (1947 to 1964), there was a severe scarcity of many agricultural produces. The administrative response to such a scarcity situation was mostly designed along the experiences and devices of the Second World War years. On the one hand, trade in many food grains and commodities, like sugar, was heavily regulated, with movement restrictions across districts in states, etc. Maximizing availability of food was the principal preoccupation, even obsession in design and working procedural content of policy. Ushering in the Green Revolution, principally in the agriculture of wheat and rice, and encouraging success in Operation Flood in the milk sector stabilized food availability in the country.

This period also witnessed the appointment of the Agricultural Pricing Commission (APC), with the aim of regulating prices that balance consumer interests and farmers' aspirations. Yet, the scarcity in pulses and oilseeds, and dependence on imports persisted and continue to haunt us even today.

The retention price mechanism may be broadly described as follows: normal average cost covering price per ton plus 24 per cent gross return on capital costs was calculated for every manufacturer. From such a price, the administered price fixed for the farmer was subtracted. The difference was paid as the subsidy payment to the manufacturer. Such a subsidy was available for only those units with a capacity utilization of 80 per cent or more of its installed/stated capacity. Evidently, this signalled understatement of installed capacity to ensure eligibility. This was often euphemistically referred to as 'gold-plated capacity'. This also implied that the actual incidence of such a subsidy scheme was only partly accruing to the farmers. However, as it was declared as a subsidy to farmers, the political label of farmers' subsidy stuck. Hence, this design became a holy cow, and any reforms or revision of the same was perceived as being anti-farmer.[3]

The period from the 1980s witnessed several important developments that triggered diversification and gradual shift in favour of high value crops. This period also witnessed the rise of horticultural and floricultural crops. The relaxation of import restrictions on several crop plantation materials for vegetables, fruits and flowers brought about a change in the quantity and quality of these crops. The oilseed mission opened up the opportunity to introduce new varieties and crops. It was during the period up to 2002 that proposals were made for reforming the system of markets of agriculture produce. However, these were less noticed and discussed, perhaps eclipsed by the euphoria about industrial delicensing that occurred concurrently. In 2002, the Task Force on Agricultural Marketing Reforms[4] recommended the abolition of several policy restrictions and barriers, including the Agricultural Produce and Livestock Market Committees (APMCs) under the Agriculture Produce Marketing (Regulation) Acts of several states. It was also followed by the Union government's appeal and attempt to liberalize agriculture in 2006 by suggesting a model act for agriculture produce that facilitated abolition of the licensing regime enjoyed by extant middlemen in APMCs, and setting up of private mandis, including farmers' mandis. It also strongly argued in favour of promoting and stabilizing forward market-based trading platforms and pointed out sudden unreasonable bans on the alleged grounds of so-called speculative trading fears. In 2003 (and again 2007, with some modifications), the model Agricultural Produce Market Committee (APMC) Act made similar suggestions for reforms in the APMC system.

Let us look at some of the burning issues that need serious attention for the decade to come, as well as reforms that can be implemented to remedy them. But before we proceed to these issues, it may be useful to note certain features of the agricultural and rural economy in India.

1. The share of agriculture in India's gross value added (GVA) is dwindling, and it is now in the vicinity of 20 per cent.[5] The population dependent on agriculture, though not strictly employed in agricultural and allied activities, is around 52 per cent.[6] Naturally, the sector engages a significantly high share of the poor population. (The estimates of rural poverty are drawn from various poverty studies, including Tendulkar and C. Rangarajan committee report of 2011–12.)
   At the same time, the farmers in several areas complain about scarcity or non-availability of labour, and the wage rates of agriculture labour have risen in many areas. This is also one of the complaints about the Mahatma Gandhi National Rural Employment Guarantee Act (MGNREGA), which exacerbates the higher wage and scarcity.[7]
2. Most of the states have been experiencing what is often called feminization of agriculture. In broad terms, this means that in operative, effective employment, the share of female labourers and labour performed by the female labourers is significantly higher. In many areas, male workers perform relatively fewer heavy-duty menial tasks and ordinarily command higher wages per day. Several other tasks are usually performed by women. The labour participation rates in officially published estimates, however, are much lower.[8]

3. Average operational land holding has been securely declining, and the numbers and proportion of small and marginal farmers have been consistently rising.[9]
4. One of the rounds by the National Sample Survey Office (NSSO) revealed that a large number of farmers desire to quit agriculture.[10]
5. With rising population, the average population size of villages has been climbing and many of them will resemble semi-urban areas in many economic characteristics. The villages with greater proximity to national or state highways exhibit different features of migration and employment preferences.
6. The cropping patterns and character of allied activities of villages in many urban peripheries have changed and show remarkable shifts in favour of non-food products.
7. Share of non-food products in the total value of output in agriculture has been rising, and it is presently estimated to be 55 to 60 per cent.[11]
8. Notwithstanding the reference to agriculture-related activities as the sovereign domain of state governments as per the Seventh Schedule of the Constitution, the market of agricultural produce has been inherently and historically national in character.

   The promulgation of the Essential Commodities Act in 1956, together with (i) the Agricultural Price Policy of the Commission for Agricultural Costs and Prices (CACP); (ii) working of the Food Corporation of India (FCI) for dual responsibility of minimum support price (MSP) policy and the public distribution system (PDS) mechanism; (iii) scheme-based planning/financing process in vogue for six decades; (iv) working of the fertilizer subsidies scheme operated by the Union government, have resulted in substantial centralization of this 'sovereign subject'. The state government has become the implementing agency of the schemes and policies that were largely defined, designed and governed by the Union government. At best, the state governments enjoy greater autonomy in land legislations governing land markets (principally, tenancy, ceiling limits and more or less non-operative anti-fragmentation/subdivision acts). Thus, common assertions in public discourse about agriculture being a sovereign domain of state governments should be taken with a sizable pinch of salt.

Major policy recommendations

Agricultural market reforms

There are three distinct yet related problems that are entangled in the current debate. There are some distinct problems that are entangled in a significant issue and the subject of many debates. The policy conception that prevailed in the early years was overshadowed by the management of challenges posed by scarcity. The APMC was thought to be an institutional structure where the supplies could more easily be monitored and their movement easily regulated, as expressed in the preamble to the APMC Act. The unintended consequence of this was the creation of an exclusive class with licence to trade in the APMC, in collusion with a political class that controlled the APMC. Such an alliance of interests and collusive oligopolistic control of trade channels and trading finances (including underground illegal usurious transactions) were quite similar to the experience in industrial licensing policy.

This was further compounded when FCI entered the scenario with PDS and a food-supply safety mandate for principal food grains. FCI was also mandated to ensure such procurement at declared MSP. This has created a totally wrong impression that an MSP-type mechanism is viable and possible for all type of crops. Hence, it is worthwhile to look at the outcomes as actually achieved in this regard.

The FCI has been principally involved in the procurement of

wheat, rice and maize, which it purchases at the MSP in some of the principal mandis in Punjab, Haryana and Western Uttar Pradesh.[12] Its operations are geographically extremely lopsided. The easiest way to appreciate this is to compare the share of Punjab–Haryana in the production of wheat and rice vis-à-vis the share of FCI procurements from these states. Moreover, excessive procurement by the FCI beyond the 'safety level norms' simply does not occur in several other mandis in other states. Most of the mandi prices remain much below the prescribed MSP level, across mandis and over the seasons, and they keep on fluctuating in response to underlying demand and supply forces.

Evidently, unless the FCI is willing and able to procure all the supply for all the weeks of the season, the MSP level can never be attained. Traders understand this elementary fact much better than those who believe that MSP can be enforced perennially for all crops. The FCI does not have the required storage facility to hold even the wheat and rice or maize it procures, and the produce continues to rot for an average of two years. The FCI routinely sells such degraded stock with the label 'unfit for human consumption,' and several animal feedstock companies purchase the same at the convenient bidder price. Thus, the FCI may be credited for at least indirectly and partially protecting the livestock of the farmers.

Due to the limited financial and storage constraints, organizations like the FCI cannot stabilize prices at levels that would simultaneously please the farmers and consumers in a reasonably efficient manner. The burden of subsidy, even grossly calculated as MSP minus fair price/ration shop prices, is bound to become larger and larger. There is enough accumulated experience over years that makes it evident that the regime of MSP and PDS as operative today is an economically flawed idea. Farmers are being fooled by this mirage, and it is even more disastrous in its fiscal implications.

Given the heavy concentration of FCI operations in a few

chosen states, the response to the 2020 farmer's agitation in most states remains lukewarm. Because the agitation is largely led by farmers from these few states, this minority have been able to supersede the other silent majority of farmers who would, in fact, welcome the freedom from the oligopolistic regime of the APMC. More curiously, the honourable Supreme Court did not even care to publish the report of the committee which it had appointed![13] It could have invited members of earlier committees, members of the chief ministers' committee to probe the truth of the claims and to voice what the other silent mass of farmers may have had to say. It could have also examined the views of the states where the regulatory regime had been partially and silently dismantled (e.g., Maharashtra). The government has shelved the bills and injured the future prospects of these overdue reforms. The bills constituted the welcome exercise of removing the dead wood of policy history. Let us hope that yet another consultation process with the provision of a joint body of the Union and state governments (something similar to the GST Council) is envisaged to effectively facilitate the open environment for trade in agricultural produce.

Let us not also ignore the fact that the basket of goods produced by the agricultural sector has undergone considerable change, and several of these goods have a flourishing market size that largely remains untouched by the APMC as well as the FCI. It would be suicidal to further perpetuate the myth of farmer prosperity through the MSP regime. The market mechanisms have discovered better pathways with very minimal regulatory intervention, as in the case of milk, fruits, eggs, etc.

The FCI is primarily responsible for procurement of farm goods at MSP. The use of such procurement for the PDS purpose is largely handled by the state government. Hence, reforms will be needed at both levels, i.e., procurement and storage by the FCI and PDS operations by the state government.

Moreover, the state governments themselves are participants

to these PDS operations, with some financial aid shared with the Centre, so that the regional and crop-wise imbalance in procurements and PDS requirements are addressed more effectively. State governments also need to look at the changing nature of crop patterns of their own states and think more carefully of their own fiscal-cum-administrative capacities (e.g., warehousing and further marketing channels necessary for the sale of procurements) before engaging in any scheme that involves support-price type interventions.

Water supply: Agriculture and non-agricultural uses

State governments are responsible for harnessing, building and conserving water resources of all types (principally groundwater and surface water resources). With rising urbanization, many states are already facing the issue of equitable water allocation between competing uses and users. Many of the surface water irrigation schemes were initially designed to cater to agricultural uses, but civic and industrial demand is expected to rise much faster. Hence, state governments should handle this responsibility with a serious examination of technological opportunities and options—recycling of water and more efficient methods of uses (e.g., micro-irrigation technologies, changes in crop patterns, etc.), institutional arrangements such as water user associations (WUAs) and, most importantly, pricing of the water delivered, which should cover operation and maintenance costs.

Some states (notably Punjab and Haryana) have exhausted their groundwater by unmindfully promoting unsustainable crop patterns (this too involves working of MSP procurement by the FCI).[14] It would be advisable to introduce a **blue-box** subsidy for not cultivating these water-table depleted lands. Blue-box subsidy in World Trade Organization (WTO) parlance means production limitations subsidy. In other words, instead of engaging in large unaffordable procurement with entire value of output, it may be wise to declare net income subsidy per hectare for not cultivating wheat or paddy, which have excess production levels.

The most important reform effort would be building the necessary administrative and commercial intelligence of the state agriculture departments. The first and foremost step would be to develop a geographic information system (GIS) of land records, terrain and soil/slope profiles at the micro level, i.e., the farm plot level. It should endeavour to generate more realistic estimates of the area under crops, crop yields and potential market arrival data in all (public and private mandis). The department, with the help of the local government, should also install, operate and monitor weather data and warning systems. This would ensure that the agriculture department has sufficient information on all fronts.

State governments should use the public–private partnership (PPP) model to promote a packaging-cum-warehousing facility (including preservation-oriented cold-chain technologies), as such arrangements will attract private sector investments, including farmer/companies, and state government resources need not be burdened and blocked for such uses.

The Union government should refrain from using quota, and it is necessary to have stable predictable export–import (EXIM) policy to develop and consolidate the export markets for agricultural products. The Union government has a habit of declaring bans and price caps to arbitrarily curb exports on the basis of alleged or real fears of rise in domestic price levels. This invariably results in induced or forced fall in domestic prices and hence loss of income to the farmers. It may be pointed out that several farmers organizations have opposed such bans exclusively.[15]

There already exists an emerging service sector in the rural areas—transport services, packaging delivery, maintenance and repair of various equipment, including vehicles. There is a rising demand for equipment that is used in various operations (such as hormone sprays).

It is expected that the volume and diversity of service sector operations and products in agriculture will rise significantly in the coming decade. Rural schools and colleges should be encouraged to add courses that provide exposure to modern agricultural methods and practices through training kiosks.

MANUFACTURING—GETTING GLOBAL SCALE

There are many who argue that India totally missed the bus in capturing the demand for outsourced manufacturing of products for the global market, while China made aggressive investments and positioned itself as the factory of the world.[16] It is true that in many areas of manufacturing, from rare earths to chemicals to electronics, China has stolen a long march over India, and in some traditional labour-oriented opportunities, such as textiles, Bangladesh, too, has shown better success. However, India has some successes and many opportunities to look forward to in this decade. India is among the world's largest producers of farm equipment. India is also among the top five in coal and iron ore production, steel and cement, and reached the top in terms of real estate construction in 2019. A spate of recent announcements with large outlays for Production Linked Incentive (PLI) schemes in key sectors also give rise to the hope that we can indeed do much better in manufacturing and capture our rightful place as the preferred 'China Plus One' partner for global manufacturing. The PLI scheme, which was notified on 24 February 2021 by the Government of India with the objective to boost domestic manufacturing, investment and export in telecommunications and networking products has now been expanded to multiple sectors and is spurring investment by global and Indian multinationals and niche companies.

In our earlier PIC publication, *Rising to the China Challenge*, we had done an assessment of global opportunity and the relative status of India and China to advocate industry-specific strategies in three broad categories of industry sectors:

- **Category 1: Huge asymmetry areas where India must progressively reduce dependence**

A case in point is rare earth metals, in which, having the largest natural availability of rare earths, China has a dominant position. With many clean energy applications and high-tech industry products, like electric and hybrid cars, dependent on rare earths, the concern of the world at this huge dependence on China is the only factor going against Chinese dominance in the future. Australia and the US will chip away at China's share. India has performed below potential in this industry in spite of significant beach sand mineral deposits. The future game plan for India has to be to make the mining and production of rare earths more attractive for the private sector and become part of at least some global supply chains in this area.

- **Category 2: Opportunities to focus on 'Aatmanirbhar' with 'Atmavishwas' and meet the domestic demand to gain technological leadership**

A classic example of such an opportunity is the telecommunications sector. The global telecommunication services market size is expected to grow from \$2.64 trillion in 2021 to \$2.86 trillion in 2022 at a compound annual growth rate (CAGR) of 8.5 per cent.[17] Rising spending on wireless communication due to shifts to cloud technologies and mobile devices is changing the complexion of this industry. India's revenues in the telecommunications sector stood at \$37.36 billion in 2021.[18] In contrast, China's telecommunication industry reported revenues of \$99.46 billion in the first five months of 2022, up 8.5 per cent compared to the same period the previous year, according to Xinhua, citing data from the Ministry of Industry and Information Technology.[19] China's telecommunications market size was \$430 billion in 2021.[20] China's success in deregulation has led to the advent of mega-companies like China Mobile, China Tower, China Telecom and China Unicom and, more recently, Huawei and ZTE.

India's opportunities for the future lie in the move from traditional copper-based networks to dense fibre optic cable networks and the entry of major private sector players, such as Reliance Jio, with a focus on 5G. In 5G, India needs to be committed to block the entry of Chinese players for both self-reliance and security reasons. There is an imperative to stem the influx of imports of optical preform, optical fibre and optical fiber cable products through safeguards and/or higher basic customs duty to encourage local capacity development. The Indian government should allocate 1 per cent of annual GDP towards publicly funded fibre infrastructure and reduce dependency on the private sector. Broadband connectivity itself has a correlation with GDP growth, so a sustained, structured programme will enable further economic growth across sectors.

It is important to underline recent developments in India in this segment. While the entire start-up investment in India was lagging behind the US and even Israel for many years, Jio's ability to raise over $20 billion at an equity valuation of $58 billion[21] demonstrates what the tremendous global tech majors and investors see in the potential of the telecommunications segment in India. In the investment announcement made by Google, who came into Jio at similar valuations to fierce tech industry rival Facebook, CEO Sundar Pichai said their excitement stemmed from the potential for millions of users in India to become owners of smartphones.[22] With the advent of 5G and the massive expansion and national push that Jio is expected to make, Google expects that new opportunities will be unlocked, powering the vibrant ecosystem of applications and pushing innovation to drive growth for the Indian economy.

- **Category 3: Global industry-building opportunities**

There are two significant areas that immediately jump out. The first is consumer electronics. The global consumer electronics industry is expected to reach $838 billion in 2020 with over $151 billion revenue generated by China. Investments in smart robotics and factory automation, extensive investments in artificial intelligence (AI) and prosperity-driving consumer appliances are all advantages for China. India needs to accelerate the rollout of 5G and internet of things (IoT) and leverage initiatives such as Digital India and the Smart Cities Mission to usher in a new era for electronic products. Tremendous opportunity has been lost in hardware even while the software and business process industries have made great strides.

While India has built an outstanding ICT industry with dominant market share in IT, engineering, BPM and product engineering services in the world, India has missed the opportunity in core ICT, where Taiwan, China and Thailand have built large industries. The core ICT layer includes base stations, routers, blade servers, phones, laptops, etc., that are built using semiconductors, like semiconductor chips, hardware processors and other components such as optoelectronics and sensors. A big frontier for core ICT systems is cloud for 5G, which will need a new class of server blades with the capability to support wireless networks with multi-gigabit per second throughputs. Important thrust areas in semiconductors include special purpose engines for deep neural networks that are capable of handling large modelling applications with large volumes of data and co-packaged optical transmissions with massive processing power (bits per second) and connectivity from a single chip. With the need to process large amounts of data and the coming capacity jumps for storage, processing and transmission with quantum computing, next generation data warehouses and 5G, these capabilities will become essential to build and sustain a digital economy.

Through core ICT, the industry will move from just software to hardware, along with embedded software and firmware, and this will be the passport for India to be a true participant in the multi-trillion-dollar global core ICT industry. In the coming decade, ICT will be the key enabler of many high-growth industries in India, including biotechnology, pharmaceuticals, advanced materials and even energy. India's best bet to enter the core ICT ecosystem is to grow new companies while expanding the existing industry efforts in this area. India requires entrepreneurial university researchers and engineers from the industry both within and outside the country. The initial opportunities for India will be in the design layer—systems and semiconductor design—where the engineering skill sets are largely available and investments are relatively smaller. However, semiconductor and other component manufacturing is important too, and careful planning will be needed to build this sector. By focussing strongly on all three layers—domain, services and core ICT—and building a new era of patents and inventions, India can truly lead the world in all aspects of ICT. A reasonable 10-year target for India in core ICT can be a 5 per cent share of global revenue, which means a $200 billion plus per annum value addition by 2030. Indian engineers have what it takes; there is now the ability to be part of a China-less supply chain, attract global venture capital and build the $200 billion core ICT capability for the country.

The second sector where India can grow and dominate is automobiles. The global automobile market has been dominated by American, European and Japanese manufacturers, though China is counted among the largest markets worldwide. China's early moves in the autonomous, electric and connected car segment and their dominance in the production of batteries for electric cars have led to projections of market leadership by 2040, which India should watch, emulate and challenge. Indian Aatmanirbhar or self-reliant production of cars conforming to all emission standards have to be ramped up and an aggressive push for exports made. All major automobile makers in Japan, Korea, the US and Europe should be incentivized to use India as the base for massive global production. Exclusive automotive special economic zones (SEZs) offering significant tax benefits and excellent infrastructure could be the way forward. India should leverage its successful IT and automobile component sectors to manage the complex systems of vehicle electronics and connected vehicles, and use the accelerating investments of global players in Indian manufacturing plants to accelerate in this critical sector. Initiatives like the Ministry of Electronics and Information Technology's (MeitY) STPI Centre of Entrepreneurship for Autonomous Connected Electric Shared Mobility need to be substantially supported through domestic research and development (R&D) and investments to enable India to take the lead in the next generation of transportation.

There are other opportunity segments and sectors too. The first is chemicals, where the global revenues reached $4.73 trillion in 2021.[23] India's revenues of $178 billion[24] places it far behind China, which became the world's largest producer in 2009 and today enjoys over 40 per cent of global industry revenue. With more than 600 chemical parks and upwards, with 60 million employed compared to India's 5 million plus,[25] China is far ahead in this sector, though given the context of oil prices moving to lower levels and Chinese labour costs rising, China's competitive advantage might be less in the future.[26] India has opportunities to leverage a China Plus One objective of many global consumers to present a real alternative destination by creating special purpose SEZs, positioning the country as a leader in certain value chains and segments, and showcasing the use of digital technologies and Industry 4.0 smart production systems as well as low-cost labour to be the destination of choice for the future.

Another opportunity sector is healthcare and pharmaceuticals. While India has done well in the pharmaceuticals segment, a large percentage of inputs to any drug manufacturing come from China. China also has one of the fastest-growing healthcare markets in the world. Global revenue in the healthcare segment has been projected by analysts to reach $59.70 billion in 2022. Revenue is expected to show an annual growth rate (CAGR 2022–2025) of 11.80 per cent, resulting in a projected market volume of $83.42 billion by 2025. China's revenue in this segment was projected to reach $18.63 billion in 2022 and show an annual growth rate (CAGR 2022–2025) of 4.47 per cent, resulting in a projected market volume of $21.24 billion by 2025.[27] In the case of India, it was projected to reach $535.90 million in 2022 and was expected to show an annual growth rate (CAGR 2022–2025) of 13.88 per cent, resulting in a projected market volume of $791.50 million by 2025.

Revenue of the worldwide pharmaceutical market in 2021 stood at $1.42 trillion with 49.1 per cent revenue share of the North American market. The pharmaceutical industry in India was valued at an estimated $42 billion in 2021.[28] According to India Ratings & Research, the Indian pharmaceutical market revenue is expected to be over 12 per cent year-on-year (YoY) in FY 2022–23. China's pharmaceutical industry saw combined business revenue climb 18.7 per cent YoY in 2021, registering a revenue of about $502 billion in that year.[29]

With a strong focus on healthcare in India and the extensive use of digital technology and services, India has an opportunity to substantially ramp up healthcare revenues and also make big impacts on the global pharmaceutical industry. There is an upside potential if Indian companies become major global producers of Covid-19 vaccines and syringes. Telehealth and wellness tourism are also significant segments to be exploited. On the pharmaceutical side, the Indian drugs industry is a heavy user of active pharmaceutical ingredients (APIs) sourced from China. In an environment where China is seen as a bad actor in the global economy, where Chinese nationalism can harm counterparties abroad, this presents a problem. India must look at diversifying our global sources of supply for APIs while boosting domestic API production and vertically integrating the pharmaceuticals industry from chemicals to APIs to formulations. Market leaders like Sun Pharmaceuticals are already doing this, but much more needs to be accomplished.

One critical point we must make is that manufacturing is no longer purely labour-intensive; it is smart manufacturing which brings in automation, robotics and other technologies in new smart manufacturing and manufacturing execution systems environments. India has recognized this, and there are many initiatives that have been researched and discussed by PIC, and the Confederation of Indian Industry is now getting into implementation with smart manufacturing initiatives commencing in key sectors of the manufacturing economy.

The Opportunities in Industry 4.0

The fourth industrial revolution, or Industry 4.0, originated in developing countries to address challenges associated with ageing demographics and high cost of labour by introducing extreme automation in industrial operations. In contrast, India has young demographics, with 60 per cent of its population under 29 and an abundant workforce needing employment. India has a unique situation to deal with—India must adopt Industry 4.0 to remain competitive while creating more and more jobs for the youth. This challenge can be converted into an opportunity by empowering the Indian workforce with new-age skills and becoming the world's talent factory.

One of the most valuable intangible assets of any country is its human capital. If India wants to be competitive in the fourth industrial revolution, it must upgrade its human capital with twenty-first-century skills. The changes caused by Industry 4.0 are likely to be radically faster than anything experienced yet. We need to create new talent and reskill and upskill the existing workforce to meet the industry's growing requirements. Like any other revolution, Industry 4.0 also demands a new type of education and skilling to achieve national competitiveness and leadership.

A number of platforms have been initiated in India to help develop indigenous manufacturing technologies by converging India's technical resources on each of them. The technology areas covered by these platforms include manufacturing, mobility, advanced materials, additive manufacturing, robotics and automation, mechatronics, sensor control and power electronics, and machine learning and AI.

India has made a good start by initiating the PLI scheme and attracting global leaders, like Apple Inc., to expand their manufacturing operations from India. Spreading this to multiple sectors where India has been trailing, like semiconductors, chemicals and APIs, will restore manufacturing to the 20 per cent-plus share of GDP it once enjoyed and make India a global manufacturing hub. These initiatives have great potential to lay a strong foundation for India's journey towards Industry 4.0 in the coming decades. Today, India has surpassed the US as the world's second-most-desired manufacturing destination, according to Cushman & Wakefield's 2021 World Manufacturing Danger Index,[30] indicating the growing interest shown by global manufacturers in India as a preferred manufacturing hub. However, the adoption of digital technologies and Industry 4.0 by Indian companies is still at a nascent stage, with only 14 per cent of the businesses in India really attempting to transform themselves.[31]

India should design and conduct a nationwide Industry 4.0 maturity assessment of large and small enterprises based on the local context across the sectors to know where India stands currently in terms of IT and operational technology (OT) systems implementation, process automation, availability of 'insightful data' to make easy and quick decisions, cost overheads, pockets of optimization (of cost of operations) and other relevant parameters. The outcome of this study will provide direction, focus and relevance to various government programmes.

The micro, small and medium enterprises (MSME) segment, which is the backbone of the Indian economy, has very little access to knowledge, digitally aware talent and technology. The future of MSMEs depends mainly on their capacity to respond to industry needs by improving industrial management processes with proper planning, optimal use of resources, controlled production and continuously evaluating operational performance to maintain a competitive advantage in the market. Adopting Industry 4.0 for MSMEs can positively impact costs, revenues, equipment maintenance, design and customer interface for their overall growth. To make MSMEs adapt to these changes and become an active part of the global supply chain, India needs a special programme dedicated only for MSMEs to mentor systematically and handhold enterprises by creating awareness, building organizational and talent capability, designing specific solutions for demonstration, and providing right digital solutions for implementation. Along with initiatives of the Indian government, in a bid to uplift and revitalize the MSME sector, the World Bank launched a $500 million programme in 2021, Raising and Accelerating Micro, Small and Medium Enterprise Performance (RAMP), aimed at improving the performance of 555,000 MSMEs, which can boost and accelerate the adoption of digital and smart manufacturing for longer-term productivity-driven growth.[32]

Before 2025, India should aim to transform a large part of Indian enterprises to reach the level of Industry 4.0 with the support of various government initiatives. In addition, India should identify 25 lighthouse projects across industry sectors to showcase successful enterprises that have adopted and benefited from Industry 4.0. The idea of lighthouse projects originated at the World Economic Forum (WEF) to show the way for the world's manufacturing companies interested in implementing Industry 4.0. The lighthouse factories should demonstrate connected and intelligent factories, interconnected supply chains and distribution networks, real-time monitoring, tracking and tracing to improve productivity and prevent downtime, machine-to-machine and machine-to-human interactions, resources optimization, and safety. India needs to create a dedicated online platform to showcase lighthouse projects and share experiences from successful manufacturing companies.

Beyond 2025, the adoption of Industry 4.0 will rise during this period. The power of Industry 4.0 lies in the integration of physical assets with digital technologies in a dynamic environment for a smart and intelligent production system. A traditional factory consists of sourcing, procurement, design, production, quality and maintenance, working in silos with limited collaboration and communication. In smart factories, these silos are integrated into one large system with benefits of reduced cost and improved efficiency, quality and productivity to stay competitive in the global market.

During this period, every significant Indian manufacturing organization needs to transform into a smart and connected enterprise by integrating horizontal data capture across manufacturing, warehousing and supply chains, using cyber-physical systems and vertically integrating companies to their supply and demand chain partner organizations. Smart analytics (prediction, intelligence, decision-making capability), simulation-based production planning and smart control (the ability to automatically and remotely control machines and production) will all play a role in bringing Indian manufacturing capability, quality and productivity to world standards.

Advancing further, enterprises need to develop capabilities in digital twin, cognitive and biointelligent systems to increase reliability, optimize the use of resources, minimize downtime, and improve performance and efficiency. As a result, large and small organizations across industries can become competitive to produce goods capable of mass customization and become part of global supply chains.

While manufacturing companies progress towards Industry 4.0, Indian IT companies can offer smart solutions to the Indian and global markets. It is estimated that smart factories could add multi-trillion dollars in value to the global economy during this period. Today, India is the world's largest sourcing destination for the IT industry, employing more than 4 million professionals. Industry 4.0 sees massive usage of IT in the manufacturing sector and requires smart solutions on assembly lines. Extending India's current strength of IT to OT would make the current IT industry reach over a trillion dollars by 2030, as the adoption will accelerate in this period.

In the long term, the goal for Indian enterprises should be to transform from a smart and connected enterprise to an intelligent, self-aware, autonomous, sustainable and networked enterprise to achieve leadership in the fourth industrial revolution. The data produced from operational and biological systems will grow exponentially, and the power of AI must multiply to make machines capable of predicting actions and be autonomous and intelligent. This growing AI capability has various benefits. Intelligent robots can manoeuvre delicate procedures and work in extreme conditions. Enterprises will be able to function autonomously, with intelligent and self-aware machines to accomplish specific tasks in the presence of uncertainty and variability, and self-simulate to adapt to novel situations. And systems will also be capable of self-diagnosis and repair.

During this period, industry structures and business models will be disrupted. The largest and most successful companies in the world during this period will be platform companies, who are able to connect all ecosystem players in an industry and enable them to share data and collaborate. In recognition of this and after the success of UPI as a payments platform par excellence, the Indian government has announced the Open Network for Digital Commerce (ONDC), which will create standards for all platforms under digital India for the future. An estimated 70 per cent of the new value created in the economy will be based on digitally enabled platform business models. The next wave of innovations for enterprises will be on the back of the platforms and ecosystem of multiple platforms. A diverse set of large-scale integrated systems that can operate independently on their own will be networked together for a common purpose. The new-age companies rely on the principle of demand economics rather than supply economics and grow through network effects.

India's prospects for the future lie in the new wave of wealth creators by unleashing India's entrepreneurial spirit. The lower costs of infrastructure and assets pave the way for more suppliers, inspiring healthy competition among businesses and promoting entrepreneurship, in turn, triggering a culture of fast-paced innovation to ensure survival. In emerging economies like India, this competition makes for a thriving market, thus pushing the economy to further growth. What's more, this trend received a boost from the pandemic, which saw the acceleration and expansion of digital technology in sectors like e-commerce, telehealth and education. Industry 4.0 is opening up new opportunities for businesses, and the innovative implementation and other technological frontiers as platforms are giving birth to new start-ups, transforming Indian economics like never before.

We must conclude this discussion on manufacturing by cautioning that Made in China 2020 has announced its targeting of 10 key sectors for additional government support. These sectors are: (1) new energy vehicles, (2) next-generation IT, (3) biotechnology, (4) new materials, (5) aerospace, (6) ocean engineering and high tech ships, (7) railway, (8) robotics, (9) power equipment, and (10) agricultural machinery. China has always supported industry creation and scaling through significant government backing, and India will have to pay heed and build active partnerships between industry and government to gain market share in these and other emerging segments.

India launched the PLI scheme in February 2021 in chosen sectors for deep investments. It is an encouraging step that the Indian government has committed $26.6 billion to address the nation's manufacturing capabilities and enhance exports across 13 sectors through PLIs.[33] These include mobile handset and components, automobiles and automobile components, solar photovoltaic (PV) modules, specialty steel makers, man-made and technical textiles, food processing, specialized pharmaceutical products, advanced chemistry cell battery and IT hardware. This scheme relies on identifying national and global champions in each sector to manufacture part of their needs and hence make India an integral part of the new supply chain. It is inherently World Trade Promotion Organization (WTPO) compliant and serves the need of those who would like to see their global value chains insulated from a possible trade war between India and China. These are small steps but could pave the way for India to become a true manufacturing powerhouse and create at least a hundred million new jobs for our youth by 2030.

SERVICES—CONSOLIDATION AND EXPANDING OUR GAINS

India's growth story in the twenty-first century is remarkable because it contradicts a seemingly iron law of development that has held true for almost 200 years since the start of the Industrial Revolution. This law—which is now conventional wisdom—says that industrialization is the only route to rapid economic development. It further states that as a result of globalization, the pace of development can be explosive. But the potential for explosive growth has, until now, been distinctive to manufacturing. This is no longer the case. India's experience suggests that latecomers to development can benefit from a global service revolution that has fundamentally changed the pattern of development.

India's experience with the service revolution offers hope that globalization can indeed be a force for development in many more developing countries. The marginalization of Africa during a period when China and other East Asian countries grew rapidly led some to wonder if latecomers to development were doomed to failure. The process of globalization in the late twentieth century led to a divergence of incomes between those who industrialized and broke into global markets and a 'bottom billion,' to use Paul Collier's phrase, of people in some 60 countries, where incomes have stagnated in this century. It seemed as if the bottom billion would have to wait their turn for development, until the giant industrializers like China become rich and uncompetitive in labour-intensive manufacturing.

The promise of the 'service revolution' is that India and other developing countries do not need to wait to get started with rapid development. There is a new boat that the latecomers can take. The globalization of service exports provides alternative opportunities for developing countries to find niches beyond manufacturing, where they can specialize, scale up and achieve explosive growth, just like the industrializers. Industrialization is *not the only* route to economic development.

The Service Revolution

Services have characteristics that differ significantly from goods. Goods are physical objects that can be put in a box and traded. They can be made anywhere, at any time and at any scale. More and more goods are produced each year as firms develop new products and as production processes are broken down into individual parts and components. With a growing number of goods, productivity can rise due to specialization (a finer division of labour) and scale economies (falling unit costs of production). This specialization in goods and the exploration of new markets allow even small countries to find a niche in global markets where they can be competitive.

Traditional services are difficult to place in a box because they are constrained by time and proximity. For example, running a restaurant, providing a haircut, setting up medical check-up centres or offering individual loans, all require face-to-face transactions. This makes it difficult to trade in traditional services. They are produced where and when demand is present.

But technological changes (telephone, internet and AI) have made many services tradable, just like manufactured goods. These services, called modern impersonal progressive services, include communication, banking, insurance, business-related services and much more. They have been created by three global forces—technology, transportability and tradability—the 3 Ts that are driving the services revolution. Technology, especially ICT, has given services a physical presence. They can be produced and stored in a digital format.

Thanks to the internet, modern services can be easily transported today over long distances with little or no degradation in quality. One indicator of the cost of transporting services is the average cost of an international telephone call to the US. For most developing countries, this has fallen by more than 80 per cent or more over the last decade,[34] a decline in cost which is much more rapid than the fall in transport costs for goods. Perhaps as important as cost is the speed, clarity and reliability with which information can now be transported. There are no borders, customs or tariffs on the international exchange of most business services. Service exports are now one of the fastest-growing components of global trade.

The digital age will continue to transform more services into modern impersonal services. The range of business processes that can be globalized and digitized is constantly expanding: processing insurance claims, desktop publishing, the remote management and maintenance of IT networks, compiling audits, completing tax returns, transcribing medical records, financial research and analysis. The list of possible activities is almost endless.

Modern impersonal services have many features in common with manufacturing. Like manufacturing, they benefit from technological advances that generate productivity growth year after year. They exhibit similar tendencies for scale as in tailoring and industrial security. Service producers can bring down unit costs by expanding operations. They benefit from being in close proximity to one another, as that creates a pool of well-trained workers and is labour-intensive. Many modern services, like some types of manufacturing, provide employment for women. Enhanced economic status for women, in turn, can create development spillovers like lower population growth rates, more emphasis on better education for children and higher household savings rates.

There is mounting empirical evidence that India and other developing countries are relying more on services and less on manufacturing as drivers of growth and job creation.[35] The relationship between income and economic structure has shifted over time, with countries across the income distribution uniformly increasing the share of labour in service sectors and an increasingly less stark relationship between manufacturing intensity and GVA per capita. While global growth convergence in manufacturing was a clear and strong trend some decades ago, it is no longer as strong in recent decades. The service sector has shown stronger growth convergence in recent decades.

Services-led Growth

Services are now the largest contributor to GDP growth in India, contributing nearly twice that of industry.[36] High service growth is associated with high service export growth, and this suggests that it is services that have been driving overall economic growth rather than vice versa. Although there is also a positive relationship between manufacturing growth and overall growth, the effect of services is much stronger than the effect of manufacturing on economic growth.

How dynamic is total factor productivity (TFP) growth of services? Services were once thought of as stagnant, with low productivity growth areas and without the dynamic externalities attributed to manufacturing. That was one reason why services were not thought of as a potential leading sector for development.

But India's growth experience shows that services have displayed significant productivity growth, approaching a healthy 2 per cent annually.[37] India's TFP growth rate in the service sector has increased at twice the rate of its TFP growth in industry, and India has outperformed China in terms of TFP growth rates in services.[38] One reason for rapid productivity growth in services is that India is starting from a low technological base compared to international best practice, and there is ample room for rapid catch-up. Beyond this, services also display potential for productivity gains from learning, networking and knowledge spillovers. As the service sector is much larger than manufacturing, heeding the needs of services growth is important for policymakers.

The ability of services growth to drive overall economic growth is a new phenomenon. Because modern services can be traded, the demand curve has become much more elastic, meaning that prices do not decline rapidly as volumes increase. This permits services to be a source of sustained growth.

Service Export

In India, the majority of foreign direct investment (FDI) inflows are concentrated in the service sector, and, in particular, modern impersonal services. For India to sustain growth over the long run, it needs to leverage the global economy. The East Asian experience of a manufacturing-led growth model has shown that domestic demand is not sufficient to sustain growth. Firms need exports to take advantage of scale and agglomeration economies. Successful growth experiences are typically associated with greater integration into the world economy, as developing countries' domestic markets are much too small to support sustained expansions of production.

The globalization of services provides new opportunities for India to find niches beyond manufacturing, where it can specialize, scale up and achieve explosive growth, just like the industrializers. As the original set of services expands in various parts of the world, they will open opportunities of related but additional services, adding much-needed foreign exchange to the country. This pace of change will be rapid and in line with the digital revolution. An indication of this revolution is that global internet usage has grown. This growth is much faster in developing countries—India alone adds one million new users every month to a booming mobile phone market.

Spatial Awakening

One source of productivity growth in services is urbanization and agglomeration of activities in select locations. Modern impersonal services tend to cluster together to take advantage of scale economies and externalities. Clustering in services can potentially be more persistent and concentrated than in manufacturing, as services are less land-intensive. A thick market for services attracts more service firms and workers. Service corridors arise just like manufacturing clusters. These benefit from externalities such as knowledge spillovers between firms, workers and universities. Productivity-enhancing externalities are far more prominent in service corridors compared to goods clusters, as services tend to be 'non-rival' goods and lend themselves to more collaboration.

It is easier for service firms to cluster than manufacturing firms. Service firms take up less space, do not cause traffic jams when shipping their goods and pollute less. This is not only true for developed countries, with notable tradable services hubs in New York, London, Silicon Valley and also in India.

Services have shown a distinctly different spatial development pattern in India. The high-density services clusters are gaining relative to those locations with slightly lower employment density. Many of the well-known IT clusters continue to benefit from agglomeration economies. For example, service employment in

Hyderabad and Chennai is growing at an annual rate of 11 and 4 per cent, respectively.[39]

A reasonable question may be whether these results are driven by particular subgroups of manufacturing or services. To answer this question, we distinguished between the formal and the informal sectors. This distinction may be relevant, since firms in the informal sector are less subject to laws and regulations, and thus, perhaps more free to operate and choose their location. Differentiating between the unorganized and the organized sectors does not change our finding. The service sector is becoming increasingly concentrated in high-density clusters, whereas in manufacturing, the picture is more mixed. We examined multiple sectors for which we had data (22 manufacturing subsectors and 12 services subsectors). Still, the main result holds. Services are becoming increasingly concentrated in high-density clusters, and this is not driven by a few subsectors. In the case of services, around 90 per cent of employment is in subsectors that exhibit increasing concentration in high-density clusters, whereas the corresponding figure in manufacturing is around 60 per cent.

The strong evidence of agglomeration economies in the service sector is consistent with findings for the US and Europe. Given the impact of ICT in India's rapidly growing service sector, this is what we would have expected. Being a 'young' industry, services benefit from knowledge spillovers, leading to the emergence of high-density service clusters. In contrast, the evidence for such agglomeration economies in manufacturing, though weaker than in services, differs from the tendency towards dispersion across the entire distribution in the case of the US and Europe. This suggests that manufacturing in India is not as mature as in the US or Europe.

Despite concentrated spatial location, the benefits of service growth appear to be widely distributed. Service growth is the largest contributor to poverty reduction globally and regionally. Globally, there is cross-country evidence from some 50 developing countries that poverty reduction is correlated more strongly with growth in the service sector than with growth in manufacturing or agriculture.[40] Regionally, it is also the case that localities with higher service sector growth exhibit lower rates of poverty. Each one percentage increase in trend growth in the service sector among Indian states is associated with a decrease in the trend of the headcount poverty rate by almost 1.5 points.[41] Some states in India, such as Karnataka, Tamil Nadu and Andhra Pradesh, have experienced a significant decrease in urban poverty that may be associated with an increase in their service sector share.

If we are to learn any lessons from the US and Europe, India's engines of growth should be its medium-density cities. The trade-off between agglomeration economies and congestion is indeed similar in India, as in China and the US.

In India, we have seen that over decades, business activity tends to gravitate towards densely populated urban centres, and the tier 2 cities have often been laggards in both growth and development. What frictions or barriers might be holding back tier 2 cities? We can obtain some suggestive evidence by controlling certain district-level characteristics—the percentage of the population with a high school degree or more and the percentage of the population with post-secondary education; household access to infrastructure (percentage of households with electricity, percentage of households with toilet, percentage of households with telecommunication services, percentage of households with tap water); travel time to a top-10 city and distance to a top-7 or a top-3 city.[42] When exploring which of these controls can explain the advantage of high-density clusters, we can rule out most. For example, being close to a major city or having access to some of the basic utilities, such as tap water or toilets, do not seem to matter. Only two variables, the percentage of the population with post-secondary education and the percentage of households with access to telecommunication services, have the potential of accounting for the relative advantage of high-density clusters.[43] Once we control either of these two variables, there is no longer evidence of high-density service clusters growing particularly fast. In other words, if all locations had the same percentage of their population with post-secondary education or if in all locations the access to telecommunication services in households were the same, then high-density service clusters would lose their attractiveness.

If part of the worse performance of India's medium-density locations is their deficient local infrastructure, it may be useful to compare India's experience not just to that of the US but also to that of the other large emerging economy, China. Our analysis shows that China looks very different from India. Once a threshold of around 150 employees per square kilometre is reached, agglomeration economies start dominating in India, whereas the opposite happens in China. For Chinese locations with a density above 150 employees per square kilometre, service employment growth strongly decreases with size, indicating important congestion costs. Along that dimension, China looks more like the US, where congestion costs also dominate for locations above the 150 employees per square kilometre threshold. Given that the overall level of local infrastructure is better in China than in India, this finding is consistent with the interpretation of frictions holding back the growth of medium-density locations in India but not in China.

The Future

What might future patterns look like? We compute the counterfactual employment growth of Indian districts if the relationship between density and growth was the one we estimated for the US. Two features stand out.

- First, many of the relatively slow-growing Indian districts would grow much faster. These correspond to medium-density places, similar in density to places such as the

Silicon Valley. As mentioned before, with few exceptions, these districts in India do not seem to be able to take advantage of the service revolution.

- Second, different areas of the country would benefit from growth in the service sector. Growth would be more concentrated in the coastal regions, especially in southern states such as Tamil Nadu and Kerala as well as in northern states such as West Bengal, Bihar and Uttar Pradesh. Of the well-known IT clusters in India, medium-density places such as Ahmedabad and Pune, and especially Bangalore, have high growth rates in the counterfactual, whereas the high-density places, such as Chennai and Mumbai, do not.

We find strong evidence that two key barriers in tier 2 cities are the small share of highly educated population and the deficient local infrastructure, in particular poor access to telecommunication services. The findings for China, an emerging economy that has suffered less from a lack of infrastructure, support this interpretation. It is not obvious to us why Indian individuals should dislike congestion less than Americans or should benefit more than Americans from agglomeration economies. These forces seem to be more technological and universal. Therefore, the likely culprits are restrictions to economic growth in intermediate-density cities or districts.

Limitations to growth in modern impersonal service are mostly on the supply side, and, in particular, the availability of employees with education and skills that meet the requirements of the global services market. The globalizing market for skills, however, allows developing countries to capitalize on their cost advantage in terms of labour and to make investments in expanding the skills of their labour forces to meet the demands of the fast-growing global IT and information technology enabled services (ITES) industries. Locations with comparatively large talent pools will have an advantage in attracting IT services and ITES companies because large companies prefer to source services from locations where scalability is feasible.

Telecommunication

India and other developing countries are well known for their poor infrastructure. But the infrastructure that matters to service trade is in better shape. India has experienced a telecommunications revolution. The sector has experienced major investment and competition, and this has improved electronic delivery of services tremendously.

Telecommunications growth is the most powerful symbol of the vitality of the service sector and is, at the same time, critical for the further development of other parts of the economy. While there has been a dramatic transformation of this sector, some policy issues remain. A key issue is the design of universal access regimes. The policy priorities should be to reform the incumbent operator; strengthen the regulator and enhance its independence from both the incumbent and the government; eliminate barriers to entry other than those dictated by say scarcity of spectrum; and establish an effective universal access scheme that widens access to services in poor and remote areas. Global and regional cooperation in telecommunications and the internet could strengthen the competitiveness of India in the services export sector.

Civil Aviation

India has marched ahead with aviation reform, especially on international routes. Landlocked countries may be victims of geography but their isolation is sometimes deepened by their own policies as well as those of their neighbours. There are three obvious priorities for policy. The first political challenge is to prepare national airlines for a more competitive environment. Serious consideration should be given to a possible joint venture with a foreign airline, which could inject the necessary capital as well as technological and managerial improvements. At the same time, policymakers can push for more liberal bilateral air service agreements that do not restrict capacity or flight frequency or even opt for more open-sky agreements. Finally, there is a need for regulatory reform, in particular, to enhance both the independence and capacity of the departments of civil aviation.

Organizing for Services

India has broken with economic convention. Its decade-long growth spurt has been largely fuelled by the global trade in services. The best-known examples are states such as Andhra Pradesh and Karnataka, which have been transformed from stagnating rural economies to dynamic service hubs. The ICT revolution has rapidly introduced a large array of new products that developing countries can produce at lower costs. What is certain is that the old idea of services as being non-tradable and non-scalable because of inelastic demands no longer holds for a host of modern progressive products.

Development is a process of organizing resources according to their best use. When that is done right, there are incentives to accumulate through investment in profitable activities. Until now, it was assumed that the critical task was how to organize for industrial growth. Even the World Bank's *Doing Business* report and its Enterprise Surveys focus exclusively on goods-producing firms, and policy prescriptions for development have focussed largely on what can help countries industrialize.

Moving forward, what is important is that countries seize opportunities in line with their comparative advantage, whether this is in services or in manufacturing. India's comparative advantage in services arose because of its history of quality higher education institutions, its English language heritage and its computer-savvy diaspora. It also arose because of the comparative disadvantage in logistics and infrastructure on which trade in goods depends. The right mix of incentives, policies and investments in education, telecommunications and connectivity can create the enabling conditions to ignite a services-led growth revolution.

What could India do?

Although the same set of general non-distortionary growth policy is as important for services as for manufacturing, specific strategies for services matter. Investments in both physical and human infrastructure matter greatly for attracting new enterprises in both the manufacturing and services industries. But unlike in the manufacturing sector, investments in human infrastructure, education and skills matter much more. Human capability plays a bigger role in services. Given its stage of development, India needs accelerated investments in both physical and human infrastructure to support new drivers of growth and job creation.

India's experience offers hope to other latercomers to development. The process of globalization in the late twentieth century led to a sharp divergence of incomes between those who industrialized and broke into global markets and the 'bottom billion' in some 60 low-income countries, where incomes stagnated. It seemed as if this stagnation would persist till opportunities arose to fill the spaces left by giant industrializers like China becoming rich and uncompetitive in labour-intensive manufacturing. This is no longer the case, and this is indeed the opportunity for India and many aspiring nations of the world.

2

THE TRILLION-DOLLAR DIGITAL ECONOMY

Ganesh Natarajan and Manoj Soman

There has been significant speculation around the attainment of the $5 trillion GDP status for India. From the time Prime Minister Narendra Modi set this target for India to achieve by 2024, we have unfortunately been buffeted by multiple setbacks that have pushed our present and future backwards. From the middle of the FY 2018–19, the economic cycles affected the manufacturing industry, and even some segments of the agriculture and service sector started slowing down. And then, Covid-19 hit, severely affecting the fortunes of the Indian economy and causing it to decline by double digits in the FY 2020–21. The impact has been severe, with the economy sinking to pre-2019 levels, and in spite of a resurgence of GDP growth in the FY 2022–23, we struggled to cross the $3 trillion mark and have many years to go before achieving the $5 trillion GDP goal, which is now certainly unachievable in the original target year of 2024. It is difficult to set a new target for attaining this milestone, though there is already talk about reaching $10 trillion GDP by 2030.

However, the waves of fortune have begun to swell again and, with the global economy limping back to life post Covid-19, the exports sectors, particularly technology services and some forms of manufacturing from India, can certainly show double-digit growth in 2022–23. India will eventually scale the $5 trillion and even $10 trillion peaks, but what is most heartening is the fact that Digital India can and will reach a tryst with a trillion-dollar milestone well before the overall economy hits the $5 trillion mark. To understand the components of this trillion-dollar figure, let us first consider the work that has already been done and the results achieved, and then look at the pathways to realizing this mission in the shortest possible time.

The nine pillars for Digital India[1] which have been defined as priority areas by the government are:

- Broadband Highways
- Universal Access to Mobile Connectivity
- Public Internet Access Programme
- e-Governance: Reforming Government through Technology
- e-Kranti: Electronic Delivery of Services
- Information for All
- Electronics Manufacturing
- IT for Jobs
- Early Harvest Programmes

All these are works in progress and present a lot of hope that we can and will achieve the goals in the near future. The purpose of this chapter is to share and develop a common understanding of what it will take and how it can be done.

The three areas to understand before we embark on defining a plan are:

1. The IT, engineering and business process services industry's stellar achievement of $200 billion for 2021–22[2] and National Association of Software and Service Companies' (NASSCOM) approach to expanding this achievement;
2. Studies done by McKinsey Global Institute (MGI) and other research agencies in India and abroad over the last three years on the opportunities and challenges in achieving a trillion-dollar Digital India;

3. The Government of India's MeitY's new commitment to achieving the milestone by 2025.

The highlights of each of these research areas are enumerated below.

SEIZING AN OPPORTUNITY TO SCALE OFFSHORE

The story of India's rise to a position of global dominance in outsourced technology services has been told many times and needs no repetition here. The key point to note from our past success, which could lead to new pathways to the future, is the seamless transitions the industry has made over almost three decades.

The early beginnings were made when one man, F.C. Kohli, at the helm of Tata Consultancy Services (TCS) realized that Indian talent could be sold in the US and Western Europe to build critical technology applications as part of the teams based within those countries. The next phase was the creation of offshore centres with visionaries like N.R. Narayana Murthy and Nandan Nilekani of Infosys investing in top-class development centres in the country. The legitimation of offshore to fix the Year 2000 (Y2K) software bug and the eventual building of capabilities in migration, implementation and maintenance from India led to a large number of companies, notably HCL, Satyam, Cognizant, etc., becoming billion-dollar corporations.[3] And the spreading of capabilities to engineering services, BPM and outsourced product development and engineering created enough pillars for the industry to approach the $200 billion level it is expected to cross in 2022–23.

The four significant components of the industry are IT services, at over 50 per cent of the total pie, followed by BPM and engineering services, and finally product and platform development, which is less than 10 per cent of industry revenues today but has maximum growth potential. If the industry grows at over 12 per cent for the next eight years (the Q2 YoY revenue growth of TCS of over 15 per cent is an encouraging beginning[4]) and the global market for cloud, AI, cyber security keeps growing, a $500 billion goal by 2030 is aspirational and definitely attainable.

For a dynamic and highly entrepreneurial industry like technology solutions from India, there is a responsibility and an opportunity to show the way for other industries eyeing global market share. New opportunities abound; increasing importance is being given to India's development by major global software firms and Fortune 500 companies alike, the engineering capabilities are increasing by the day in India and the Business-to-Business Software as a Service (B2B SaaS) opportunity is being pursued as the next big white space by many entrepreneurs in India today. The flood of money into Indian edtech and fintech start-ups in India, the burgeoning number of unicorns and the rocketing share value of all tech firms are pointers to a future that can truly be much bigger than the past or present if the game is played the right way.

The IT and ITES industry, which can grow to $350 to $400 billion, still leaves a gap of $600–$650 billion. What would be the other components of a trillion-dollar Digital India of the future? These are to be served by digitally enabled businesses and 'born in digital' platforms and products that can change the consumption landscape in the country.

BUILDING A DIGITAL INDIA

The MGI study titled 'Digital India – Technology to transform a connected nation'[5] published in March 2019 enumerates some broad themes which can enable the achievement of this lofty mission. Some of the points made by this study and material drawn from other research provide adequate pointers to the successes and challenges of the past and pathways to the future for Digital India.

Growth of Digital Consumers

The adoption of digital across the spectrum of Indian smartphone owners has been truly prolific. Crossing 600 million internet subscribers a year ago, India is second only to China in terms of subscriber volume. With data consumption per capita at the higher end of the spectrum of global users, the higher proliferation of both mobile phones and internet bandwidth that is expected in the next few years can see internet usage, apps download and overall digital comfort accelerate even faster in the Indian market.

Nothing illustrates the craze for data more than a recent incident that happened at 3.00 a.m. in the morning on the pavement in front of Ganesh's home on Bandra Bandstand in Mumbai. Disturbed by the persistent wailing of a child, he went down on the street to find a woman curled up on the pavement with an infant near her so absorbed in a movie she had downloaded that the wailing child had little or no impact on her sensibilities. With the promise of 5G and cheaper access to the internet through a new generation of Jio phones and network, India's track record as a fast-growing internet nation, along with Indonesia, is only expected to increase its pace.

Dual Engines of Digital Growth

Successive governments and public and private sectors are both responsible for the steady push in internet proliferation and digital consumption growth. A defining moment in the country was probably the induction of IT industry czar Nandan Nilekani into the government to set up the Unique Identity programme, also known as Aadhaar. This came at a time when mobile phones had begun to proliferate and the Modi government launched the Jan Dhan initiative that envisaged bank accounts for all the citizens of the country. The JAM trinity can truly be credited for sparking off this wave. Over a billion Indians have enrolled into the Aadhaar programme and over ten million businesses have been brought on to a common digital platform through the Goods and Services Tax (GST).

After lagging behind China for a long time, the telecommunications industry is finally coming of age with Jio and other firms marching ahead with their 5G launches and lowering the cost of data, both of which will play a major role in bridging the digital divide in the country. The MGI projection is for India's lower-income states to grow faster than higher-income ones in internet infrastructure and subscriptions, the number of internet users to scale by about 40 per cent to between 750 million and 800 million, and the number of smartphones to double between 650 million and 700 million by 2023. This will provide an amazing infrastructure base for the internet economy to surge forward in the country.

Digital Adoption in Businesses

Businesses have been fascinated by digital ever since the great promise of cloud computing to transition costs, from capital expenditures to operating expenses, brought digital transformation into sharp focus not only for CIOs but also CMOs, COOs and even CEOs of medium-to-large organizations. In an earlier book written by Ganesh and his colleagues at 5F World, *Accelerating Digital Success: Reimagining Organisations for a Post-Covid-19 World,* the authors, in building a model for digital success, have discussed how wave upon wave of digital technologies, from the SMAC stack (social, mobility, analytics and cloud) to AI and machine learning to edge applications such as augmented and virtual reality, and IoT. They have forced a complete reengineering of the way businesses run. Multiple customer journeys, many enabled by digital touch points have been reimagined; business and manufacturing processes have been reengineered around new technology functionality; predictive and prescriptive analytics models have enabled actionable insights to become mainstream in corporate thinking. Every employee has had to be reskilled and upskilled to cater to the insatiable demand of digital immigrants and natives on their journey to product discovery, comparison and purchase.

However, not all firms who have been enthusiastic about digital become successful adopters of the new way of engaging with customers and other stakeholders, and attaining success. The MGI survey of more than 600 firms shows uneven digital adoption across sectors and sharp differences between the speed of adoption of core applications like enterprise resource planning (ERP) and customer relationship management (CRM), while success stories in full implementation of Industry 4.0 and smart manufacturing applications are still at a very nascent stage. Predictably, it is the leaders in every segment, such as State Bank of India, Bajaj Finance, Siemens, Flipkart, etc., who are also excellent adopters of digital technology. While large firms tend to invest more in central technology and digital applications, democratization of digital has happened through multiple fintech start-ups such as Zerodha, digital payment platforms like Paytm, digital marketing service providers like Kalzoom Advisors, data privacy pioneers like Arrka Software and cyber security solutions firms like K7 Computing. Thanks to the pandemic, digital adoption in collaboration and learning has accelerated substantially, and the increasing demand for digital talent is also expected to drive digital within educational institutions and skills development platforms and institutes.

Citizen-centric Digital Applications

The proliferation of digital inside homes and society has gone through three phases of applications and companies coming forward to offer distinctive solutions. The first was the use of digital to reduce cost with market makers such as Google, Facebook, Amazon, Alibaba and India's own Flipkart; these did a great job initially of getting customers used to convenience and low costs. The era of Netflix and Apple's myriad products introduced the concept of superior experience to a ready customer, and, finally, the platform economy has created phenomenal success stories like Airbnb, Uber and Byju's in India, which have demonstrated that asset ownership is not as important as having the right resource available on a pay-per-use model as and when needed.

This is where the big opportunity exists to build core ICT businesses as well as IT-enabled platforms and services that can contribute $600 to $650 billion to the trillion-dollar agenda. On the core ICT side, it is not just semiconductor manufacturing (mentioned later in this chapter) but multiple hardware components to support digital applications could proliferate across most sectors of India's economy. With the April 2020 announcement of PLIs, the opportunity to play in the multi-trillion-dollar core ICT space, including both manufacturing and the more adjacent design engineering services, can yield at least $100 to $150 billion to the trillion-dollar story in 2025. Added to the core digital sectors such as IT and BPM, product engineering and digital communication services, the current $200 billion revenue could more than double by that year and rapidly expand thereafter to give India competitive positioning in multiple areas of ICT and digital technology.

The other half of the trillion will come from the platforms. As mentioned earlier, the JAM story and the adoption of payment platforms by all segments of the economy has blazed a trail that can be followed by platforms for agricultural markets, skills and education, healthcare services, SMEs and even employment. Newly digitizing sectors, including agriculture, education, energy, financial services, healthcare, logistics and retail, as well as government services and labour markets, could each create $10 billion to $150 billion of incremental economic value in 2025 as digital applications in these sectors help raise output, save costs and time, reduce fraud and improve matching of demand and supply. The math can surely add up to the balance $500 billion in 2025 and position India to be the crucible of innovation for digital technology development as well as digital application to all fields of citizen success.

A trillion-dollar digital India also has the potential to create 60 million to 65 million jobs by 2025, many of them requiring functional digital skills, according to the MGI estimates. Retraining and redeployment will be essential to help 40 million to 45 million workers whose jobs could be displaced or transformed. Technology industry association NASSCOM, which created the industry-wide FutureSkills Platform for employees in organizations to upskill and reskill themselves, has shown the way by launching a partnership with MeitY for the benefit of all citizens in the country in November 2020.[6] As Yuval Noah Harari has said in his book *Homo Deus*, citizens will have to re-educate and reskill themselves to participate in boom cycles every 15 years or so, and the availability of reskilling platforms for every new job category will surely be a prerequisite for active citizen participation in the digital economy.

A successful and growing digital economy has tremendous advantages for the whole country and will also necessitate the creation of strong ecosystems. Slowly but inexorably, as is happening with successful digital businesses in recrafting new journeys for all stakeholders, traditional roles and relationships between players in the economy will undergo changes. Traditional interactions between consumers and producers in core sectors of retail, logistics, healthcare and agriculture will change with the use of platforms. Large players in each of these segments are experimenting with digital for all customer touch points, process reengineering and extensive use of data to make the customer interaction more meaningful and mutually beneficial.

The changing roles of the store in the larger retail customer journey management, the medical practitioner in telehealth, remote diagnostics and cognitive logistics supply chains will all need new participation modes of all stakeholders. The role of the government will primarily lie in the provision and management of digital pipes and other infrastructures and investing in public data platforms, while executives in the private and public sectors will need to take a holistic view of digital transformation and the judicious mix of technologies, processes, data and analytics, and reskilling of employees for an 'always on' digital culture leading to digital success.

Apart from the restructuring of businesses to optimally enable new customer, business partner and employee journeys, every citizen of a true digital nation will need to be informed and willingly embrace the culture and skills needed to participate and benefit from the digital economy.

Artificial Intelligence—The Game Changer

AI has the potential to add multiple jobs and also accelerate progress in discovery as well as citizen-centric innovations in every industry and every walk of life, although Einstein had said, 'Artificial Intelligence is no match for natural stupidity',[7] and many sceptics argue that putting AI at the centre of decision-making will only lead to reinforcement of biases and a denial of opportunity for human intelligence to explore new ways of thinking.

AI has increasingly been seen as a key creator of competitor advantage—for firms, societies and nations. An *IndustryWeek* report suggests that AI could add 15 trillion to the global economy by 2030, which is more than the reported current GDP of China.[8] China has made aggressive plans for AI, and India has developed a plan to add $957 billion, which could be 10 per cent of India's economy if India can touch a $10 trillion level in its GDP by 2030.

In *Rising to the China Challenge*, we have called out the woeful inadequacy of India's investments in high-quality research, education and innovation in the past, and this is one malaise that could affect AI too, with the threat that AI could also remain a hype component of seminars and rhetoric, with very little real action on the ground. On the contrary, both the US and China are in a head-to-head battle for leadership in AI, and China's investment in AI-enabled processes and even AI applications in smaller cities like Tianjin speaks to their ambition to succeed in this area. China introduced the New Generation Artificial Intelligence Development Plan in July 2017, called AIDP 2017, laying out a three-step plan to bring China's AI industry in line with global competitors in 2020 and reach global leadership status in many AI fields by 2025 and, finally, become the primary centre for AI innovation by 2030. The AIDP has some very specific initiatives—the development of intelligent and networked products like vehicles, service robots and identification systems; creation of a comprehensive support system, including intelligent sensors and neural network chips; development of intelligent manufacturing, which has always been China's forte; and investing in industry training and testing resources, and extensive cyber security. China, at this stage, is miles ahead of India in AI, and the controlled environment created by the administration is enabling the country to become a leading hub for AI developments.

Other G20 countries are also marching ahead. For instance, Japan unveiled an overarching AI strategy in 2017 for building its tech-infused, ultra-smart 'Society 5.0'. The manufacturing hub in Germany's Stuttgart-Tübingen area is transforming itself into an AI research hub, with critical support from the country's industrial giants like Daimler, BMW and Bosch. In 2017, Amazon committed to contribute $1.5 million to this collaborative research effort and a further $500,000 to fund individual research.[9] The European Commission's SPARC and Germany's Cyber Valley collaboration attract high levels of private sector funding and participation to execute the region's vision on AI.

India has to take wise and conscious steps towards building an AI economy, having lost some time in the past worrying about AI eliminating jobs, with the realization that assistive and augmentative AI can benefit the country substantially than autonomous AI. The trillion-dollar AI dream can be realized if AI adds 1.3 per cent to GDP growth annually and a scenario develops of AI applications in every segment of the economy, augmenting human work, adding autonomous value through the creation of new products and services, and enabling new shared platforms for education, healthcare, financial services, supply chains and government. MGI has pointed out that there are anecdotal examples of Indian companies quickly adopting AI and integrating it into their business, like Ola, which is now tracking traffic and attempting to improve customer experience; Myntra for fashion data and trend prediction; Urban Ladder for optimizing intra-city logistics and predicting product demand and returns; and Paytm for fraud detection and prevention. Our belief is that many of these successful case studies underline the power of augmentative AI, which enhances the capability of human beings rather than autonomous AI that could lead to large-scale loss of jobs.

The MeitY, working with NASSCOM, has recently created a 'policy group' to work out a policy framework and road map for emerging technologies, including AI, block chain and big data analytics. The Ministry of Commerce and Industry has constituted a task force on AI to explore possibilities for leveraging AI for development across various fields in manufacturing and services. In India, Niti Aayog, working with all the ministries on their AI strategy, called for leveraging AI not only for economic and military growth but also for social inclusion and touched upon all the hot topics of skills for youth, research investments and developing Indian-made AI solutions for the world. Key sectors for focus are healthcare, agriculture, education, smart cities and infrastructure, smart mobility, and transportation, all of which are excellent policy areas. The objective is to establish the country as an 'AI garage' to enable development of scalable solutions for India that can be implanted across all developing and emerging economies of the world.

Predictably, where the Indian agenda falls short is the absence of concrete plans and investments that will be so essential to create a trillion-dollar business opportunity. While China plans on competing with the West through civil–military fusion and large central and independent city investments, India expects that tighter collaboration between private, government, non-profits and educational institutions will provide a strong AI focus on social development and inclusive growth. India can hope that the fondness for India as a natural consequence of the reluctance to engage more with China will enable us to attract foreign partners and investors, and support future development. But the ecosystem must develop, and we have to create legal and even philosophical reasons to pursue the AI path. If the environment is right, the choices are well-made and investments are done in accordance with the needs of the community rather than the wants of a few, AI can truly hasten the linkages of digital progress with the real needs of the country, now and in the future!

Government Response—Positive Moves

Realizing the importance of achieving the trillion-dollar Digital India as an industry segment and as an enabler for growth in the rest of the economy has encouraged MeitY to chalk out a 1,000-day agenda in September 2021. A recent change of guard to the visionary leadership of Minister Ashwini Vaishnaw and Minister of State Rajeev Chandrasekhar, and the continuity provided in the bureaucracy by Secretary Ajay Sawhney give confidence that serious steps will be taken and an enabling environment be created in the country.

The key focus areas the ministry is expected to push are policy for encouraging investments, infrastructure readiness, including the much-delayed National Optical Fibre Network (NOFN) and talent to fuel India's big push to digitize every process and value-creating sector.

NASSCOM research studies and reports since 2019 have suggested multiple areas where government initiatives can help to accelerate the progress towards Digital India. Some of these include taking steps like a strong data protection bill that could increase global investor and customer confidence. Revamping the Information Technology Act 2000 and easing labour laws for the industry in key states and, finally, the ability for companies to easily exit from SEZs to higher taxation areas when the situation calls for it, would all make it easier for the industry to operate and companies to flourish.

Industry would also greatly benefit if the government embarks on a major brand-building agenda and showcases Indian capabilities in all embassies and trade fairs abroad. The engineering and R&D industry segments would particularly benefit from large government-supported 'show and tell' events in Germany, Japan and the US.

At a domestic level, on the lines of the famous STPI scheme and the easing of hardware imports in an earlier era that enabled the software services industry to really take off, the government could consider clear and consistent treatment of transfer pricing, clarification of GST treatment for R&D exports, and simplification of the import and export of equipment for R&D and prototyping.

In December 2021, the government announced a whopping $10 billion incentive plan to build the microprocessor industry in India.[10] While it is early days yet to predict which major initiative can lead to true success, the intent is clear and can be translated into robust action.

Imperatives for Digital India

India is well-positioned for the digital revolution if we can move on four fronts. First, investments made in digital connectivity need to be linked with its fast pace of urbanization. City planners can use modern technology to better manage congestion and pollution. Cities of all sizes need to better understand the opportunities provided by modern technologies. Advances in wireless sensor systems, ICT and infrastructure allow cities to collect and curate massive amounts of data capable of sustaining and improving urban life, thanks to the new and ever-growing web of connected technology—IoT. The linkages between urbanization and new technologies should be socially inclusive, which optimizes the use and minimizes the cost of digital technology in meeting the urban development goals.

Second, the focus of fiscal policy needs to be scaled up towards digital infrastructure investments. A vast majority of public investment in India still goes into traditional infrastructure (roads and highways), and truly little into digital infrastructure despite a much higher rate of return on investments in digital infrastructure.[11] This is unlike in China and the US, which have rapidly expanded its investments in digital infrastructure. The key to the digital foundation lies in increased access to dependable and less erratic electricity supply. Digital investments will need to be scaled up from billions to trillions to expand digital reach, digital depth and digital value.

Third, policymakers will need to promote a more competitive digital economy to ensure that innovative technologies do not become the province of a few firms that come first and it becomes a winner-takes-all story. Digital entrepreneurship can be scaled up by promoting the interoperability and data mobility across different enterprises, just like it was done with the traditional telephone system. This will enable consumers to use multiple digital data services and switch from an inferior digital service provider to a superior one. Providing greater choices to consumers will enable many more new digital enterprises to enter, promote innovation, improve efficiency and create more jobs.

Fourth, policymakers need to promote protection of personal data, and freedom of expression and opinion. Digital enterprises use personal data to develop descriptive, predictive and prescriptive analytics models that are able to provide more targeted recommendations to customers. This improves productivity but also creates huge downside risks. Personal data collected for one purpose has the potential of being misused for purposes that can harm individuals and societies. The more data are reused, the greater is this downside risk of data misuse. Protecting personal data can be challenging at the country level, given that digital data can move globally. A country-wide cooperation may be needed to support policies that secure both people and digital enterprises on which they depend.

The Digital Divide Concern

The potential downside of an accelerating Digital India is the possibility of a widening chasm between the digital haves and have-nots. We are already seeing situations in urban homes where the young internet hobbyist has become the choice maker and the procurer during the Covid-19 pandemic, when people did not venture out of their homes. As increasing adoption of digital technologies for more aspects of work and life becomes apparent, divides could happen within families, within organizations and across segments of society, with the younger digital adopters finding significant opportunities to succeed while the rest get or feel left behind.

One way of addressing this on a national basis is to ensure that there is widespread availability of digital education in the country. These could be provided through universities and colleges, skills lighthouses in urban slums and even common service centres in villages. The imperative must be to democratize digital access and ensure that digital facilities and platforms are accessible by all.

Another significant concern would be that of data and cyber security as platforms spring up for multiple needs and data starts flowing across the digital grid, getting stored centrally and locally in many clusters. It is extremely critical that security awareness and adequate tools and technologies proliferate in a fast-digitizing country, and every citizen has the confidence to leave old practices behind and embrace the digital.

PATHWAYS TO DIGITAL INDIA

The optional pathways to achieving the Digital India goals are the $1 trillion contribution to national GDP, the enabling of industry and society, the creation of new business and social models and the increase in prosperity for hundreds of millions of Indians.

The vision is clear and the opportunity is huge. If one takes stock of the pathways that open before a post-Covid-19 world, with all the credentials already established and the potential roadblocks identified, one can look at five open paths that the trillion-dollar journey can choose to take:

1. Spreading the depth and width of technology products and the service sector;
2. Growing the hardware and microprocessor industries;
3. Creating the platform economy for domestic and global success;
4. Developing globally capable talent; and
5. Unleashing entrepreneurship for the digital economy.

Spreading the tech products and services industry

The NASSCOM study[12] on the trillion-dollar opportunity has identified areas where some intense work is needed to accelerate the growth of the three key segments of IT and BPM services, engineering and R&D, and the nascent products segment of the industry. Some of these are essential points worth mentioning here.

In IT and ITES, Covid-19 has opened the opportunity for remote working, and with the government and private sector promise of spreading easy-connectivity buying in the key IT cities, it is very conceivable that at least 15 to 20 new cities can emerge where at least a few hundred thousand jobs can be created. These will also enable small entrepreneurs to create firms that support larger companies, and women and differently abled folks to participate in a much bigger way in the workforce. With some government support, the industry could also substantially enhance the quality of faculty development in the major colleges and universities, and provide digital platforms for skills upgradation for individuals and classroom participants to upgrade the capabilities to the new needs of product development and deep technology capabilities.

In the engineering and R&D space, a strong focus on smart manufacturing and industry partnerships would enable clusters of capability to emerge that would benefit both the engineering services and core manufacturing industry within each segment. Centres of excellence in areas such as alternative energy, connected and electric vehicles, and digital health could come up as virtual superclusters in various parts of the country, encouraging both domestic and global industry consumption. Talent development would be a logical extension of this initiative, with apprenticeships at the entry level and industry-supported industrial masters and doctoral programmes, enabling India to emulate the best of American and Chinese practices in these areas.

In the product space, there is a clear need for government–industry–academia partnerships to shift the focus away from just programming and software services skills to product design and engineering, and building talent with deep technical and management skills for product development. India must also participate in and eventually lead the booming demand for B2B SaaS companies. According to a 2021 report compiled by McKinsey & Company and SaasBOOMi, a community of industry leaders, the Indian SaaS industry could itself have a trillion-dollar potential by 2030 and create half a million new jobs. There are nearly a thousand such start-ups already in India, 10 of which are unicorns with over a billion-dollar value each, with the industry mascot being Freshworks, with a successful IPO end of 2020 and a multi-billion-dollar valuation.[13]

The potential to dominate the SaaS marketplace stems from the same reason that built the IT and BPM services industry—the availability of a large pool of technically competent English-speaking talent in the country at relatively low cost. This enables SaaS companies to serve both small and large companies in global markets and, unlike India's oldest unicorns InMobi and Flipkart, which have focussed on the domestic market, have an enormous global market to serve with their products and platforms.

Core ICT Services—Hardware and Semiconductors

Beyond the tremendous hype created by the traditional industry, which has been discussed in the earlier section, lies an enormous opportunity that has been talked about but has not received the leadership attention or investments it deserves. The success of countries like Taiwan, Thailand and China and the recent problem of chip supplies for major corporations, including the automotive sector, underscores the enormous significance of the core electronics industry that is at the heart of virtually all smart devices and processes. The critical element of this new frontier dream is to build the ecosystem for electronics and semiconductor chip design and manufacturing. Today, India imports 100 per cent of the chips, memories, microprocessors and other components required by its electronics industry, and this has serious implications for India's economy and national security.[14]

The total available market (TAM) for the global core electronics industry (also called core ICT) has been pegged at $1.78 trillion and expected to grow to $5 trillion by 2030. The core ICT is organized into two layers.[15]

1. **Design companies:** These companies architect and design semiconductor chips and create IPs and build electronic systems using them. Semiconductors include processors, wireless chips, AI engines, chipsets, etc. Systems include

mobiles, computers, routers, server farms, data centres, storage, wireless base stations, etc. Design companies contribute to total $1 trillion, of which semiconductors contribute $350 billion and systems $650 billion.

2. **Manufacturing companies:** This is where the semiconductor chips are designed and IPs get fabricated, and the products from the system companies get manufactured and put together as end products. Manufacturing companies contribute a total of $780 billion, which include semiconductor fabrication, components, and assembly and test, contributing $550 billion, $150 billion and $80 billion, respectively.

The layer 1 companies do not actually need their own fabrication facilities. They are called 'fabless' design companies and contribute a significant $1 trillion out of the $1.78 trillion TAM. The manufacturing of semiconductors is outsourced to dedicated pure-play fabrication facilities (called fabs), such as Taiwan Semiconductor Manufacturing Company Limited (TSMC), GlobalFoundries Inc. (GF), etc. Fabs contribute to $550 billion of the TAM. There are a few design companies who also have captive fabrication facility, called integrated device manufacturer (IDM). Many IDM companies have been moving to the fabless model over the last two decades due to extremely high costs involved in owning, maintaining and periodically upgrading their foundries.

What does India need to be successful in this vital sector and where are we placed?

- **Competent workforce of semiconductor technologists and engineers supported by good universities/institutions for both training manpower and research.** India is very well placed on this, with the presence of top semiconductor chip companies' design centres like Texas Instruments, Broadcom, Intel, Qualcomm, etc., with highly trained engineers for more than two decades now. There is also the presence of semiconductor product companies such as Cisco. India contributes a staggering 20 per cent of the global semiconductor workforce![16] However, unlike the IT services industry where many entrepreneurs created large companies with significant support from industry association and favourable policies created by the then Department of Electronics, which morphed into the MeitY, the aspirations on semiconductor professionals have remained stranded without a real industry structure created to help them to scale. We must translate the capabilities of these professionals into business opportunities.

- **Critical mass of fabless semiconductor companies with expertise in commercial chip development activities.** India has many chip start-up companies, but they are spread too thin in many areas with inadequate critical mass, leaving gaps and poor synergies. We must systematically nurture and leverage the above-mentioned talent and aspiration combination, and turn it into a large number of fabless start-up opportunities for them.
- **Strong domestic demand for semiconductor chips for local consumption and solving India-specific problems.** Despite high consumption of semiconductor chips, we do not define our own specifications but only use whatever is available internationally. We need to start driving India-centric chip specifications.
- **Predictable and semiconductor-sector-friendly policies and incentives from the central and state governments.** Lot of work is being done by the Government of India currently, but we need to accelerate it into the fabless space.
- **Expertise in planning and executing complex mega-projects.** Process plants, technical expertise, management of an ecosystem for procurement of raw materials, chemicals, etc., as chipmaking is less about electronics and more about chemistry, raw materials, process mastery,

heavy equipment and supply chain. India has both public as well as private companies with strong expertise in this area, albeit in the non-semiconductor space, which can be leveraged for the semiconductor fab domain through joint ventures.

- **Semiconductor fabs and allied capabilities such as assembly, testing and IC packaging, etc.** There are just a few government-funded fabs such as the Semi-Conductor Laboratory (SCL), but they are not state-of-the-art. A few companies exist in the testing and packaging space. India has the opportunity to leverage and strengthen its new-found political proximity to Taiwan.

It is clear that fabless design is a strong driver and high-impact component in building the overall ecosystem. Fabless activity needs much lower capital investment and higher return-on-investment (ROI). The focus on fabless activity will help India move up in the value chain much faster, with much higher ROI. The PLI schemes are already attracting global smartphone manufacturers to India and can potentially catalyse other ecosystem activities, including fabless semiconductor design, if suitable policy and incentive structures are put in place.

Electronics Manufacturing

We have had a great start with the PLI scheme for smartphones by attracting many mobile manufacturers so far. Given that India, with its billion-strong population, is one of the leading consumers of mobile phones, the immediate focus can be on PLI schemes for original design manufacturers (ODMs), original equipment manufacturers (OEMs) for the manufacture of mobile phones and its components and subsystems such as BTLE/GPS/NavIC, Li-Ion batteries, power management integrated circuits (PMIC), mobile sensors and associated electronics, wireless connectivity, audio subsystems and creative wearable devices. This will provide large employment opportunities for skilled and unskilled labour. This prong will also accelerate the development of specialized start-up clusters around various ODMs/OEMs.

In an announcement made in December 2021, the Government of India pledged ₹76,000 crore of incentives for fab semiconductor investors in India.[17] This is part of the Modi government's bid to make the country a hub for electronics. The announcement came almost a year after the government sought expressions of interest from companies to this effect.

Smartphone OEMs work with a variety of ODMs for their subsystems, such as app processor subsystems, radio and modems, sensors, battery, PMIC, display, peripherals, cameras, audio subsystems, etc. ODMs are in charge of the subsystems—specs, design and sourcing—and can potentially work with local IC suppliers for their design requirements. Hence, we can leverage the existing PLI engagements and give surgical focus to the ODMs and OEMs to enable and accelerate the growth of local fabless companies. The Government of India needs to target the selected subsystems and provide the right policies and irresistible incentives to those ODMs to set up their shops in India. After this, one can rope in relevant fabless companies to support the ODMs in close proximity by setting up design clusters.

Workspaces where multiple start-ups can share common resources, collaborate and potentially build on each other's strengths are highly beneficial. One way to do this is to create start-up accelerator clusters. For every cluster, we can establish an experts committee to identify and nurture selected start-ups, provide initial funding and business-related mentoring (approx. ₹1–2 crore per design start-up), make available fab technology process design kits (PDKs) and electronic design automation (EDA) tools for a few years, provide test chip fabrication, prototyping and prototesting financial support and also support patents and IP creation, and make business networks available to the start-ups to facilitate venture capital connections. Opening up state-owned fabs like SCL/Indian Space Research Organisation (ISRO) to private players/start-ups for design-in and shuttle programmes can be of great mutual benefit to both start-ups and foundries.

The workforce for these initiatives can be built by creating policies and a conducive environment for talented engineers showing strong entrepreneurial aspirations to venture into start-ups. This can be achieved by creating a support system to address their concerns, such as covering their livelihood, business funding, policies, overall environment to get commercial success. This should also include overseas Indian chip experts who are interested in setting up start-ups in India. Strengthening collaboration with top engineering institutions/universities will help tap into the research faculties and students to participate in real industry problems early on. Formation of centres of excellence for R&D in targeted domains will help in this regard. The creation of a repository of key problems in electronics our nation needs to solve—requirements, specifications, sponsors—can feed into the centres of excellence to work on, and eventually some of them might turn into viable start-ups.

On the funding side, it is good to see government-backed initiatives such as the Karnataka Semiconductor Venture Capital Fund (KARSEMVEN Fund), but it has a very small corpus. It is crucial to encourage the big private players of the Indian industry who have the venture capital funds in different technology areas to participate in truly scaling up the semiconductor fabless activity by introducing their semiconductor-specific venture capital funds. The government needs to address their concerns and incentivize the private players to bring out such semiconductor venture funds.

Building the Ecosystem

There is a unique geopolitical transition happening in India's favour, offering a window of opportunity to build and strengthen India's semiconductor ecosystem and eventually become a key player in the global semiconductor industry. Foremost is India's rising international image—there are issues the world is facing with China on the supply chain side, and there is urgency for geographical de-risking of the fabs, which are presently geographically concentrated. While India is already developing proximity to Taiwan, the nation is also aggressively focussing on Digital India and 'Aatmanirbhar Bharat' and has launched PLI schemes for electronics and mobile manufacturing. India needs to take the fullest advantage of these unique geopolitical transitions.

It is imperative to create an autonomous, deep-expertise and high-powered semiconductor nodal agency that will oversee the semiconductor ecosystem development—identify weak areas, and synergize and engage with the right institutions, companies and government departments to first build and strengthen a fabless design ecosystem, followed by mini-fabs and then, ultimately, indigenous fabs. This initiative, in congruence with an expanding investor base in other areas of hardware and electronics, can deliver half a trillion itself in the next 10 years. Let us not miss the bus this time.

Creating the Platform Economy

The areas of opportunity we have indicated, focussed on capability building across all ends of the ICT spectrum, can push global solutions developed in India to well over a half a trillion-dollar level by 2026 and will push up industry employment to over 10 million. But the country still needs over 300 million fresh jobs to be created and existing industries brought to world-class capability by 2030. Here, digital enablement has a key role in the creation and proliferation of digital platforms, each of which could add $50 to $150 billion to the economy.

A digital platform in its simplest definition uses a core product or series of connected products to build a multi-user environment that can enable a seamless and effective 'pay-per-use' economy. The current hype over B2B SaaS is itself a by-product of the realization that ownership of software assets is a phenomenon of the past, and it is access to the latest and most user-friendly tools and processes that will drive usage and collaboration.

As mentioned elsewhere, UPI as a platform for payments and uncomplicated financial transactions on the internet has been a pioneer for the platform economy in India. In fact, UPI, along with Aadhaar for over a billion Indian citizens and residents, and CoWIN, the app created for tracking and registering citizens in Covid-19 times, have been hailed as the three largest digital platforms in the world.[18]

The evolution of Digital India will happen through the availability of digital infrastructure from powerful quantum computing and 5G hubs through the major metros and smaller towns to the panchayats and villages in every district in the country. The obvious advantages of a homogeneous availability of connectivity is what the technology services industry has already seen—the redistribution of jobs from larger cities to smaller locations and the ability of every citizen to access a variety of services and products from wherever they are in the country.

In productive sectors of the economy, platforms will be all-pervasive in the following fields:

- **Manufacturing:** With smart manufacturing and Industry 4.0 solutions helping large companies to integrate information flows from manufacturing execution systems, IoT and enterprise resource planning systems, the reach out to first- and second-tier suppliers has already started, and supply and demand chains are being optimized. However, the big benefit of digital manufacturing platforms will be the potential collaboration within and between SME clusters. In this regard, a role model is DIGICOR, which is a consortium of eleven organizations from Germany, Netherlands, Greece, United Kingdom, Czech Republic and Italy. DIGICOR provides tools, platforms, consulting and digital services that enable collaborative networks to be formed and succeed through innovation. Smaller companies are also enabled to cater to the demand of large OEMs.

The ability for SMEs to collaborate with information that is beneficial to a community rather than just one firm and to find matches with similar entities or with those higher or lower in the product value chain assists in the development of synergistic supply chains that can greatly reduce costs in the system. With India having traditionally suffered in comparison to China in terms of logistics and transportation, digital manufacturing platforms will enable us to catch up and ensure the participation of large numbers of companies in every manufacturing sector.

- **Agriculture:** India watchers and industry participants will remember the successful experiment of e-Choupal that one of our successful companies, ITC, had launched decades ago in 2000. With the new agriculture laws creating their own sense of uncertainty about the future of farming and the nature of industry participants in the sector, the availability of digital portals accessible to every farmer and participant in the vast ecosystem of agriculture in the country will greatly increase product and information availability, and enable informed choices on what to grow, how best to do it and how to distribute agricultural produce to the consumer in new 'farm to fork' supply chain models.
- **Healthcare:** Telehealth and digital solutions for diagnostics and remote treatment have already been legitimized and brought into the mainstream by the distancing imperatives of Covid-19. As the initiatives under Ayushman Bharat progress, and primary, secondary and tertiary healthcare providers integrate their service delivery across the length and breadth of the country, national- and district-level digital platforms can integrate all product and service providers and enable every citizen to access healthcare

in an efficient and timely manner.

- **Entertainment:** The proliferation of entertainment options such as Netflix, Amazon Prime, Voot and SonyLiv has already brought entertainment with amazing customer experience to the screens of consumers and made the need to travel for a cinema or theatre a non-essential activity, although connoisseurs of good art and theatre will always still prefer the experience of going to a concert or show. The recent announcement of Meta and the immersive experiences promised by Facebook, and the enormous potential of augmented, virtual and mixed reality for both education and entertainment are likely to see the launch of entertainment communities similar to online gaming around the world that will change the face of media and entertainment in significant ways.

  One of India's most successful digital history and culture companies—LHI (Live History India) Digital has begun to curate personalized experiences that enable their prime customers to have immersive experiences of places and historical happenings. These will soon become the norm in the digital world.

  Digital platforms are the future, and the country can easily generate the half a billion new capabilities needed to make the trillion-dollar Digital India agenda successful, if platforms are conceptualized thoughtfully, implemented wisely and used effectively.

Building globally capable talent

This is addressed in detail in a later chapter. As the MeitY and NASSCOM have shown with the successful launch of FutureSkills Prime for technology skills, providing platforms where skills providers can deliver solutions and aspirants can access from a wide variety of options will be critical to the success of a digitally enabled India.

Entrepreneurship unleashed

This is also addressed in detail in a later chapter. With the prime minister of India exhorting youth to be job givers and not takers and the 'Start Up India Stand Up India' slogan resonating well with the youth, digital platforms for identification and enabling entrepreneurs to take flight in millions across the country will be one of the big pillars on which the India of 2030 can and should be built.

CONCLUSION

How does a country with challenges of poverty, excessive urban congestion and an escalating sense of digital divide embark on a robust strategy to accomplish first a trillion-dollar digital economy and, finally, a true digital nation where every process and every citizen is empowered digitally? Keeping in mind the imperatives mentioned above, the recent steps announced by the MeitY are welcome because they will pave the way to digital infrastructure, including the completion of last-mile internet connectivity with the NOFN, and a robust open data policy that will ensure that safe exchange and interchange of data is possible for core needs of the citizens, like healthcare, education, skills and employment.

The rest will be the responsibility of the smart cities and smart villages czars, in the public and private sector, who must pitch in to build platforms for the ecosystem to come together. The path has already been lit by Aadhaar and UPI, with payment platforms now being adopted even by small retailers in urban and semi-rural locations. Many more digital platforms for agriculture, healthcare, SMEs in industry and employment will need to come up, and with the rapid spread of mobile phones, potentially accelerated further by 5G and quantum computing, it is conceivable that every child will enjoy blended learning that lifts education beyond the capability of mediocre schools, and every youth will be able to choose their vocation and get the skills needed to enter employment or entrepreneurship for a sustainable livelihood, with every vocation empowered through easy access, analytics and opportunity enhancement.

The five pathways we have advocated in this chapter will get us to the trillion-dollar Digital India—by 2026, if we are able to accelerate the deployment of digital infrastructure. The youth of the nation will work towards digital success if the ecosystem is built to support them.

3

NEW MODEL FOR URBAN DEVELOPMENT IN INDIA

Ejaz Ghani

There are two schools of thought globally and specifically in India on which way our growth should be—should we continue to accelerate the process of urbanization and let large aggregations of people and commerce in the top 50 to 100 urban locations become the key engines of growth? Or should we aggressively pursue a path of moving businesses and jobs from urban to rural India and ensure that the digital divide is reduced and every Indian gets a chance to participate in the future growth and success of the economy?

At the risk of making a sweeping generalization, one could argue that the world's two leading powers of the day, China and the US, have chosen different paths to reach the level of success they have achieved. China has invested heavily in their large cities, incidentally in the Yangtze and Pearl Deltas and, later, even in the heartland of the country. All of their megacities—Shanghai, Beijing, Shenzhen, Tianjin, to name just a few—have large budgets and a concrete plan to become world-class investment destinations. The city mayors are fully empowered, their investments in technology and even new initiatives like AI are sometimes more than what other countries in the region invest nationally, and they have made their cities the true engines of their growth story. In the US, however, regions like Silicon Valley and full states like New York and Illinois have been developed, and citizens living in small towns in these states enjoy the same level of digital, physical and social infrastructure that people living in San Francisco, Washington DC, Chicago or New York City would.[1]

India has a choice to make—to accelerate the process of job redistribution and ensure that the NOFN and empowerment of all rural areas are taken up in mission mode and completed, or just take the enormous urban sprawls like Mumbai, Delhi, Kolkata and Bengaluru and substantially improve infrastructure and mobility in these cities and enable a hundred more smart cities to develop and compete for global investment attention.

THE CASE FOR URBANIZATION

By 2030, India's urban population will increase to 600 million people, twice the current size of the US. The pace of India's urbanization will be 100 times the speed of the first country in the world to urbanize, the United Kingdom.[2] India has the benefit of being a latecomer to urbanization, to improve the economic and social landscape for economic growth, job creation, congestion management and climate change. Technological innovations will enable latecomers to urbanization leapfrog and benefit from the fourth industrial revolution and the spread of AI in urban management, and innovations in construction material and new modes of transport to improve mobility. Connectivity, proximity and diversity will accelerate knowledge diffusion, spark innovation and enhance productivity and job growth. Unlike other countries that are confronting an ageing population, India's urbanization will benefit from a young population.

While India's vision of urbanization is filled with promises, urbanization also poses enormous challenges—how to make cities more competitive, manage congestion and pollution, and make urbanization more inclusive. How India manages urbanization will influence its future economic and social growth trajectory. Policymakers and urban planners need better insights on how urbanization and industrialization interact. What makes cities more entrepreneurial and attract more entrepreneurs? Do cities go through specialization or diversification? Which cities will create more jobs? How will urbanization impact India's climate change agenda?

URBANIZATION AND INDUSTRIALIZATION

Urbanization has long been recognized as a key ingredient in industrialization and growth. Urbanization and industrialization are meant to go hand in hand. Structural transformation shifts growth and jobs out of agriculture in the rural areas and into manufacturing in the urban areas. But this transformation has now been threatened by the demons of congestion and high land costs in cities.

In the early 1990s, India's manufacturing sector walked hand in hand with urbanization. This process has reversed from 2000 onwards, with the pace of de-urbanization of manufacturing gathering momentum. India's pace of urbanization and industrialization have diverged.

India has experienced what some have called premature de-industrialization or a secular slowdown in the manufacturing trend. The share of the organized manufacturing sector in urban employment has declined dramatically. The organized manufacturing sector, which accounts for over 80 per cent of India's manufacturing output, has also become more rural.

This de-urbanization of manufacturing is more pronounced in large-scale manufacturing industries that are more land-intensive. Informal enterprises, which are less land-intensive, are moving into urban locations in search of a better physical infrastructure.[3]

The divergence between urbanization and industrialization has the potential to transform rural areas into urban areas and give birth to tier 2 and 3 cities. This has the potential to generate 70 per cent of the country's new jobs and drive a four-fold increase in per capita incomes.[4] This will be associated with more efficient allocation of industry between urban and rural settings. Empirical evidence has shown that India has experienced a decline in spatial mismatch since the early 1990s.[5] Districts with large initial spatial mismatch have experienced reduced mismatch over time. Districts with a more educated workforce and better physical infrastructure have shown stronger declines in spatial mismatch.

This improvement in spatial location mismatch has improved the allocation of enterprises across both the organized and unorganized sectors. The reduction in spatial mismatch amongst small enterprises was much faster than in large enterprises. It is very important for policymakers to recognize that much of the urbanization that is occurring in India is in the unorganized sector, and this trend needs to be integrated into urban plans, land allocation, zoning regulations, and in government procurement schemes and policymaking processes. The more that Indian cities recognize this influx and design appropriate policies and investments to support it, the more effective the policy interventions will be. The spatial relocation of manufacturing into rural areas raises big questions. Is rural development just about raising agriculture productivity or should it be broader in its scope to also promote industrialization and urbanization?

SPECIALIZATION OR DIVERSIFICATION?

Should cities grow through specialization or diversification? This is not a new debate, as it dates back to Alfred Marshall and Jane Jacobs. A city becomes more specialized when the degree to which one industry concentrated in that city is much higher compared to the national average. The diversity of a city measures its industrial composition by looking across all industries in that city and the degree to which the city resembles the national average.

Is India's urbanization being driven by specialization or

diversification? Are Indian cities more specialized or diversified compared to the US? In 1991, around the time of India's economic liberalization, the manufacturing sector displayed greater specialization. It also showed greater spatial variation in specialization across cities. These trends have changed over time. Cities have become more diversified and their spatial variation has diluted.

Of the 600 districts in India, some districts have chosen to specialize in specific products. Examples are Kavaratti (water transport), Darjeeling (paper products), Panchkula (office accounting and computing machinery) and Wokha (wood products).[6] Other districts that also stand out in specialization include Dhubri, Bhopal, Gorakhpur, Saharsa and Jamnagar. The least specialized districts are Bhiwani and Nellore.[7]

The districts that are more diversified include Mahbubnagar, Palghat, Trichur, Jalna, Sivaganga, Parganas, Hugli and Neemuch. The least diversified districts are Nizamabad and Bhavnagar. Some major urban centres, such as Mumbai and Bangalore, have experienced the largest declines in specialization and diversified rapidly.

An industry-oriented perspective to specialization and diversification can provide deeper insights into how technological changes could impact future patterns of urbanization. Specialization tends to be much higher in traditional industries compared to modern industries. Roughly three-quarters of districts in India that have higher specialization levels have relied on traditional industry. Some modern industries—such as back office, accounting and computing machinery, and radio, television and communication equipment and apparatus—also tend to be located in more specialized districts.

Although India's specialization levels were much higher than in the US in the early 1990s, it has converged over time. India's urbanization pattern is now comparable to specialization and diversification levels observed in the US.

INCREASING JOBS

What about the link between urbanization and jobs? Evidence suggests that job growth is linked more to diversification than specialization. Cities and districts that are more diversified have experienced greater employment growth. Initial clusters of modern services have also experienced abnormally high employment growth post 2000.

The strongest expressions of job growth due to diversification are in settings not often linked to the benefits of diversity. These effects are much sharper in rural areas of the districts and among small enterprises. India's emerging urbanization trends highlight the inclusive nature of its urban awakening. The local reach of urban diversity to job creation is much deeper in India than previously expected. Evidence also shows that high growth rates fuelling greater poverty reduction are also concentrated in the rural areas of these districts.

A case in point is one of the fast-growing tier 2 cities, Pune, which has a total population now in excess of 6 million, with a diversified focus on manufacturing, technology centres, and scientific research and entrepreneurship. The city, which is not a state capital, being the largest urban centre in the country, has the disadvantages of poor urban transport systems, a military airport that serves to handle the fast-growing civilian traffic and two inadequately funded municipal corporations. Much of the infrastructure creation that has happened has been pushed either by the builders of the city or by the demands of multinationals who have ensured that new manufacturing areas like Chakan and technology areas like Hinjewadi get the support they need to enable industry to come in and grow. The city is still able to grow and succeed because it has great institutions in education and skills. Education is through the ancient Pune University and many new private universities, such Symbiosis, MIT, FLAME, etc., which have ensured that supply of talent for the city's fast-growing new industry sectors is excellent.

On the skills side, a unique public-private partnership between the Pune and Pimpri Chinchwad Municipal Corporations (PMC and PCMC) with a local entity, Pune City Connect, has seen tens of thousands of youth from the slums acquire a sense of agency or responsibility for their own livelihoods, acquire English conversational competence and digital literacy, and their empowerment and embarking on a skills journey of their own choosing, leading to entrepreneurship or jobs. The success of this venture can be attributed partly to the meticulous design of the intervention personalized to every individual's want and partly to the collaborative model where the government provides the capital expenditure, philanthropic organizations and corporate social responsibility (CSR) provide the operating expenses and the entire skills ecosystem of the city finds a place in providing their content to youth who choose their skill area.

The complementarity of the formal university education system with the industrial training institutes that provide blue-collar skills and the skills lighthouses that prepare youth for multiple service sector jobs has enabled Pune to rise above its infrastructural limitations and become an aspirational city for people to live and work in. Potentially, at least 60 cities could follow this model, and it is not surprising that Pune City Connect in a new avatar of Lighthouse Communities Foundation is now setting up skills lighthouses in the key cities of Delhi and Odisha, and plans to spread the public-private partnership model across Maharashtra, Karnataka, Telangana and the Northeastern states in the next five years. Will we see a model emerge by 2030 where not just the capital cities of all the states but a few dozen more would choose a development and infrastructure strengthening model that enables no child or youth to be left behind? That would truly be an interesting outcome.

URBANIZATION AND CLIMATE CHANGE

India's manufacturing sector is spatially dispersing, and low-density manufacturing districts are growing faster than high-density large cities. Both trade and transport connectivity seem to be playing important roles in spatial development.

How has the migration of manufacturing plants out of urban sectors into rural areas impacted climate change? As major cities de-industrialize, how much has local particulate matter, ambient sulfur dioxide and water pollution decreased? For growing factories located in the exporting cities, is their energy consumption per worker growing faster than the average factory? What are the greenhouse gas emissions implications of a geographical shift in the location of industrial production? If land and energy inputs are complements, has industrial sector development in India and electricity consumption increased because firms are moving to areas where land is cheaper?

Based on an emissions inventory for major cities in India, industry is responsible for 70 per cent of local air pollution. Empirical work in the US and Eastern Europe has highlighted how local air pollution declines as de-industrialization takes place.[8] We recognize that there are other major pollution sources in developing countries, including vehicle growth.[9]

Our empirical methodology is focussed on estimating pollution production regressions in a similar spirit as Kahn's (1999) study of US counties.[10] The unit of analysis was the city's ambient air pollution measured either as sulfur dioxide or particulate concentrations. Industries can contribute to local pollution either from the direct emissions they produce or by consuming ample amounts of electricity that is generated using nearby coal-fired power plants. Estimates of this ambient pollution production function can be used to study how industrial contraction improves a city's ambient air quality. Estimating this pollution production function requires data on ambient pollution, information on the geography and scale, and attributes of manufacturing activity.

Our analysis exploited the plant-level data for India and on the spatial nature of Indian manufacturing and environmental quality (ambient air quality) in the post-globalization era at the district level. The unit of our ambient air quality data was the city, but that of the manufacturing data is the district. In the ASI unit-level data for India, the factory code contains the location characteristics, including the state, district and urban/rural. The data contains information on each plant's industrial code, location and scale of economic activity, and use of key inputs such as labour, energy and electricity. We matched our city-level ambient environmental quality data to the corresponding district-level data in the state in order to build our final database with trade, manufacturing and air quality information.

City-level annual pollution data are available for air quality for the last two decades in India. The four air pollutants of SOx, NOx (sulphur oxides and nitrogen oxides), suspended particulate matter (SPM) and PM10 (particulate matter with a diameter of 10 microns or less) are monitored more regularly, and information on some additional pollutants (e.g., respirable lead, ammonia) is available for some years for major cities. The Indian apex environmental agency, Central Pollution Control Board, initiated air quality monitoring in 1984 under the National Ambient Air Quality Monitoring Programme (subsequently renamed National Air Monitoring Programme) starting with seven cities, and the network now covers 344 cities and towns.[11] The ambient air quality data is available as annual average with standard deviation, reported separately for each pollutant for the cities. This is the most extensive environmental quality data available for India. The data covers 127 cities across 26 Indian states now (less for the earlier years), so they correspond to a subset of the total number of districts in India (640).[12] Recent public health studies have measured how exposure to particulate matter is associated with elevated mortality rates.[13] These figures can be used to estimate how many statistical lives are saved because of the migration of industrial activity away from major cities.

Consider the following algebra example. Consider a city with 10 million people. If industrial migration away from this city reduces particulate matter by 5 units and if each unit of particulates raises the probability of death by 1 in 100,000, then the emissions reduction saves 500 lives in this city. As India's economy grows, the value of a statistical life increases,[14] and the social benefits of this industrial shift grow.

A potentially valid concern is that a type of 'zero sum' game emerges as heavy industries close in major cities and reopen in areas with a comparative advantage in exporting to other nations. Such destination areas would experience economic growth and pollution growth, and thus, their net standard of living would be overstated by regional gross national product (GNP) growth. Environmental economists have emphasized two counterpoints in the face of this criticism. First, new capital tends to be cleaner than older capital because they go into the 'green' economy. This is the 'technique effect', where emissions per unit of output are lower for newer factories. It is true that this is less likely to be the case if the export regions are poor and do not enforce environmental regulations. This has been borne out in China, where there has been negative correlation between FDI flows to Chinese cities and local air pollution. While in the past, scholars have argued that FDI is positively correlated with local pollution (because more inflows of capital are used to build dirty factories), Zhang et al. argue that China's cities receiving FDI are also receiving better information to build cleaner factories.[15] In the case of India, we will test this hypothesis using panel data across India to test for pollution increases in geographic areas experiencing industrial production growth.

In the case of India's cities, we can test for whether new factories lead to less pollution degradation (for the same level of production) in cities where the factories have been opened relative to the pollution impact from older factories in the same industries located in other cities. The simple way to test this is for us to create a measure of industrial activity for industry l in city j at time t from new factories versus old factories. In the regression equation, one of the key variables in the X vector will be total electricity consumption in location j at time t. As industry moves to the region, this will increase. Since much of India's power is generated using coal, which is a dirty fossil fuel, increased coal consumption will increase local pollution indicators such as particulates and sulfur dioxide.

This discussion highlights the importance of measuring how much a district's total electricity consumption increases as it becomes an export hub. This question can be answered by using data from two firm-level surveys, the Annual Survey of Industries (ASI) and the one conducted by the National Sample Survey Organization (NSSO).[15] The ASI survey has information on the so-called organized manufacturing sector (essentially comprising firms with electricity and more than 10 workers), whereas the NSSO covers the unorganized manufacturing sector and the service sector. Both surveys overlap for the fiscal years 1989–90, 1994–95, 2000–01, 2005–06, and 2010–11. This data can be used to test whether growing factories located in the export cities are consuming more energy per worker than the average factory in non-export cities in the rest of the nation.

What are the implications in terms of greenhouse gas emissions of the geographical shift in the location of industrial production? Using manufacturing plant-level data, we can observe the energy consumption of each factory and its geographic location. If land and energy are complements in production, then export factories that move to locations where land is cheaper should consume more energy (holding the vintage of the factory constant). The greenhouse gas implications of this 'industrial sprawl' hinge on the carbon emissions factor of the region's power plants. Intuitively, if coal is the energy source at power plants, then the carbon implications of this industrial production will be much larger than if natural gas or renewables are used. These issues have been examined in China and the US.[16]

Where are nascent green technology export industries clustering? With the focus on renewables, India has been importing renewable power equipment such as wind turbines and solar panels mainly from the US. While early work in the area of green technology proliferation has focussed on the country aggregate, microdata is now available in various parts of the country on the increased focus of the green tech sector. Just as California is an important hub for green tech, what is the equivalent in India? As we anticipate increased growth of such industries, which parts of India will specialize in these? Policymakers need to understand the root causes of this trade and geographical comparative advantage to draw policy lessons on the role of human capital, strategic subsidies and path dependence.

THE FUTURE OF URBANIZATION

India has experienced a slowdown in the growth of the manufacturing sector, much like the rest of the world. But this has not restrained the pace and scale of urbanization and economic growth. Urbanization has accelerated, especially in districts with access to better infrastructure. Key to the pace and scale of urbanization are investments in infrastructure. A majority of people in the developing world live without access to electricity and roads, and more than half a billion people lack access to drinking water in the developing world.

The future of India's urban awakening will be shaped by investments in roads, electricity and water. This will require improving the efficiency of public spending as well as increasing private investments. Infrastructure investments offer an opportunity to resolve the global disconnect between high-income countries with an ageing population and excess savings in search of higher yields, and low-income countries with a younger population and growing infrastructure investment needs.

Less than one per cent of $68 trillion global funds managed by pension funds, life insurance and others go towards infrastructure investments.[17] City governments and municipalities will encounter challenges in mobilizing private investments due to the small size of projects and low risk appetite among investors. But these challenges can be countered with local visionary leadership. City governments will need to identify infrastructure projects that promote entrepreneurship, make cities more competitive and ramp up spatial development through increased urban–rural connectivity. Local governments can attract private investments by leveraging assets, including land, mobilizing user revenue and modifying financial regulations/incentives to increase the risk appetite of investors. They will also need to build technical and financial capacity. Access to better infrastructure will enable millions more entrepreneurs, especially women-headed small enterprises, to benefit from the urban awakening.

The movement of economic activity in Indian manufacturing between urban to rural areas has strategic implications. Different parts of India's manufacturing sector are moving in different directions. While the organized sector is becoming less urbanized, the unorganized sector is becoming more urbanized. This process has been most closely linked to greater urbanization changes in districts with high education levels; a second role is mostly evident for public infrastructure as well. On the whole, these urbanization changes have improved modestly the urban–rural allocation of industries within India's districts.

However, the movement of organized sector plants in manufacturing to rural areas is surprising, given the relative youth of India's manufacturing sector. Perceived wisdom is that this sluggishness, in part, is due to the limits imposed by India's poor infrastructure and weaker education levels, among other factors like strict building regulations.[18] Our work supports these claims. Continued investment in these factors, beyond their direct effects for Indian businesses, will also provide beneficial effects from an urbanization and spatial allocation perspective.

Policymakers should take an inclusionary rather than exclusionary approach to the urban informal economy. It is very important to recognize that much of the urbanization is in the unorganized sector. Moreover, education and infrastructure investments, regardless of original motivation, are primarily operating through the unorganized sector. There should be adequate provision of urban infrastructure for the informal sectors to develop. The more Indian cities recognize this influx and design appropriate policies and investments to support it, the more effective the policy interventions will be. Urban planners need to scale up the emphasis on informal livelihood, which is neither taxed nor monitored by the government, and integrate it into urban plans, land allocation and zoning regulations to ensure that the urban informal workforce can gain access to urban infrastructures and markets. The organizations of urban informal enterprises can be invited to participate in policy forums and government procurement schemes.

Sharper differences in urban–rural wage levels will decrease the pace of India's urbanization. These effects are most pronounced in the unorganized sector. District land area and urban population are not important. Higher build-up area is strongly associated with increased urbanization. Cost factors in the real estate market may also be present in labour markets.

The multiple layers of central, state and municipal urban regulations that can contribute to an artificial urban land shortage in India will need to be streamlined. Urban land prices are abnormally high in relation to India's household income, and households consume less floor space than they could afford if the regulatory environment were reformed. In addition, some regulations have a negative impact on the spatial structure of cities. By unreasonably reducing the amount of floor space that can be built in centrally located areas, and by making land recycling difficult, some regulations tend to 'push' urban development towards the periphery. As a result, commuting trips become longer, public transport becomes difficult to operate and urban infrastructure has to be extended further than what would have been the case if land supply had been unconstrained.

Infrastructure investment in India remains low in comparison to international standards and currently cannot support a fast pace of urbanization. The private sector, rather than the government, now needs to take a lead role in identifying and developing projects. In practice, many public authorities across the world resort to unique selling points (USPs) motivated by the perspective of solving the challenges brought by their lack of capacity to identify and develop projects. However, many projects that originate as USPs experience challenges, including diverting public resources away from the strategic plans of the government, providing poor value for money and leading to patronage and lack of transparency, particularly in developing countries. To ensure governments can mobilize the strengths of the private sector while protecting the public interest, USPs, when accepted, should be managed and used with caution as an exception to the public procurement method.

India needs to ramp up infrastructure investments to scale up urbanization and make cities more competitive. India has a huge potential to benefit from urbanization, given the size of India's urban demographic dividend, with 12 million new people joining the labour force every year.[19]

THE REVERSE ARGUMENT: DE-URBANIZATION AND THE GROWTH OF 'BHARAT'

The case for the next big phase of growth of India can clearly be based on three current realities:

1. The Covid-19-induced 'work from home' option enabling millions of people to move back to small towns and even villages.
2. The climate change-induced flooding and problems in cities that is encouraging more and more people to move back to smaller locations in the country.
3. The imperative for redistributing jobs and improving physical, digital and social infrastructure to a level when all Indian citizens can work from anywhere and enjoy the same benefits of economic growth.

A strong argument in favour of distribution of jobs comes from the IT services industry in India. During the early days of offshore outsourcing, American and European corporations were reluctant to permit software professionals working on their projects to work outside secured software campuses in the seven large IT cities of Bengaluru, NCR, Chennai, Hyderabad, Pune, Mumbai and Hyderabad. Data and information security, and the perception that teams should be able to work together drove that anxiety. However after a year of Covid-19, when all their employees worked on projects from homes and home offices all over the country, and given the alacrity shown by large Indian companies to move seamlessly to a 'work from home' model for all their employees, large corporations were quite open to their outsourcing partners also having employees working from anywhere so long as the project outcomes were met.

This opens up opportunities for firms to rapidly expand their workforces for global clients and also substantially cut their costs on two counts. This first is the reduction of expensive office space in the big cities and the second is the lower cost of employees in tier 2 and 3 locations, and much better retention opportunities. Already recruiting New Direction (ND) skills companies who partner with large software majors have starting opening 'Hire, Train and Deploy' bases in small towns like Salem and Trichy, and preparing candidates from all over the country to participate in the next phase of the IT, BPM and engineering services revolution.

Once this model is created and large-scale urbanization is enabled, it will create at least a couple of hundred million new jobs, employing many who would have been unemployed or underemployed in the rural parts of the country. The collateral benefit of this will be a rethink of agriculture and cottage industries in 'Bharat' or rural India. Through this process, a new productive country with sustainable livelihoods for all can be attained at least by the time India celebrates 100 years of her independence in 2047.

4

THE FUTURE OF MOBILITY AND SUSTAINABILITY

Ravi Pandit and Kaustubh Pathak

The progress of humanity is inextricably linked to the progress of human mobility—from the tree to the ground, from Africa to the rest of the world, from the bottom of the sea and into space, human progress has been reflected in our mobility.

Mobility is also the lifeline of any economy, and the mobility industry is one of the highest contributors to GDP and to employment. The way the human body depends on blood vessels, in the same way, several industries depend on the mobility industry.

Unfortunately, the mobility sector is a major consumer of fossil fuels and hence one of the highest contributors to environmental damage. In India, the transportation sector accounts for a third of the pollution in the country.[1]

World over, mobility is in the state of unprecedented transformation. Let us look at how these changes are likely to happen because this will define the future of mobility in our $5 trillion economy.

Mobility enables the transportation of goods and people from one place to another. With the advancement in the field of telecommunication, the need for transformation of people is being revisited globally, especially after the Covid-19 pandemic. Most of the service industry, including IT, banking, consulting, etc., are now finding it convenient to function online and are allowing people to work from home. With reliable, high-speed internet, people are preferring meeting virtually than meeting in-person. The development of technology is opening up new dimensions for people to communicate. The evolution of mobile phones over the last 10 years has changed the way we live and communicate today, virtually shrinking the world into the palm of a hand. And this is just the beginning—with concepts like the metaverse becoming a reality, people will get an immersive experience in virtual reality where they can interact and collaborate in 3D digital avatars. As Microsoft's CEO Satya Nadella mentioned while speaking at Microsoft Ignite 2021 conference, 'It is no longer just looking at a camera view of a factory floor, you can be on the floor. It's no longer just video conferencing with colleagues, you can be with them in the same room. It's no longer just playing a game with friends; you can be in the game with them.'[2] Such life-like communication experiences will totally transform the need for mobility.

In a similar fashion, advancements in technology will transform the mobility of goods significantly. Concepts like city-based vertical vegetable farms will reduce the need for transportation of farm produce to a great extent. Technology like 3D printing will allow manufacturing of finished products near the point of use. This will increase the efficiency of goods transport significantly. The movement towards localization will promote the localized economy by giving preference to use of locally produced goods over the ones imported from distant places. This can be seen from the fact that local mobile producers in India and China have taken massive market share by moving towards regional supply chains that produce locally for local markets. This is partly because heavy things are more expensive to move, so localized production of large products, such as vehicles, fabrications, etc., is much more cost-effective.[3]

It is much more effective to transport an electron than a molecule or matter, so a strong telecommunication network can support a reduction in the mobility of people and goods. It follows that growing the size of the economy fivefold will not require a corresponding growth of the mobility sector.

While the need for mobility will be reduced, new technologies will also make mobility more efficient, in environmental and economical terms. A variety of transport modes such as drones, air taxies, bullet trains and hyperloop capsules, which were considered only a part of science fiction, are now becoming a reality. With the successful flights of SpaceX, Virgin Galactic and Blue Origin into space, the era of commercial space travel has begun. Though this is still futuristic for India today, the country will have a big role to play in terms of research, technology development and manufacturing. Many Indian companies have already initiated their work in this domain. Agnikul Cosmos, Skyroot Aerospace, Dhruva Space, SatSure and Pixxel are some of the Indian start-ups working in this domain.[4] Around 60 start-ups have registered with ISRO since 'unlocking' of the Indian space sector.[5] Flying taxis or urban air mobility (UAM) vehicles is another domain that will redefine urban mobility. Morgan Stanley, a US investment company, predicted that the global UAM market will grow at CAGR of 30 per cent, reaching $1.5 trillion by 2040.[6] This is sure to affect city planning, building architecture and transport infrastructure development in the near future.

On-road mobility is also going through a transformation years after Henry Ford introduced Model T to the world. The new revolution is being called 'CASE,' which is an acronym for Connected, Autonomous, Shared and Electric. The new mobility will be largely electric, completely connected, significantly autonomous and will be increasingly used in shared format.

MOBILITY IN INDIA

India has one of the largest mobility systems in the world, mainly comprising road transport followed by railways. Lack of adequate public transportation in the country is one of the significant reasons for the large growth in privately owned vehicles in the past decade, causing frequent traffic congestions in many cities. This has contributed to an increase in the pollution levels of the country. As per the World Air Quality Report published by IQAir, India is home to 35 of the world's 50 most polluted cities.[7]

With the growth of the mobility sector, oil import of the country is increasing. In FY 2020–21 (before the Covid-19 pandemic), India imported ~220 metric tonne crude oil worth $102 billion.[8] Most of the fuel demand comes from the mobility sector. According to a report submitted to the Petroleum Planning and Analysis Cell (PPAC), 70 per cent of diesel and 99.6 per cent petrol is consumed by the mobility sector alone. [9]

The ways in which the mobility sector is currently functioning in the country are not sustainable, both from the perspective of environment as well as national economy. There is, hence, a need to make a transformational change in the Indian mobility sector.

Luckily, this need has not gone unnoticed by our government and the policymakers. More than 20 cities in the country are building metro rail systems for rapid public transportation. Many cities in India have started using battery electric buses. With tax incentives and special schemes like FAME (Faster Adoption and Manufacturing of [Hybrid &] Electric Vehicles in India) and FAME-2, use of electric mobility is encouraged even in case of two-wheelers, three-wheelers and cars. On 15 August 2021, the government launched Hydrogen Mission for the country, which will play a significant role in promoting fuel cell vehicles in the country. We are seeing the dawn of a new world.

The government is also keeping pace with the new developmental trends in the mobility sector.

Indian Railways is working on the Mumbai–Ahmedabad high-speed railway (bullet train) project. The high-speed train will operate at a speed of 320 km/hr, reducing the travel time from seven to less than three hours. The first phase of the project is expected to be completed by 2026. The government also plans to have a bullet train service connecting Delhi and Varanasi by 2030.

Another futuristic concept that the country is currently working on is the hyperloop. It is basically a sealed tube or system of tubes with low air pressure through which a pod may travel substantially free of air resistance or friction. This will allow passengers to travel probably at the speed of an airplane at the cost of road travel. The project is expected to be ready for demonstration within the next three years.

A high-speed transportation network will reduce travel time and provide better connectivity, thereby giving boost to business, tourism and overall development in a region.

It is predicted that globally, the industry will see more than 100,000 drones deployed for commercial use every year over the next four years.[10] The drones will be used for surveillance (in military, agriculture, traffic monitoring, etc.), aerial photography, supply of essentials and medicals, disaster management, etc. Considering this, the Ministry of Civil Aviation in India recently announced the Drone Rules 2021, which will provide a massive boost for private investment, R&D, innovation in technology development, testing, training and manufacturing. This reflects the intent of the government to facilitate growth of this industry in the country. India will also be one of the biggest users of drones. With the growth in this space, there will be high demand for trained and certified drone pilots in the near future.

Clearly, the mobility sector is in for a transformational change as we commence our journey for the $5 trillion economy.

MAKING THE TRANSFORMATIONAL CHANGE

The Three Shifts in Urban Mobility

Urban mobility covers a range of modes of transport, including walking on foot, bicycles, mechanical two-wheelers, shared three-wheelers, personal cars, shared transport such as buses, metros, railways and commercial vehicles.

We believe that the movement will be largely from (i) diesel/petrol to electric, (ii) from personal to shared, and (iii) from physical movement to digital movement. These three big shifts will dominate the future of urban mobility. This will be because there will be a significant groundswell for pollution-free, non-congested transportation funded through private as well as public investment.

We believe that most of the electric transportation will run on batteries. In the next five to 10 years, the incremental vehicle population in the country will be almost 30 per cent battery electric.[11] In our opinion, the current battery technologies are changing by the day. New chemistries such as sodium, new technologies such as solid state, and new manufacturing methodologies will all make battery electric vehicles cheaper than the polluting diesel/petrol vehicles.

Despite the current blip caused by Covid-19, people will move towards shared transport rather than personally owned transport. Cab services such as Ola and Uber are going to bring an increasingly larger share of vehicles on the road. Autonomous vehicles, especially on fixed routes, will make vehicle sharing even more attractive. A large part of goods delivery and last-mile connectivity will be shared.

The third dimension of change will be from physical to digital. As we see in most of the service industries, people are working from home because of Covid-19. But it would be wrong to think that we will go back to our old ways when Covid-19 becomes history. According to the survey conducted by real estate firm CBRE South Asia Private Limited, over 73 per cent of firms in India are planning hybrid working arrangements.[12] Also, in case of the US, it is observed that the organizations are more inclined towards the work from home culture.[13]

STEP: An Enabling Framework

Radical yet sustainable transformational change requires a systematic model. An earlier publication from two of the contributors to this book, *From Leapfrogging to Pole-Vaulting,*[14] postulates that transformational change involves the application of four levers to make the transformation radical yet sustainable. The four levers are STEP, as detailed below, along with the public action required for each.

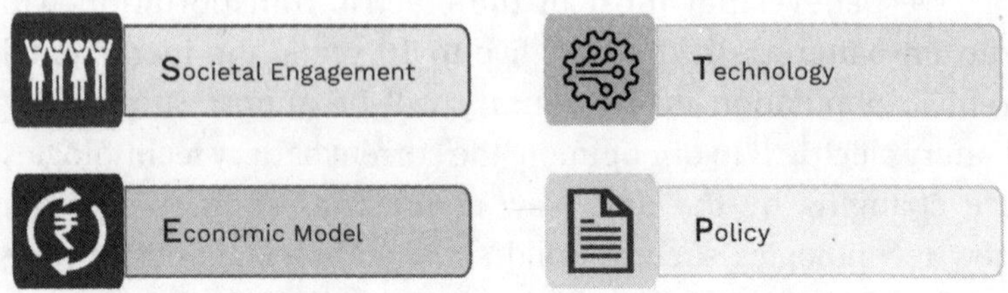

- **Social engagement:** No transformation will last if it is not accepted by people at large. It is, thus, necessary to convince people to be a part of transformation by spreading knowledge about the impact of the transformation.
  The three big shifts are largely born out of deep societal changes. Awareness about the ill effects of pollution on health has triggered the first shift from fossil fuel to electric. Change in the perception of the younger generation towards mobility makes private cars no longer an 'object of desire', causing the second shift—going from private to public transportation. Increasing preference for virtual meets over in-person meetings to save the time and energy needed for travel has caused the third shift—from physical to digital. All three shifts have significant societal tailwinds.
- **Technology:** Technological advancement plays a pivotal role in any transformational change. Key technological innovations have always formed the foundation of any revolution around the world.

These shifts are also driven by emerging technologies. Steep falls in the cost of clean energy generated through solar and wind energy has made renewable energy affordable. Changes happening in the energy storage technologies will further encourage use of this energy for mobility application. Technologies relating to AI and machine learning will make shared and autonomous transportation even easier. New manufacturing technologies such as 3D printing and robotics are changing the world of manufacturing. Finally, the telecommunication technologies, including 5G and 6G, are creating a cloud of information across large geographies that can help coordinate the movement of people and goods. We see an increasing rate of acceleration in the change of technologies. We are at the cusp of a cleaner, safer and better transportation.

- **Economic model:** A sustainable transformation needs to be economically viable. Such economic viability brings in private capital and reduces the need for concessional public funding, which is always scarce.

  The three shifts will essentially substitute the current ecosystem with a completely new ecosystem of transportation. Clearly, this needs significant investments. We see investments happening through private as well as public sources. Moreover, consumer preferences help in increasing revenues, whereas technology advancements help in reducing costs. There is certainly a need for public funding till the new ecosystem crosses the tipping point. We shall come to that in the last lever, P, namely policy.
- **Policy:** Transformational changes need to be anchored in sound long-term policy. Policies provide a systematic set of guidelines for implementing change over a period of time. In order to promote use of clean and shared mobility, the solutions in-line with the objectives should be incentivized, and others should be taxed in order to discourage their

usage. For example, implementing variable tolls for private vehicles will help in reducing the less-essential car trips or in shifting towards public transportation, thereby controlling road congestions. Premium tax rates on the purchase of conventionally fuelled vehicles and tax exemption for clean mobility solutions will also aid in the transformation. It is also essential to phase out the incentives gradually as the transformation gains more and more acceptance from society.

Additionally, a large number of investments will be required to cater to the growing demand for batteries in the country. India has set an ambitious target of achieving 30 per cent electric vehicles sales by 2030 across all modes.[15] Battery demand in the country is, thus, expected to grow at the rate of 12 per cent CAGR over the next five years, estimated to reach market value of $4 billion by 2026.[16]

The Indian government has already implemented many schemes and has brought policy reforms that are necessary for transforming urban mobility. These include the FAME and FAME-2, the 100 Smart Cities project, a PLI scheme for Advanced Chemistry Cells of ₹18,100 crore and the Vehicle Scrappage Policy. The government has also made provisions in September 2021 of ₹120 crore to encourage production of drones and their parts. In addition to these, we have some more suggestions as listed below:

- Corporates should be encouraged to move towards electric mobility to transport goods and people. This can be done by covering the differential expenditure incurred in this transition under CSR by considering it under conservation of environment, as per Section 135 (schedule-VII, subclause-iv) of the Companies Act.
- Development of indigenous technologies and local manufacturing will help in reducing the costs. This can

be encouraged by floating innovation challenges, bringing PLI schemes for setting up local manufacturing units, etc.

- Converting existing vehicles into electric ones should be encouraged by the government, as it will cost far less compared to the new ones and accelerate the transformation significantly.

Rethinking Intercity Mobility

While the transformation of urban mobility will be governed by battery electric vehicles, the solution will not be suitable for long-distance intercity mobility, as weight and charging requirement will constrain the load-carrying capacity and travelling range of the vehicle. This challenge can be addressed by using hydrogen fuel cell vehicles, as they are five times more efficient than the conventionally fuelled vehicles and cause practically zero pollution.

Governments, industries and researchers around the world have realized the potential of hydrogen as a clean energy source of the future and thus are focussing on exploiting it. Many countries, including Germany, South Korea, Spain, Japan, UK, etc., have committed significant resources in using hydrogen as fuel for transportation.[17]

In Europe, an initiative called 'Hydrogen Mobility Europe' (H2ME) was launched to provide fuel cell electric vehicles (FCEVs) access to the first truly pan-European network of hydrogen refuelling stations. This has resulted in 1,400 FCEVs operating in Europe supported through 49 hydrogen stations till date.[18]

Japan has set an ambitious target of having 200,000 FCEVs on the road by 2025, while the number was only about 3,600 in 2019. It also intends to make 320 hydrogen filling stations available to the public under its third Strategic Roadmap for Hydrogen and Fuel Cells.

In the US, key hydrogen developments are taking place across several states. California can be considered as a representative example, which already has about 7,800+ cars and a few dozen buses powered by hydrogen on its roads, supported by a relatively small network of 54 hydrogen refuelling stations.[19]

Though most of the advancements in utilizing hydrogen fuel cell technology for transportation are seen in the case of road transport, efforts are also being taken to explore the use of fuel cells in other modes of transportation. The Coradia iLint™ is the world's first passenger train powered by a hydrogen fuel cell. The train is developed by Alstom and has been in commercial service in Germany since 2018. Planes like ZeroAvia, DLR-HY4 and Aerodelft's Phoenix PT have demonstrated the possibility of using fuel cells for air travel.

India is blessed with natural resources like solar and wind power, and biomass, which can be utilized to generate green hydrogen in abundance. Shifting towards the hydrogen economy will help India reduce its oil import bill significantly. Hydrogen being clean fuel, it will also reduce the pollution levels of the country, which is also in line with India's United Nations Climate Change Conference COP (Conference of Parties) commitments.

A BRIGHT FUTURE

So far, we have talked about how road transportation in the country can be transformed. Most of these points also apply to other modes of transportation, including railways, metros, ships, and short-distance air travel. Many private companies across the globe have already started working in these areas, and some of them also have prototypes ready for demonstration. Currently, Indian Railways and a ship-building company from the country have expressed their interest in exploring the possibility of using hydrogen and fuel cells for their respective mobility application areas. Though this is just a beginning, with adequate investments and support from the government, one can expect transformation in these sectors over a period of next 20–30 years.

With the developments happening in the field of mobility, we are certain that the future is very exciting. Advancement in the fields of telecommunication, digital technologies and clean energy solutions will play a crucial role in transforming mobility as well. This will make transportation connected, safe and intelligent. In the next 30 years, mobility will see the greatest transformation in the history of humanity.

Hydrogen will have a major role to play in this transformation. Implementing the hydrogen economy can cut down India's fossil fuel imports at least by $18 billion,[20] corresponding to transportation application. Displacing fossil fuels by hydrogen will also help in meeting 30 per cent of India's United Nations Climate Change Conference COP commitments. Using biomass to generate hydrogen will potentially create 500,000+ jobs in hydrogen-generation plants, supply chain management for the skilled/unskilled workforce and opportunities of rural entrepreneurship, and will also help increase farmers' income. At full scale, the hydrogen economy can increase India's GDP by ₹12 lakh crore (6.2 per cent).[21]

The invention of the internal combustion engine was the first big revolution that transformed the mobility sector. The second revolution was the introduction of battery electric vehicles. The invention of hydrogen fuel cells is the third revolution in the field of mobility, which is just around the corner. Though India could not contribute in the former two, we are confident that India can lead the third revolution. From the invention of zero to Mangalyaan and vaccines for all during Covid-19, India has showcased its ability to innovate and contribute to the world's progress in the recent past. Similarly, India can also set an example for innovation and mass-scale adoption of FCEVs by making them cost-competitive to the conventional vehicles.

5

THE SEAMLESS INTERCONNECT OF SCIENCE, TECHNOLOGY AND INNOVATION

Raghunath Mashelkar

Science provides the base for technology, which, in turn, triggers technology-led innovation. Potentially, science solves problems, technology transforms and innovation impacts.

The power of the idea that science, technology and innovation (STI) need to be seamlessly integrated has been driving the innovation to create social and economic transformation and has been well-recognized. In fact, innovation has become a tool for competitiveness as well as accelerated growth. There is a growing realization in India that research and innovation must go together. After all, research converts money into knowledge, but it is innovation that converts knowledge into money and social good.

HISTORICAL PERSPECTIVE

Well-known scientist Dr Jayant Narlikar, in his book *Scientific Edge*[1] gives a list of what he considers as top 10 achievements of Indian science and technology in the twentieth century. Dr Narlikar's listing has been chosen in that he is the only one who has, through his own astute understanding of what constitutes real excellence in science, pinpointed big milestones of individual or institutional achievements.

We note that in Narlikar's list of 10 achievements in the twentieth century, there is none that came from industry.

In the pre-Independence era, the first on his list was Srinivasa Ramanujan, who opened so many new doors, some even well after his untimely death in 1920. The second was Meghnad Saha's ionisation equation (1920), which opened the door to stellar astrophysics. The third was S.N. Bose's work on particle statistics (c. 1924), which clarified the behaviour of photons and opened the door to new ideas on statistics of microsystems that obey the rules of quantum theory. The fourth was C.V. Raman's discovery that molecules scatter light (c. 1928), the Raman Effect, which opened the doors for a new way to study the internal structure of molecules. The fifth was G.N. Ramachandran's pioneering work in structural molecular biology (c. mid-1960s), which created the Ramachandran Map, which, even today, is at the very heart of elucidation of all protein structures; leave alone his breakthrough on collagen triple helix.

Post-Independence, Narlikar listed another five. The first was the development of nuclear power and capability (founded in the 1950s). The second was the Green Revolution in agriculture (the 1960s and 1970s). The third was the Indian space programme and satellite fabrication, with satellite vehicle launching capability (from the late 1970s). The fourth was the work in high-temperature superconductivity (since the late 1980s). The fifth was the transformation of the chain of 40 laboratories of the Council for Scientific & Industrial Research (CSIR) towards an industry-oriented, performance-driven and accountable organization (in the late 1990s).

In the post-1950 list of achievements, there is none that came from industry. The only place where industrial R&D figures in is in the 1990s, during the transformation of CSIR, which, incidentally, the author was privileged to lead. All the achievements in the list, like that in agriculture, space, nuclear technology, etc., were driven by organized mission-driven research funded by the government. As regards excellence at an individual level, to use Narlikar's words, there was no 'Nobel Prize worthy' breakthrough in science, as existed in the first half of the twentieth century. The sum and substance are that although India's averages have risen as seen by its third rank after the US and China, it has not created those Everest-like peaks achieved in the pre-Independence era. Later in this chapter, we will deal with this aspect exclusively.

The recent book by Hari Pulakkat[2] gives an engaging perspective of what was achieved in the post-Independence era. He also highlights space science and technology, and molecular biophysics, but he adds achievements in industrial research too. One is the prowess in innovative chemical process development that led India to become the pharmacy of the world. The other is the green technology developed in the leather processing industry. Interestingly, CSIR played a major role in both.

SUCCESS STORIES

The last two to three years have brought a lot of cheer to Indian STI.

India's rank in science is rapidly rising. It is now the world's third-largest publisher of peer-reviewed scientific research papers, after China and the US. Between 2008 and 2018, India had an average annual growth rate in terms of scientific papers published of 10.73 per cent, as against China's 7.81 per cent and the US's 0.71 per cent.[3] India became the first country in the world to reach Mars in its maiden attempt, spending just one-tenth of the budget that National Aeronautics and Space Administration (NASA) used. The Indian Space Research Organisation (ISRO) successfully launched a record 104 satellites on a single rocket.

Although 2020 will be known as the year of the pandemic, it can be called the year of Indian science as well—so magnificent was the response by the scientific community on taking on the challenge of the pandemic.

When the pandemic arrived in India, we had negligible diagnostic capability, no point-of-care diagnostics, no vaccines, no therapeutics, and the biology and mechanism of action of the virus was unknown. Our scientists delivered on all this and more.

Several innovative solutions like AI-powered contact-free health monitor and step-down ICU, multiplex RT-PCR kit, 'saline gargle RT-PCR method' for testing Covid-19 samples, 3D-printed masks coated with anti-viral agents and high-purity oxygen concentrator were developed.

Great progress was made in the field of diagnostics. The cost of RT-PCR test was brought down from ₹3,000 to ₹350![4] The Institute of Genomics and Integrated Biology even made the expensive Q-PCR machine redundant. It created a rapid diagnostic kit, with high affordability, relative ease, yet using cutting-edge CRISPR technology for detection of genomic sequence of novel coronavirus.

With vaccines, Indian scientists got into the act with multiple strategies for vaccine development. Bharat Biotech used inactivated virus to develop their vaccine, and its Covaxin has been used to vaccinate millions around the world. Zydus is using spiked protein. Gennova has developed mRNA-based vaccine.

All this was possible due to the investments in STI over decades, which went on creating robust physical and intellectual infrastructures.

This is a near-term view. But let's now reflect on how Indian STI has performed, as well as failed to perform, and also the lessons that we can draw from this journey.

DEVELOPMENT AND DENIAL

Indian technology grew in a denial-driven mode in the post-Independence era, where for love or for money, no technology was available to India.

Foreign technologies were denied because of lack of resource as well as a closed economy in the pre-liberalized era. They were also denied due to security and strategic reasons. It was through the path of 'technonationalism' that India developed self-reliance through its own technologies in both civilian sectors as well as strategic sectors such as space, defence, nuclear energy and supercomputers.

Take defence. India developed diverse missiles and rocket systems, remotely piloted vehicles, light combat aircraft, etc. Brahmos is a great example of Indian prowess in strategic technology.

Take nuclear energy. The entire range of technologies, from the prospecting of raw materials to the design and construction of large nuclear reactors was developed on a self-reliant basis. India's nuclear fast-breeder reactors emerged from its thrust towards technonationalism.

Look at space technology—from indigenous development to satellites to launch vehicles, from SLV to ASLV to PSLV to GSLV. India's first moon orbiter project, Chandrayaan-1, Mars Orbiter Mission or even the recent simultaneous launch of 104 satellites are brilliant examples. No wonder, India is now ranked amongst a handful of nations of the world that have a credible capability in space technology.

Strength respects strength. It is the growing technological strength of a nation that increases its access to technology that has been denied to it. The technology denial regime itself underwent a change as technonationalism gave India a strong technological foundation.

A case study of India's forays into the field of high-performance supercomputers is provided below.

DENIAL-DRIVEN INNOVATION

Technonationalism is always driven by technology denial. But the denial regime itself undergoes a change as technonationalism gives the country a strong technological foundation. When technology can't be obtained for love or for money, there is no other way but to develop it on one's own. When someone says I won't give you the technology, one says thank you and develops it on their own. Denial has been a big driving force for India.

The author[5] provides a powerful example of this by illustrating India's forays into supercomputers, which today are being increasingly regarded as a strategic resource.

India's supercomputer journey began when a Cray supercomputer was denied to India in the mid-1980s. India's response was to launch the Centre for Development of Advanced Computing (C-DAC) in 1987 in Pune. In 1991–92, India developed its first supercomputer, PARAM 8000.

But PARAM by C-DAC was not the only response by India to technology denial. There was 'Flosolver' by National Aerospace Laboratories (NAL), ANUPAM by Bhabha Atomic Research Centre (BARC), and Advanced Numerical Research and Analysis Group (ANURAG) by Defence Research and Development Organization (DRDO). And then came EKA, built by Tata's Computational Research Laboratories, which at a point in time was ranked the fourth-fastest supercomputer in the world.

The long voyage in high-performance computing was not smooth sailing by any reckoning. It was plagued by several difficulties, including embargoes on critical components, architectural debates, make-versus-buy debates, loss of key talent to multinationals and bureaucratic hurdles.

Interestingly though, a direct correlation can be found between India's forays into supercomputers and the technology denial play. After C-DAC successfully demonstrated the PARAM-8000 in 1990, the Los Alamos (Worlton) report concluded that supercomputers were not necessary to design nuclear weapons.

In 1991–92, C-DAC exported PARAM to Canada, Germany and Russia, while others, such as NAL's Flosolver Mark III, and DRDOs' PACE, matched the capabilities of US-made, mid-range workstations.

In December 1992, the US Office of Naval Research sent an official to Bangalore to assess Indian capabilities in supercomputing. In 1993, the US authorized the licensed conditional export of high-performance computers to several Indian institutions.

In April 1995, India placed parallel processing supercomputing on its list of items requiring an Indian export licence. In July 1995, the US began to review its supercomputers export controls and, in October 1995, further relaxed the export of computers to India.

In 1998, C-DAC launched PARAM 10000, which demonstrated India's capacity to build 100-gigaflop machines. In response, the US further relaxed its export controls. During the same year, Cray established a subsidiary in India; the same company had denied India supercomputers in 1980s!

INDIA AS A GLOBAL DESTINATION FOR R&D

In 1995, the author, in his Lala Karamchand Thapar Memorial Lecture titled 'India's Emergence as a Global R&D Platform: The New Challenges and Opportunities,' had predicted that skill-based competition rather than product-based competition will become the key—products are actually transient mechanisms by which the market derives value from a company's skill base and the company derives value from the market. With the abundance of highly skilled talent being available in India, companies will shift their R&D to India.

Dr Manmohan Singh, the then finance minister of India, presided over the lecture. There were not many takers for the dream shared in that lecture. Today, that prediction has come true, with over 1,100 multinational R&D centres coming up in India, employing over 300,000 scientists, engineers and technologists doing cutting-edge research, design and development.[6] It is Indian talent, Indian IQ that is generating significant fraction of their global intellectual property (IP) for these multinational companies.

The real driver for these companies to set up their R&D centres in India is, of course, the fact that they get highest intellectual capital for a dollar in India. The following table provides a quantitative calculation by looking at the 2020 research publications produced per dollar of R&D invested.[7]

Country	GDP (current US$ Trillions), 2018	R&D Expenditure (% of GDP)	R&D Spending (US$ Billions), 2018	Publications Count, 2018	Publications Count per Billion US$ R&D Spending
India	2.7	0.66%	17.82	1,35,788	7,620
UK	2.9	1.70%	49.30	97,681	1,981
China	13.9	2.14%	297.46	5,28,263	1,776
Germany	3.98	3.11%	123.78	1,04,396	843
USA	20.52	3.00%	615.60	4,22,808	687
Japan	5.04	3.22%	162.29	98,793	609

Leave alone the comparison with advanced nations, even compared to China, India is about four times better in terms of research publications per dollar. This driver will continue to push more companies to set up their R&D centres in India. One might argue that it is Indian IQ that is producing IP for multinational companies. What is the gain for India? Yes, there is a big gain.

This has also led to the phenomenon of brain drain turning to brain gain to brain circulation. A number of Indian scientists employed by these centres are returnees from abroad, who, after acquiring high-level research experience, have moved on to serve in the Indian industry or institutions. Indian STI has, thus, benefited.

LEADING INCLUSIVE INNOVATION

Indian industry has done well in some sectors. For example, India's dominance in generic drugs has given it the reputation of being the pharmacy of the world. The automobile industry is another example.

The Indian way of innovation has led to the introduction of new nomenclatures in the dictionary of innovation! These include phrases like frugal innovation, Gandhian innovation, MLM (more from less for more), reverse innovation, nanovation and even Indovation!

Some Indian innovations were driven by the powerful combination of scarcity and aspiration.

Some of these have been truly game-changing and are taught as case studies in leading business schools of the world. Aravind Eye Hospital doing high-quality cataract eye surgery at one-hundredth the cost for the same procedure in the US or the fact that Narayana Health can do a high-quality heart surgery at one-fiftieth the cost prevailing in the US,[8] thanks to 'workflow innovation', are just as well-known as the Jaipur foot example of a high-performing $20 foot, which became a *Time* magazine cover story.

But some of the recent examples are even more stunning. These are innovations that already exist.[9]

- Can we make high-quality but simple breast cancer screening available to every woman, at an extremely affordable cost of $1 per scan?
- Can we make a portable, high-tech ECG machine that can

provide reports immediately and at a cost of ₹5 a test?

- Can we make a robust test for mosquito-borne dengue, which can detect the disease in 15 minutes at a cost of $2 per test?

Another huge success was the unified payments interface, or UPI, which is the simplest, cheapest and most reliable peer-to-peer financial transaction mechanism. It was India's lifeline during the Covid-19 lockdowns.

These examples show that India has the potential to be a leader in frugal innovation through the creation of public platforms, which prevents end-to-end monopoly and enhances the ability of start-ups to build specialized applications meeting the needs of specific segments of users.

These public digital platforms have not been built by traditional public sector agencies but by groups of technical experts on a low-cost and largely pro bono basis. The end product is inclusive public good, which is then managed and maintained by a government agency. The next generation of inclusive innovation will be triggered by creating the framework or scaffolding.

Inclusive innovation in India is truly diverse. An important component of this is innovation by the people for the people—grassroots innovation. Prof. Anil Gupta has been a pioneer of the grassroots innovation movement, and his book *Grassroots Innovation*[10] describes the power and impact of grassroots innovation. What is critical is that the formal science and technology innovation being developed in the laboratories of universities and national organizations must partner with the grassroots innovation being developed by the people working in the laboratories of their life, be they farmers, artisans or school dropouts. This can be done if there is a strong faith in the concept that everyone is someone, and minds on the margin are not marginal minds. India has an opportunity to become a global leader in global grassroots innovation.

ENHANCING R&D INTENSITY AND INVESTMENT BY INDUSTRY

The share of the R&D investments by the private sector in the overall R&D spend remains low, with majority of investments, close to 70–75 per cent, coming from the government.[11] These proportions are nearly reverse not only in advanced countries but also in countries like Korea, China, etc.

For India, 'make in India' has meant 'assembled in India' and not 'invent and make in India'. The Chinese plan, on the other hand, has been not just 'make in China' but 'create in China'. Indian industry has paid for this lack of innovation and aggressive innovation by China while competing right here in India. Let's take a recent example.

Indian mobile phone manufacturers had begun dominating the domestic market in 2015, when home-grown brands held a 45 per cent smartphone market share. But from a mere 9 per cent market share in 2015, the Chinese brands reached 68 per cent share by the end of 2019, while the Indian brands plummeted to a mere 7.5 per cent by 2019.[12] How did Indian brands lose their home turf despite having early movers' advantages in a short span of four years?

Indian companies largely adopted a mere assembling and trading business model with no research or innovation. The Chinese undertook aggressive innovations, localization to reduce their tariff tax and transportation cost, innovative customization for local customers and large economies of scale. The lesson for us is simple—innovate or perish.

PATENTS AND TRANSLATIONAL RESEARCH

In 1895, Sir J.C. Bose invented the wireless. When asked to take patents, he refused to take them, saying that knowledge should be free. Marconi, who came much later, took patents. In 1998, an American company filed a patent on Basmati. Incidentally, the author led the team that fought the battle and got the patent revoked. Therefore, as far as India is concerned, the journey from Bose to Basmati, from 1895 to 1998, showed lack of understanding and preparedness of diverse aspects of intellectual property rights (IPR).[13]

The J.C. Bose case shows a lack of awareness of the importance of patenting. The Basmati case battle was a classic case of biopiracy, for which India had not taken safeguards in IPR terms, until the author came out with the TKDL Basmati battle on the wrong patent given to the US, which was fought under his leadership, following the earlier turmeric battle that he had led.

The Indian economy opened up only in 1991. Until then, India did just import substitution, copying and reverse engineering. No capacity in IPR creation and protection was developed. India's lack of creation of original innovations has also shown up in the below-par performance in the creation of competitive IPR.[14] For example, for the past few years, the Indian patents list is dominated by foreign companies.

In doing successful translational research, which is essential for completing a successful journey from mind to marketplace, India could have done better.

There are some exceptions. For instance, the development of the pharmaceutical sector demonstrates the successful translation of pharmacology as a science to the production of important and useful drugs. Not only indigenous manufacture based on imported technology but also manufacture based on the indigenous development of Covid-19 vaccines is a case in point. The emerging digital start-up ecosystem is also a strong example of scientific developments being applied to useful technologies.

By and large, India has not done well. The author, in his book *Reinventing India*, has given several examples of such missed opportunities. For instance, Ashok Jhunjhunwala of IIT Madras developed wireless local loop technology. It got implemented first in Madagascar, Angola and Brazil before it was accepted in India. And there are several other examples, where discoveries made in India have created wealth, but not in India.

Why has India not done so well in the journey from mind to marketplace? It is because India lacks a robust national innovation ecosystem. Essential elements of a powerful innovation ecosystem comprise physical, intellectual and cultural constructs. Beyond mere research labs, it includes idea incubators, technology parks, a conducive IPR regime, enlightened public procurement systems, rigorous yet facilitating regulatory systems, academics who believe in not just 'publish or perish' but 'patent, publish and prosper', potent inventor–investor engagement, venture capital and passionate innovation leaders. Although late, by appreciating these weaknesses, an earnest effort in building a robust innovation ecosystem with all these building blocks has already started.

REGAINING STI LEADERSHIP

Before laying down a proposed pathway to regain Indian leadership in STI, we must get some first principles right. The author has dealt with the subject of the pathways for India to emerge as a global leader in STI.[15]

First, there is a mindset change that is required among all the players. That involves the government, R&D institutions and industry.

The decision-makers in both public and private sectors generally believe that India should wait till new technologies developed by global players reach a high level of maturity and scale so that India can then jump in and deploy them successfully without 'wasting' funds on potential failures. The general thinking is: let others make mistakes so that we will only use the most successful ones and thereby never fail. Unless this mindset changes fundamentally at the highest level of decision-making,

STI in India will remain poorly valued and poorly funded.

India must move from the penchant of doing 'first to India' to 'first to the world.' For instance, in the case of drug development, move from 'fastest copier of molecules discovered abroad' to 'fastest creator of new molecules.' This type of original and breakthrough research in every field will also lead to India moving up the IPR ladder.

Second, Aatmanirbhar Bharat, meaning 'self-reliant India,' is a national mandate today. And Aatmanirbhar Bharat would mean India becoming a part of the global supply chain and competing with the world by creating products that are made in India but also for the world. Our vision should move from 'technological self-reliance' to creating technology dominance in strategic areas, be it quantum computing or Web 3.0 or 6G or next generation green hydrogen technology. Aatmanirbhar with Atmavishwas, meaning self-reliance with self-confidence, with self-dignity, should be the focus.

Third, India must raise its aspirations far higher to create rapid and not gradual transformation. In the book *From Leapfrogging to Pole-Vaulting,* there is an emphasis for India to shift from reactive leapfrogging to proactive pole-vaulting through radical and sustainable transformation of an enterprise. India has been able to demonstrate that it can do it in some cases. We need more of these.

TEN TENETS FOR A GLOBAL STI SYSTEM

Can India pole-vault as a leading nation in STI? It certainly can. Following are the 10 tenets to make this happen.

1. Strengthening Foundational (Interdisciplinary) Science
2. Creating World Class IPR System
3. Enhancing the Ease of STI in India
4. Enhancing Investment in STI

5. Embracing Risk for Derisking our Future
6. Assuring Success through ASSURED Total Innovation
7. Building Science- and Technology-led Entrepreneurship
8. Leveraging Talent, Technology and Trust
9. Building Scientific Temper
10. Clever Balancing of Technology Options

Strengthening Foundational (Interdisciplinary) Science

Basic science matters for economic growth, and, indeed, there is ample evidence that public investment in basic research pays for itself. India must continuously raise the funding for basic science, for which the support must go up by an order of magnitude from the present levels. A Nobel Prize for work done in India was won by Sir C.V. Raman in 1930, and there has been none after that. But look at the other honours that are counted after the Nobel Prize, such as the Wolf Prize, Fields Medal, etc. These have eluded India as well. Even if we consider the next level of honours, such as election as Fellow of the Royal Society, Fellow of the US National Academy of Science, they are so few. For instance, in engineering, where India is supposed to be strong, in the last 360 years of the history of the Royal Society, only three Indians have been elected for doing research in India, namely Prof. M.M. Sharma, Late Prof. R. Narasimha and the author!

A large enough or *impactful size of resources* is critical for success. Appropriate rewards for excellence achieved at a global level of accomplishment are equally critical.

Creating a World-Class IPR System

We have to recognize that IPR-driven industries contribute to national GDP in a significant manner. A European study has found that IPR-intensive industries in Europe generated around

30 per cent jobs during 2014–16 and contributed about 44.8 per cent to GDP.[16]

Skills in filing, reading and exploiting patents will be most crucial in the years to come. We need to properly protect our inventions. We need to understand the implications of the patents granted to our competitors. Many of the patents written by our professionals could be easily circumvented.[17]

A robust IPR regime is needed for publicly funded academic research, which invariably has a public interest character, whereas industrial in-house R&D is primarily done by industry for private good. In the US, the Bayh–Dole Act (1980) showed a new direction for the results of the basic research produced in academic institutions. This was done, first, by creating the rights of patents (like property rights) based on the outcome of the academic research, which not only created new knowledge but also potentially commercializable knowledge. And second, by granting these rights through exclusive licences provided to for-profit firms. This significantly changed the relationship between the agents involved in the innovation ecosystem. The long-pending bills on the 'Protection and Utilization of Public Funded Intellectual Property' need to be passed, with the necessary provisions put in place that will promote the creation of wealth from the scientific research done in academic institutions.

Patenting is expensive. So, there must be dedicated national funds as well as special allocations to institutions. Skills in patent-related endeavours are very special. For example, interpreting patent data for identifying the areas where there is a freedom to operate, writing patents professionally so that the competitors will not easily bypass them, assessing the potential current and future value of an IP, etc., are all highly professional jobs. IP analytics is emerging as 'the data science of analysing large amount of IP information, to discover relationships, trends and patterns for decision making'. There is increasing use of IP analytics methods, i.e., AI methods, machine learning and deep learning, to analyse intellectual property data. The major areas of impact are 'knowledge management, technology management, economic value, and extraction and effective management of information.'[18]

There is a need for integrated IP asset management by taking a look at all the rights in a holistic manner—looking at patents, copyrights, trademarks, designs, domain names, trade secrets, etc.

The pace of technical change is so high that there is not enough time to get ROI, and you have to extract value directly from IP quickly and inexpensively by proactively licensing non-core, non-strategic IP that has tactical value.

The IP strategy has to be aligned with corporate strategy. Our companies should embed intellectual assets and intellectual asset management into the organizational culture.

Enhancing the Ease of STI in India

The reality of India's STI today is that it is shackled by bureaucracy. This situation was recognized with a promise to correct it in the speeches at the Indian Science Congress by successive prime ministers in the years 2000, 2011 and 2015, to which this author has been a personal witness.[19] But despite these honest and good intentions by the top leadership, bureaucracy has stayed its course over the years.

The fundamental principle of bureaucracy is more about appearing to be right, process being more important than the performance, and also mistrust rather than trust. This creates overemphasis on and overburdening of processes, assuming that it will necessarily lead to desired outcomes. Overemphasis of procedures comes at the cost of speed. Indian scientists have to wait for many weeks to buy simple consumables and many months to buy equipment.[20]

The disbursement of research funding is almost always slow and often unreasonable. The problem gets compounded when one wants to do translational research that always requires speed and larger quantum of funding. Therefore, while the government wants scientific institutions to undertake useful research that can deliver visible and impactful outcomes with speed, the government's bureaucracy makes it difficult to achieve these objectives.

Rigid and obtrusive regulatory systems, which are also non-efficient at the same time, can cause impediments in moving science-led innovation forward. Some companies have had to shift clinical research abroad, thus losing altogether India's cost advantage in clinical trials. Similar is the case in other areas of life sciences; for example, in plant science, the research leading to genetically modified crops is getting held up due to the lack of a precautionary but a promotional regime. Strengthening of these regulatory systems, such that they do not compromise on standards and safety of people (patient first) but at the same time recognize the importance of maintaining India's comparative advantage (India first) should be always borne in mind.

Science, which is an exploration at times, cannot be audited with the current systems that are used for infrastructure projects. An audit system that insists that each patent should be commercialized inhibits the patenting initiative. On the other hand, an overdrive on patenting systems will lead to unwarranted secrecy amongst the scientific community in free idea exchange, which is a hallmark of the true spirit behind open science. Therefore, a National Oversight Board with wise thought leaders of eminence, which is able to look at such issues 'holistically', should be put in place.

Enhancing Investment in STI

As mentioned earlier, India's investment in R&D as a percentage of GDP has remained at around 0.7 per cent during the past three decades. This has to be enhanced to the often-promised 2 per cent before 2030.

The most significant development in 2021 is the setting up

of the National Research Foundation, with an allocation of ₹50 billion for five years with a focus on promotion of research in universities and colleges. Hopefully, the individual science and tech agencies such as CSIR, Department of Science and Technology (DST), Department of Biotechnology (DBT), etc., will be allowed to continue to fund additional sector-specific research.

In order to boost innovation, the Union government needs to increase the weighted tax deduction. In 2018, the government reduced the weighted deduction on R&D from 200 per cent to 150 per cent, laying out an eventual plan of phasing out. This has made the industry unhappy.[21]

Recently, the GST Council decided to do away with concessional GST rate of 5 per cent applicable to scientific equipment and increasing it to 'applicable rates', meaning anywhere between 12 and 18 per cent. This has made scientists unhappy, since this means further reduction in budgets.[22]

While reversing such undesirable measures, the government must introduce other means such as target-based tax incentives, remodelling of patent tax box regimes, including incremental R&D-based tax incentives, and expatriate tax regimes must be introduced.

Prime Minister Narendra Modi has recently added the slogan 'Jai Anusandhan', meaning celebration of achievements in research. We are sure that measures such as the above, and more, will be taken to support research strongly at a national level.

Microfinancing through crowdfunding and philanthropic sources should be encouraged and incentivized, especially for supporting grassroots and frugal innovation-related projects and start-up enterprises.

Direct financial support to industry MSMEs with a mix of loan, equity, grants, matching grants, small business innovation grants (under fast-track mode), innovation vouchers, risk guarantees with special focus on high-risk projects must also be introduced.

Embracing Risk for Derisking Our Future

In science-led innovation, when a new idea is born, which leads to the design and development of a new product that the present market has not seen before, the ready provision of early-stage financing is crucial. Risk-financing in the form of venture capital, which acts as an intermediary for long-term investment and supports young start-ups, becomes critical. Such 'ad'-venture capital created must support the young firms from their creation till they mature. India lacks such funds.

Governments elsewhere are known to take bold initiatives. For example, in the US, every department has to set aside 2.5 per cent of the funds to support innovative programmes—the US's Small Business Innovation Research (SBIR)[23] by National Institutes of Health and Department of Defense are classic cases.[24] These grants run up to $1 million or more. Many small start-ups are catalysed through such funding. The DBT, through its Biotechnology Industry Research Assistance Council (BIRAC) programme, has been a huge propellant for the biotechnology industry. Other departments and ministries need to introduce systems that will support really high-risk cutting-edge science-based innovation. The New Millennium Indian Technology Leadership Initiative (NMITLI) launched by CSIR, in the year 2000, focussed on creating entirely new technology leading to new products with an aim to create new markets. This was India's biggest public–private partnership in post-independent India.

Assuring Success through ASSURED Total Innovation

Further, what we require is not just technology innovation but 'total' innovation. This must include technology innovation, business model innovation, workflow innovation, system delivery innovation, process innovation, organizational innovation and policy innovation. In fact, it is the innovative combination of these that create scalable and sustainable businesses.

Building Science- and Technology-Led Entrepreneurship

Science- and technology-led entrepreneurship is not only critical for creating, shaping and sustaining the future industrial sectors of the nation but also for delivering the benefits of scientific research and development to society at large.

Every effort must be made to create a nurturing and supportive environment for entrepreneurs and entrepreneurial ideas to flourish and thrive. Towards this end, it should be the endeavour to encourage entrepreneurs by reducing systemic risks, uncertainties and barriers for new businesses, incentivize private investment in new ventures, develop a rich and supportive innovation ecosystem, and provide funding support for early-stage innovation.

Leveraging Talent, Technology and Trust

World-class talent in STI will require high-class training in science, technology, engineering and maths (STEM). Further, India will have to substantially increase the number of full-time equivalents such as doctoral, post-doctoral students committed to research, and that will require enhancing the talent pool by including significantly more women in STEM training.

There is a need for rapid capacity-building in exponential technology, from applied AI to blockchain to quantum computing to edge computing to affective computing, which is emerging as an interdisciplinary field that interfaces computer science, psychology and cognitive science. The same is the case with technologies in new biology, new energy, new materials, etc.

As regards talent and technology, young start-ups are turning out to be a valuable resource for talent and technology, provided they are backed up with trust. The government has created laudable initiatives to support the start-up ecosystem within the country. One of the key drivers and motivators should be creating bold public procurement systems for start-ups in government purchases. 'The Swiss Challenge' approach to such procurement is one such enabler. It is a method of bidding, often used in public projects, in which an interested party initiates a proposal for a contract or the bid for a project. The government then puts the details of the project out in the public and invites proposals from others interested in executing it. On the receipt of these bids, the original contractor gets an opportunity to match the best bid.[25]

We have seen some of the progressive steps that some states have taken in terms of mandating government departments with public procurement from start-ups, easing the tendering processes, etc. These need to be widespread.

Indian start-ups are doing very well. To the last count, there were 106 unicorns,[26] which means a market capitalization crossing $1 billion.[27] What is encouraging is that almost half of these unicorns are by founders who have not studied in Ivy League institutions. They come from institutions from tier 2 or tier 3 cities, and some are even college dropouts. This implies a democratization of opportunity.

However, most of the start-ups appear to be on consumer tech and not deep tech. A recent study highlighted that only 4 per cent of the investments have been in deep tech start-ups. This needs to change. The challenges faced by start-ups exploring high science- or technology-led innovation are described by the author.[28] They need to be addressed.

The government must have tax exemption policies, excise duty reductions, policies to provide massive public procurement support for the early-stage market seeding and market expansion of such products. Amitabh Kant has edited a book titled *The Path Ahead: Transformative Ideas for India*[29] on transformative ideas that can change India. In that book, the author has provided a framework for such a bold and visionary public procurement policy.

The recent steps to create city-specific knowledge clusters, such as the Pune Knowledge Cluster, are very welcome. These innovation clusters are sector-specific and bring all innovation players with domain expertise—from academy, industry, finance, etc.—together. There should be hundreds of research or technology parks funded through public-private partnerships.

Building Scientific Temper

Progress in STI will mean nothing if India continues to be plagued by superstition and dogmas. India must adopt a scientific temper as a way of life, in terms of both thinking and acting. It must encompass individual, societal and political levels. It must consistently use the principles embodied in scientific method, involving the application of logic. Discussion, argument and analysis have to become vital parts of this scientific temper. Elements of fairness, equality and democracy have to be integrally built into it.

The assertions about scientific temper continue to find a place in every STI policy. Most recently, there was a reassertion of this in the Scientific Social Responsibility Policy brought out by the present government in September 2019.[30] It made a specific statement on scientific temperament committing to 'an approach to human and social existence that rejects dogma or assertion that contradicts empirical evidence or lacks a scientific basis, that habit surely questions everything, that privileges logic and rationality and is consistently self-critical.'

The question is what actions will make this possible. For India@2030 to become a nation with a fully scientifically tempered population, the author proposes five transformational tenets that can be made actionable in the decade of the 2020s.

- For students: from treating science as a subject to science as a way of life, and also not just remaining students of science but becoming ambassadors of science in society.
- For citizens: not just remaining consumers but promoting and practising citizen science.

- For civil society: changing the role from delivering services to spreading scientific temper.
- For media: changing from sensationalism to sensible science journalism.
- For cultural transformation: changing from obedience to openness and also from censorship to freedom of expression.

Clever Balancing of Technology Options

In India, we always considered the 'make' or 'buy' options, which unfortunately got converted to 'importing' and 'import substituting' in the closed economy that we had. India has to carefully consider not just the two options of 'making' or 'buying' but also 'buying to make better', 'making to buy better' and 'making it together'.

'Making' has been a preferred course of action, but one cannot make everything. Also, if one has to reach a high rate of economic growth, then other alternatives have to be sought.

'Buying' the knowledge embedded in a technology or a machinery is possible when the owner is willing to part with it. Technological advancement is a continuous process. The base technology is designated as Mark I. Incorporation of advanced performance features raises it to Mark II. State-of-the-art technology with the most advanced features makes it into a Mark III technology, which gives the owner a competitive advantage. Even in the post liberalization era, India has realized that when Mark III technologies are available with the owner, one has managed to discuss only Mark II and one has been lucky to get Mark I, since no one wants to give away a competitive advantage. Let us realize that India is not being looked at as a bottomless pit of demand but as a global competitor.

Smart countries like Japan opted for the third option of 'buying to make better' route. They acquired knowledge through licensing, absorbed it and developed superior products, which competed with the best in the world. India did not do that; we kept on buying and buying.

We have not always followed the fourth option of 'making to buy better'. Familiarity with a knowledge or a technology domain gives one an advantage in negotiations, strategic positioning and so on. It is only then one can negotiate for Mark III and get it from a position of strength.

For India, 'making it together' is the preferred option in the long run. This means creating knowledge networks between all knowledge centres in the academic world, national laboratories, etc., and our productive sector.

India must have a short-, medium- and long-term plan on what is the dynamic mix that they will create of the five options, namely buy, make, buy to make better, make to buy better and making it together.

FINAL WORDS

If the 10 pathways elaborated above are followed, Indian STI@2030 would have the following 10 features:

- India will create science that will provide solutions, technology that will bring transformation and innovation that will have impact.
- India will create science that will lead and not follow.
- Indian innovations will be disruptive and not always incremental.
- India will not be just a land of ideas but also a land of opportunities, and therefore, it would move from the current state of brain drain to brain gain to brain circulation.
- Indian STI will be risk-taking and not just risk averse.
- Make in India will not just mean assembled in India but invented and made in India, and not just for India, but for the world.

- India will create products with unprecedented cost/performance features and not just marginal cost or future improvements.
- India will create 'next practice' in STI, which others will follow, and it will not just opt for 'best practice', following others.
- Indian STI will dedicate itself to making sure that no one is left behind. It will become a global leader in disruptive and inclusive innovation, which can bring in rapid and radical yet sustainable transformation in India.
- In India's STI journey, it has moved from a follower to a fast follower so far. From there, it will not just leapfrog but pole-vault to a new future as a proud leading nation in STI.

6

INTERNATIONAL TRADE POLICY

Harsha Vardhana Singh

International trade policy has evolved to include policy measures both at the border and inside the border. The major significance of global value chains (GVCs) has transformed conventional trade policy into an industrial policy, which involves a strategic assessment of suitable policy initiatives. A close link of FDI with GVCs means considering trade and investment policy as two sides of the same coin. The fact that GVCs combine goods, services and technology further expands the toolbox of international trade policy.

Competition in GVCs takes place in terms of three different performance parameters, each of which is crucial. These include (i) timeliness of turnaround time for imports to be processed and further exported, (ii) cost-effective production of output that goes into the GVC, and (iii) consistent quality of domestic products with other parts of the GVC so that smooth operations of the GVC can be maintained. Thus, trade facilitation and consistent standards become crucial for enabling trade growth. Furthermore, experience shows that countries that have achieved a rapid growth in trade have interacted closely with the firm that manages the GVC, i.e., the 'lead firm'. This firm becomes a crucial interlocutor in the policy dialogue, and in several cases, the process of interaction must be based on identifying the priority sectors that need to be emphasized. Combine that with the aspirations of a nation and its firms to climb up the value chain and provide a larger part of the value within the GVC. This implies a vast array of issues and policy initiatives that need to be considered within an operational and practical framework of analysis. The purpose of this chapter is to provide such a framework with its key elements, explain the implications of different policies that need to be emphasized and draw the conclusions together within a coherent approach.

India's aspiration for a huge increase in GDP this decade requires a major rise in exports, a point that has been recognized in an important speech on 6 August 2021 by Prime Minister Narendra Modi. Recalling the distant past, he stated: 'When we had the highest share in the global economy, it was due to robust trade and exports... Today, as we try to reclaim that old stake in the global economy, the role of our exports is very important.'[1] Significantly, among the top 20 economies in 2020 (India is one of them), except the US, the ratio of merchandise exports to GDP of all other economies is higher than India.[2]

China is a major example of a large economy whose export growth has powered its GDP rise. In fact, both China and India's exports have grown comparatively much more rapidly than their GDP (see Table 1). China's more rapid growth of exports compared to India has contributed to a relatively higher growth of its GDP, as shown by the ratios of China and India in Table 1 below. Table 1 also shows an important point that is well-known but often overlooked in the discussion of the contribution of trade to economic growth. It is that imports are a very important part of the story of contribution of trade to economic growth. China's merchandise imports have grown more rapidly than those of India, over time, and have played a very significant role in enabling its export growth. This reflects the integral role of imports in GVCs, which involves imports being processed and exported further to another country.

Table 1. Ratio of China to India's Performance: GDP, Merchandise Trade and FDI, 1980 to 2021

	1980	1990	2000	2010	2020	2021
Ratio of China's GDP to India's GDP	1.03	1.12	2.59	3.63	5.51	5.59
Ratio of China's Merchandise Exports to India's Merchandise Exports	2.11	3.46	5.88	6.97	9.37	8.51
Ratio of China's Merchandise Imports to India's Merchandise Imports	1.34	2.26	4.37	3.99	5.54	4.69
Ratio of China's Annual FDI Inflows to India's Annual FDI Inflows	0.72	14.73	11.35	4.18	2.33	4.05
Ratio of China's Inward FDI Stock to India's Stock	2.4	12.5	11.8	2.9	4.0	4.0
Ratio of China's Merchandise Exports to GDP (%)	9.5%	17.2%	20.6%	25.9%	17.6%	19.0%
Ratio of India's Merchandise Exports to GDP (%)	4.6%	5.6%	9.0%	13.5%	10.4%	12.5%

Source: The World Bank, WTO and United Nations Conference for Trade and Development (UNCTD)

FDI inflows also play an important role in the growth of international trade, especially given that most GVCs are coordinated by transnational corporations (TNCs).[3] Table 1 shows that India's inward FDI has improved, especially after 2000, though its inflow and stock are still significantly less than China. India's FDI and its important role in GVCs and international trade policy are being emphasized much more recently than earlier.[4] Recognizing the importance of GVCs, PM Modi emphasized the need 'to increase India's share in the global supply chain in exports manifold' in the 6 August 2021 speech. This change in approach suggests that India's policy perspective is evolving towards the policies adopted by China and Vietnam during the past decades, but there are still important differences (see Table 2 below).

An important difference between Indian policymaking and that of other major economies is that the others develop their policy initiatives based on strategic evaluation and approach. India does not appear to do so. A strategic approach identifies key objectives, policy measures to achieve them effectively, prioritization amongst objectives and sectoral initiatives, monitoring and improvement of policy initiatives to enhance effectiveness, close consultation with domestic producers (including FDI), reducing obstacles to operational difficulties, and an approach to augment access to global markets. An understanding of the impact of policies on key objectives helps prepare the relevant approach to trade policy, based on policies and experience of countries that have successfully emerged as major exporters in several sectors.

The discussion in this chapter primarily addresses the trade policy issues relevant for the non-agriculture sector. While several of the policy insights of the chapter are relevant also for agriculture trade, agriculture trade policies are more complex and require a separate treatment. It is significant, nonetheless, that the points made here will apply to a very large part of India's international trade, since non-agriculture trade account for almost 90 per cent of India's merchandise exports and 94 per cent of its merchandise imports.

POLICY ASPECTS OF SUCCESSFUL EXPORT STRATEGY

The analysis in this chapter has illustrated several important points contrasting the experience of India with China and Vietnam, two of its main competing economies. Table 2 shows that both the approach and content of certain important policies differ amongst India, China and Vietnam. While Vietnam's general approach is broadly similar to that of China, it considers a longer period for achieving its objectives due to its lower resource and skill base.

Table 2. Significant Features of Policy Approaches of India, China and Vietnam

	India	**China**	**Vietnam**
Policy Focus on: ↓			
Exports →	Yes, but incomplete facilitation	Yes. Focussed support especially for major global firms	Yes. Focussed support especially for major global firms
Imports →	Lukewarm to obstructionist	Facilitative, especially if imports are part of supply chain of exports	Facilitative, especially if imports are part of supply chain of exports
Coordinating policy support for supply chain →	Partial	Full support, provided in discussion with the major company concerned	Aim for full support, provided in discussion with the major company concerned

Scale →	Low to medium importance	High importance	Medium to high importance
Emphasis on domestic content: ↓ →	High	High	Medium
Time profile →	Achieve high domestic value addition early, e.g. three to five years	Medium term, five to ten years	Medium to long term, ten or more years
Policy approach →	Requirement to meet domestic content ratio	Engaging through building strong production linkages and broad-ranging policy support to build domestic content	Engaging through production linkages and policy support for domestic firms supplying priority export sector
Policy emphasis on scale as a factor→	Domestic content ratio is the main focus of policy requirement	Begin with scale and then achieve domestic content ratio (DC) over time, i.e. focus on aggregate DC first	Same as China, though with a longer time perspective

Practices of successful countries show that the overall impact of policy initiative depends on three inter-related aspects:

1. The **policy measures** used for guiding/supporting trade performance in the next 10 years.
2. **Effective monitoring** to ensure that the policy measures are successfully implemented.

3. The **substantive policy approach** emphasized by the government, e.g., import substitution or export promotion.

The policy approach drives the other two aspects because it determines the content and impact of the other two. If the dominant policy approach emphasizes limiting imports and does not focus on enabling exports, then trade policy will basically focus on limiting imports and not on facilitating exports. Likewise, if the supply chain is not considered as an integral basis for trade policy, then the policy focus will become the responsibility of limited parts of the government, e.g., the Ministry of Commerce and Industry. The important aspect of overall coordination emphasized by other major exporting countries is not yet given due emphasis in India. Therefore, in many instances, the approach adopted to implement policy works contrary to the objective to be achieved by the policy. In this context, some points which are often overlooked and need to be kept in mind are discussed below.

- **Major focus on import substitution blinkers out a consideration of interlinked policy impact**: All competing economies use financial incentives and emphasize reducing the regulatory burden, but they differ from India in terms of their tariff policies. India's approach to trade policy is a combination of reducing the regulatory burden, raising tariffs to attract FDI and domestic investment in the sector, and incentivizing investment through subsidies such as PLI schemes.

  A point often missed in this context is that higher tariffs on inputs raise costs and thus reduce the effective support provided through PLI. Table 3 shows that India's average tariffs on non-agricultural products are the highest amongst various competing nations. Further, India has the lowest openness of its trade regime in terms of the proportion of its tariff lines with zero tariffs. In contrast, competing Asian countries that have made special efforts to become significant parts of the GVC have a large portion of their tariff lines with zero tariffs. Higher tariffs orient production and sales towards the domestic market and away from global markets, i.e., they discourage exports.

Table 3. Non-Agriculture Most Favoured Nation (MFN) Tariffs and Duty-Free Lines of India and Selected Other Countries

	Simple Average MFN Tariff (%)			Percentage of Tariff Lines with Zero Tariffs (%)		
	2010	**2015**	**2021**	**2010**	**2015**	**2021**
India	9.8	10.1	14.9	3.1	2.5	1.8
China	8.8	9	6.5	7.7	6.9	8.6
European Union	4	4.2	4.1	26.7	26.5	28.6
Malaysia	5.8	5.5#	5.2	63.2	65#	65.2
Philippines	5.8	5.7	5.5	2.7	3.9	14.3
South Korea	6.6	6.8	6.6	17.2	16.7	18.9
Taiwan	4.5	4.8	4.8	31.6	31.1	32.2
Thailand	8	7.7	8.4	24.2	39.2	40.9
USA	3.3	3.2	3.1	47.6	48.4	50
Vietnam	8.7	8.4	8.4	40.2	38.8	38.6

Source: WTO

Note: # = Estimate is for 2014

- **Key role of large-scale operations is not yet recognized in policy**: Scale of investment and production plays a very important role in improving costs of operations and competitiveness, creating a possibility for longer production runs, supplying larger export orders and attracting more established global brands as buyers. Supporting scale implies a focus on certain policy steps to develop industrial capacity, together with a policy approach encouraging a larger domestic ecosystem and easier establishment of contract suppliers or Tier 1 to 3 suppliers to lead firms in GVCs. This, in turn, over time, paves the way for a larger domestic value added (DVA) and greater participation by the domestic producers in GVCs. Figure 1 below illustrates the links between scale and exports as well as DVA.

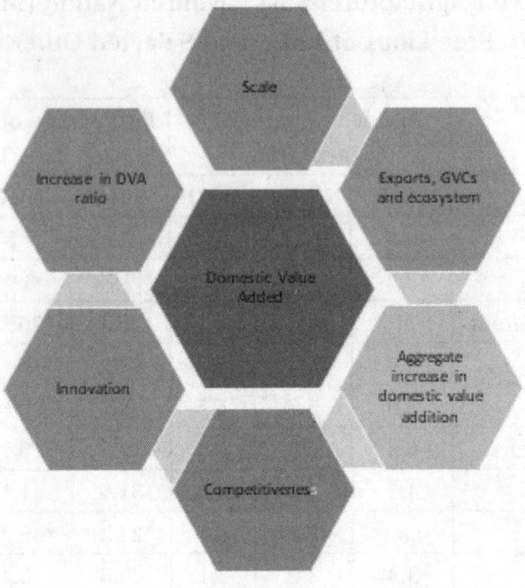

Figure 1. Sequential links between scale, exports, competitiveness and domestic value addition. (Source: https://bit.ly/3f9vlB9)

An important point in this context is that relatively high tariffs limit the scale of operations by shifting attention towards the domestic market and away from global markets. An increase in scale is essential to achieve a higher share of global markets through rapid export growth across a range of goods, as shown by the successful export economies (Table 4).

Table 4. Ratio of Exports in Competing Economy to India's Exports (2001, 2010 and 2020)

	2001	2010	2020
Electronics Exports			
Ratio of China's Electronics Exports to Indian Exports	52.9	78.2	81.2
Ratio of Vietnam's Electronics Exports to Indian Exports	0.8	1.0	11.3
Clothing Exports			
Ratio of China's Clothing Exports to Indian Exports	6.7	11.6	10.9
Ratio of Bangladesh's Clothing Exports to Indian Exports	0.9	1.3	2.1
Ratio of Vietnam's Clothing Exports to Indian Exports	0.3	0.9	2.2

Source: WTO and ITC Trade Map

- **Achieving higher DVA requires a focus on aggregate DVA rather than specifying a requirement for DVA ratio:** Increasing DVA (or reducing import content) is an important objective of India. It has begun introducing DVA ratio as a requirement for receiving financial incentives for certain sectors. This creates difficulties for three reasons. One, such a policy violates the WTO provisions and may lead to other nations imposing restrictions on Indian exports. Two, it takes a long time to increase DVA ratio as is evident, for example, from the experience of the Indian automotive sector and China's experience. The Indian DVA requirement policy, in contrast, focusses on a relatively short period of time, which creates operational difficulties if adequate technological capacity is not present in India to competitively replace imports by domestic content. Three, the DVA ratio tends to decline rather than increase if the production technology shifts to higher levels of complexity (which happens in several sectors). Insisting on raising the DVA ratio in such sectors would bind production in India to lower technology or higher cost operations, with adverse implications for export performance. That is the reason for Figure 1 to focus first on increasing the aggregate DVA, and at a later stage, on increasing the DVA ratio.

Table 2 above indicated that competing countries like China and Vietnam also emphasize DVA but have a longer time horizon than India. Their initial focus is on increasing the scale of production and establishing the domestic ecosystem, which increases aggregate DVA through a larger level of domestic output. This is a more efficient way of achieving higher total DVA in the country than an insistence on timebound DVA ratio. An approach focussing on scale and larger aggregate of production also provides a stronger basis for the FDI to connect with an increasing base of domestic producers in their supply chain. That helps to increase both the aggregate and the ratio of DVA over the medium term, i.e., three to five years.

Other Key Conceptual Aspects of Trade Policy

- **Trade policy is industrial policy**: International trade policy, whether relating to goods or services, involves policies both at the border (e.g., tariffs, import quotas) and inside the border (e.g., standards, regulatory policy, trade facilitation). Thus, trade policy is essentially industrial policy.
- **Trade policy must be devised as a national-level policy**: GVCs involve multiple goods and services, and hence policies relevant to them involve multiple ministries and departments. An important corollary is that trade policy is an important national-level policy and, in terms of importance, should be treated as a government-wide initiative.

- **GVCs show trade and investment policies are two sides of the same coin**: GVCs, which are a very important feature of trade, involve products from a number of different countries. The operations of GVCs are normally coordinated by a major firm (usually a multinational), which is referred to as a lead firm. Several countries have interacted closely with lead firms to develop their strategic trade policy approaches. Since the structure and linkages within GVCs are not the same in different industries, close consultation and consideration of the key requirements of GVCs is an important part of trade policy initiatives.
- **Competing in GVCs requires timely decisions (including import/export clearances) and quality/standards consistent with major global markets**: Competitiveness in GVCs depends on the time taken for processing the inputs (including imported inputs) and exporting products that meet the quality requirements of the GVC. Thus, competition within GVCs takes place in terms of timely clearance at the border (imports and exports), a quick turnaround of the product for exports by the firm processing the imported input and consistent quality of the product at a competitive price.

Some Other Policy-Related Factors

Higher global competitiveness requires both making appropriate policies and maintaining policy stability. Policy stability is important to create reliable business plans and to reduce uncertainty for investors.[5] It encompasses two aspects. One, to not change policy measures frequently or without due notice, and second, to not adopt WTO inconsistent policies, i.e., policies likely to be challenged at the WTO.

Stability of policies that help firms to reduce costs and improve quality of products is essential for competing in global markets. Similarly, tariffs on inputs increase costs of operations. Thus, policies such as tariffs that increase operational costs should be a secondary choice and that too as a temporary option, if at all it is needed.

The evolution of regulatory regimes facing Indian exports is another important factor to consider. Changes in regulatory regimes take place through changes through the WTO and free trade agreements (FTAs).[6] They change the prevailing global competition conditions and must be an important consideration for policy formulation.

Competitiveness is also affected due to technological developments that change both the operational conditions and the underlying basis of trade policy because they may alter the mode of conducting trade itself. Developments in digital trade are a prime example, and domestic policies must be developed to take account of such changes.

International Trade—Successes and Shortcomings

India's merchandise exports are almost two-thirds of its goods and services exports, and remain the main focus of policymakers to reduce India's trade deficit. In 2021, India was the sixth-largest economy, the eighteenth-largest merchandise exporter and tenth-largest merchandise importer in the world.[7] India was the eighth-largest exporter and tenth-largest importer of commercial services in 2021.[8]

- **Merchandise exports**: For merchandise exports, India entered the group of top 20 exporters in 2010 and has stayed close to the bottom of this group (Table 5). In 2019, Vietnam was a potential newcomer having become the twenty-third-largest merchandise exporter in the world. In 2020, Vietnam became the twentieth-largest exporter, with India's position lower at the twenty-first rank, though India's GDP is 7.6 times that of Vietnam.[9] However, this ranking changed in 2021, when India became the eighteenth-largest exporter and Vietnam dropped to the twenty-third position. It is, however, noteworthy how much Vietnam has improved its position compared to the others (Table 5 below).

Despite being in the lower segment of the top 20 merchandise exporters, India has performed relatively well over time. For example, India achieved very impressive growth in merchandise exports between 2000 and 2011. With two exceptions (2001 and 2009), India's merchandise exports increased annually by double-digit rates between 2000 and 2011.[10] India's rank as exporter improved from thirty-second to nineteenth, and its share in global merchandise trade rose from 0.7 to 1.7 per cent over this period. Since then, till 2020, however, India's share of annual global merchandise exports has ranged between 1.6 and 1.7 per cent. In 2021, the exceptional increase in India's exports led to this share reaching about 1.8 per cent. China and Vietnam are examples of a spectacular rise in merchandise exports ranking. China became the largest exporter in the world in 2009 and has remained at that level since that year (Table 5).[11] Vietnam rose to become the twentieth-largest exporter of merchandise in the world in 2020, from a rank of fiftieth-largest exporter in 2008 (Table 5).

- **Merchandise imports**: India's merchandise imports were the fourteenth-largest in the world in 2020, up from twenty-fifth rank in 2000 (Table 6). Since 2009, China has remained the second-largest importer of merchandise since 2009. Vietnam was the nineteenth-largest merchandise importer in 2020, up from forty-second-largest in 2008 (Table 6). India has been among the top importers of merchandise for several years now, and its rank as importer has been higher than its rank as exporter (Tables 5 and 6). This situation reflects the Indian government's focus on improving exports while limiting imports. However, the experience of Vietnam, with its rise in the ranks for both exports and imports since 2008, shows that imports play a very significant role in the growth of exports (Tables 5 and 6). A similar broad picture emerges for India during 2000 to 2011 when its exports were increasing rapidly, and for China, when its trade rank started growing strongly from 1997 onwards, with the improved ranking in imports preceding that for its exports (Tables 5 and 6).

In 2020, while India's merchandise imports became 7.2 times the level in 2000, imports of China and Vietnam increased at a faster rate to become, respectively, 9.2 and 16.8 times their imports in 2000. The significance of imports for export growth of Vietnam can be seen in another way, namely that Vietnam's merchandise imports were 30 per cent of India's imports in 2000, and reached about 70 per cent of India's merchandise imports in 2020.

- **Trade deficit:** India has registered a trade deficit every year since 1973. In 2021, its trade deficit was about 45 per cent of its merchandise exports. Thus, trade deficit remains a major concern for the policymakers despite India's current account deficit being much lower than the trade deficit because of its surplus on the invisible account. One reason is that this deficit has remained consistently high for a long period of time: since 2005, the ratio of India's annual trade deficit to its exports has ranged between 35 per cent (in 2020) to 65 per cent (in 2012). In contrast, China and Vietnam managed to convert their trade deficit into a surplus. China has registered a trade surplus each year since 1994, and Vietnam has had a trade surplus each year since 2016. These nations have achieved this with comparatively lower tariffs than India.

Table 5. Global Rank of India, China and Vietnam in Global Merchandise Exports, 1995 to 2020

	2008	2009	2010	2011	2012	2013	2014	2015	2016	2017	2018	2019	2020
China	2	1	1	1	1	1	1	1	1	1	1	1	1
India	23	21	19	19	20	20	19	20	20	20	19	19	21
Vietnam	50	40	40	41	37	34	32	27	27	27	26	23	20
	1995	**1996**	**1997**	**1998**	**1999**	**2000**	**2001**	**2002**	**2003**	**2004**	**2005**	**2006**	**2007**
China	11	11	10	9	9	7	6	5	4	3	3	3	2
India	31	32	32	32	33	32	31	31	31	30	29	28	26
Vietnam	61	58	54	53	52	50	49	48	50	50	49	49	50

Source: WTO

Table 6. Global Rank of India, China and Vietnam in Global Merchandise Imports, 1995 to 2020

	2008	2009	2010	2011	2012	2013	2014	2015	2016	2017	2018	2019	2020
China	3	2	2	2	2	2	2	2	2	2	2	2	2
India	14	14	13	12	10	12	12	13	14	11	10	10	14
Vietnam	42	37	34	33	33	32	32	28	25	25	23	22	19
	1995	**1996**	**1997**	**1998**	**1999**	**2000**	**2001**	**2002**	**2003**	**2004**	**2005**	**2006**	**2007**
China	12	12	12	11	10	8	6	6	3	3	3	3	3
India	28	28	29	28	24	25	26	24	24	22	17	17	16
Vietnam	57	51	52	52	49	45	46	43	42	44	44	45	41

Source: WTO.

- **India's tariffs** are much higher than its competing economies, as discussed above. An important point in this context is that even though the applied MFN tariff for Vietnam has not changed much since 2010, its actual applied tariffs in recent years are much lower due to the several FTAs concluded by it. In 2020, over 80 per cent of Vietnam's imports were from its FTA countries, while only about 27 per cent imports of India came from countries with which India has FTAs. Likewise, in 2020, about 64 per cent of the exports of Vietnam went to countries with which it has FTAs, while the corresponding share for India was 35 per cent.
- **India's non-tariff measures (NTMs)** are in general less in number than its competing economies. However, the incidence of these measures depends on the number as well as how the NTMs are implemented. Recent developments show that the implementation of NTMs in India has become considerably more restrictive in the past few years, particularly due to a greater emphasis on import substitution.
- **Trade facilitation** is a very important part of trade policy, especially for GVCs. India has improved its performance in a number of areas. However, in some important areas, including procedures and fees and charges, India's performance needs to improve in comparison to its competing economies (Table 7). Of particular relevance would be to prioritize the areas where Vietnam is better than India, namely procedures, documents, and fees and charges.

All economies have a range of incentive schemes to attract FDI and promote specific target sectors. India, too, has such schemes, a recent example being PLIs for a number of sectors.

India has fewer FTAs, compared to several of its competing

economies, and in general, its FTAs are not as deep as others, e.g., they have a smaller number of tariff lines at zero duty. In addition, India's FTAs do not have the mechanisms that deeper FTAs have for addressing concerns about NTMs faced by exports. This means that some competing economies such as Vietnam have additional access to important export markets compared to Indian exporters. India has now begun focussing on FTAs. It will have to find ways to politically achieve a reduction in its tariffs on over 90 per cent of the tariff lines.[12] For this, a toolbox of solutions to India's concerns will need to be developed.

Table 7. Trade Facilitation Areas in Which Certain Competing Economies are Better than India, 2019 (Economies compared are India, China, Malaysia, Thailand and Vietnam)

Indicator	Countries Performing Better Than India
Advance rulings; appeal procedures; procedures	China, Malaysia, Thailand, Vietnam
Involvement of the trade community	China, Malaysia, Thailand
Fees and charges	China, Malaysia, Vietnam
Documents	China, Thailand, Vietnam
Automation	Thailand
Governance and impartiality	China

Source: 'Compare your country: Trade Facilitation Indicators,' https://bit.ly/3BFPt60. Accessed on 14 September 2022.

PATHWAY OPTIONS AND IMPERATIVES

The extensive scope of the relevant issues implies that more than one group would have to host the initiatives for a trade policy reform party. The main initiative would be that of the government with the private sector (domestic/FDI and industry associations).

This would include the officials of Indian Missions abroad.

Two other supplementary initiatives would be required. One, with the government and policy agencies of the main trading partners of India for improving bilateral access to foreign markets. The other would be to provide focussed attention by the industry associations, with the help of the government.

Below are outlined some of the choices and necessities for India, given the circumstances:

- **Need for strategic clarity:** India needs to develop a coherent strategic approach that identifies the main objectives and policies to achieve them effectively. This would involve prioritization amongst objectives and sectoral initiatives; effective implementation through monitoring and coordination mechanisms, involving close consultation with domestic producers to address operational difficulties; and developing domestic capabilities as well as increasing the access of Indian exporters to global markets.
- **Need to focus on the main objectives of trade policy**: In terms of international trade, the main objectives can be summarized as increasing trade activity with higher exports based on increased competitiveness (coupled with lower imports or a reduction in trade deficit). Another important objective of the Indian government should be to increase domestic participation in GVCs through higher DVA. In Table 8 below, reduction of imports is captured in terms of improved competitiveness and increased domestic market access for the domestic industry. Likewise, the objective of increasing exports is captured in Table 8 in terms of improved competitiveness and improved foreign market access. With an increase in competitiveness and scale of operations, DVA would also rise over time. Thus, broadly three types of policy initiatives become relevant for trade policy initiatives—improving competitiveness, increasing

access to domestic markets and access to foreign markets.

- **Need to think in terms of timelines beyond the short term**: The relevant focus of policy has to go beyond the short term to include likely impact over a three- to five-year period because in many instances, improvement in operational capabilities tend to begin with an increase in imports followed by higher exports in due time. A medium-term perspective is required also for achieving the objective of increasing DVA in the activities established through FDIs. Sustaining this objective over time requires improving competitiveness over the medium to long term.
- **Need to clarify the impact of major policy initiatives on the major objectives**: Based on policies emphasized in India and the main competing economies, Table 8 shows a list of key policy initiatives and their likely impact on the major objectives in the short term (one to two years) and long term (three to five years).[13]

A number of policies are likely to have a positive impact on all the relevant objectives considered in Table 8. Amongst these, policies from numbers 1 to 4 would have a quicker response. These four policies are, thus, very important policy initiatives and should be implemented across the board. The next four policies in Table 8, i.e., numbers 5 to 8, also have a positive impact on all the objectives but their impact is likely to take some more time, say one to two years. They, too, require a general supportive approach, but the nature of these policy initiatives is such that the government would need to identify and prioritize specific sectors for particular focus. These policy initiatives are required, especially for quicker establishment of export activities or GVC hubs, and are discussed in some more detail below.

The importance of encouraging a design ecosystem is often not given the priority it deserves. However, discussions with domestic industries and experience of economies that have emerged as successful exporting nations show that the design ecosystem plays a very important role in increasing the share of domestic producers in GVCs on a sustained basis. It creates positive benefits in terms of quality, efficiency and higher value-added activity. A beginning in terms of focus on this aspect could be considered for the priority sectors identified for policy support. The impact of improvement in design capability, though very significant, will take more than two years to become evident.

The policies mentioned at numbers 9 to 12 in Table 8 are the more conventional trade policies which are most often a focus of attention. One policy among these, i.e., tariff on inputs, does not give any positive result and should be avoided. Emphasis on not raising costs of inputs will also encourage a consideration of policy in terms of impact on the supply chain as a whole.

Tariffs and subsidies have different impacts, as shown in Tables 8 and 9. These differences are addressed in some more detail below (Table 9), because their implications involve a phased approach that needs to be kept in mind for improving competitiveness over time.

'Bilateral agreements' mentioned in Table 8 include both FTAs as well as limited initiatives, such as bilateral regulatory arrangements with specific nations, and effectively using established institutional mechanisms such a bilateral trade policy forums.[14]

Table 8. Impact of Policy Initiatives on Key Objectives

	Policy Improves →	Competitiveness – Short Term Impact	Competitiveness – Long Term Impact	Domestic Market Access	Foreign Market Access
1	Reduce regulatory burden/ operational time	Yes*	Yes	Yes	Yes
2	Reduce regulatory/operational cost	Yes*	Yes	Yes	Yes
3	Improve consistency of standards/ quality with global markets	Yes*	Yes	Yes	Yes
4	Easier access to finance	Yes*	Yes	Yes	Yes
5	Discussion/coordination with lead firms	Yes	Yes	Yes	Yes
6	Encourage establishment of contract suppliers to lead firms	Yes	Yes	Yes	Yes
7	Encourage scale of operation	Yes	Yes	Yes	Yes
8	Encourage establishment of design ecosystem		Yes	Yes	Yes
9	Subsidy	Yes	**No**	Yes	Yes
10	Tariff on finished good	**No**	**No**	Yes	**No**
11	Tariff on inputs	**No**	**No**	**No**	**No**
12	Bilateral/plurilateral trade agreements	Yes	Yes	**No**	Yes

* = Impact of the policy will take place relatively quickly, i.e., within the first six months to a year after implementation of the policy initiative

Table 9. Illustration of Likely Different Impacts of Tariffs and Subsidies

Policy Measure	Reduces ↓	Increases ↓	Impact on Competitiveness ↓
Tariffs →	- Imports - Domestic output if tariff imposed on inputs	- Domestic price - Domestic output, if tariff not imposed on inputs of the product	**Reduces** competitiveness This results in: - **Lower** ability to export; - **Lower** possibility of large-scale investment
Subsidy →	- Imports - Domestic price	Domestic output	1. **Increases** competitiveness in the **short term**, which results in: - **Higher** ability to export in this period; - **Increased** possibility of large-scale investment 2. **Reduces** competitiveness in the **medium to long term** by lowering incentives for innovation, which results in: - **Decreasing** ability to export; - **Reduced** possibility of sustaining large-scale investment

The different impacts of tariffs and subsidies shown in Table 8 are further illustrated in Table 9. Tariffs improve only domestic market access for domestic producers and not foreign market access (exports) and thus are not a useful instrument to increase exports. Subsidies help gain export market as well as domestic market share, though this momentum may be lost in the medium to long term. Thus, as shown in Tables 8 and 9, the impact of subsidies is different in the short term and over a longer period.

Both tariffs and subsidies have a negative impact on longer-term competitiveness because they disincentivize sustained improvements in efficiency. Thus, if implemented, these policies should be temporary, with a timeline announced for their phase out.

Moreover, since both tariffs and subsidies result in additional rents (profits) for domestic producers, they would press for their continuation when the phase-out period approaches. Therefore, there is pressure for both these policies to get a life of their own. If the timeline for phasing out these policies is not followed, they will lead to both a loss of competitiveness over time, with tariffs leading to this negative effect even within the shorter term. Further, continuing the subsidies for long will add pressure on public finances and create fiscal difficulties. To increase the pressure on domestic producers to incrementally work towards improving competitiveness after a short breathing period, together with the announcement of a time limit for these policies, they should be implemented in a degressive manner, i.e., the support provided by the policy should be reduced with time.

Tariffs are relatively easier to implement. However, specific focus is required for effectively implementing subsidy policy. Three points are particularly relevant in this context in addition to those mentioned in the subsection on 'consultation, monitoring and improving implementation of policy'. One, special attention must be paid to provide the incentives in a timely manner, without undue delay, as was seen with previous schemes, such as Modified Special Incentive Package Scheme (M-SIPS), which showed poor implementation and delays. Two, the procedures of verification during the implementation period should not become too burdensome. Three, care should be given to ensure that WTO-inconsistent conditions are not attached as a requirement for the incentive. It was WTO inconsistency of a previous incentive scheme, Merchandise Exports from India Scheme, which led to it being phased out.

- **The need for priority ordering**: The above discussion shows a need to prioritize policies and sectors on which they focus. Table 10 suggests a framework for such prioritization.
- **The need for coordination of policy initiatives**: Both production for exports and improving links to GVCs involve supply chains that cover multiple products or sectors. Thus, the relevant policies to improve performance will need to be coordinated across different ministries. Unless the political leadership gets actively involved with periodic oversight, the coordination effort will not succeed because the different functional priorities of ministries could work against a common effort towards improving trade and investment. Any differences need to be addressed at a high level of policy and decision-making. Structured coordination mechanisms would be needed at the senior bureaucratic level, the ministerial level, and one for oversight by the PM or a minister designated by him. The key ministries/departments for coordination at the Centre would include Commerce, Industry, Finance and any others as required, such as External Affairs, and the ministry/department directly dealing with the industry concerned.

Table 10. A Suggested Matrix for Prioritizing Improvement of Policies

	Large Impact of Policy ↓	**Small Impact of Policy ↓**
Quick result of policy initiative likely (6 to 12 months) →	Priority 1	Priority 2
Impact will take more than one year and sector is covered by PLI →	Priority 2	Not a Priority
Impact will take more than one year and sector is not covered by PLI →	Priority 3	Not a Priority

- **The need for effective policy implementation:** This is an important point of general relevance. India has announced a number of good policy initiatives but feedback from exporters suggests that implementation is not satisfactory, with major gaps between performance and intent in many cases. This requires a specific mechanism to improve efficiency of implementation.
- **The need for consultation, monitoring and improving policy implementation**: Policy initiatives would include either new policy measures to fill an identified policy gap or steps required to improve existing policy by removing obstacles to effective policy implementation. Both these require periodic consultations with industry on an ongoing basis every four to six months to identify major priority gaps or areas for improvement. The process should include the following:

    i. Information should be collected on the major policy-related obstacles that need to be addressed, preferably the top three or five priority policy concerns of each industry.[15]

ii. A time-bound programme to address these concerns should be implemented.
iii. A management information system (MIS) should be used to keep track of the extent of improvement that occurs by the time of the next meeting with industry (held every four or six months).
iv. The MIS information sheet should be put up on a website.
v. If the issue is not addressed in six months, it should be taken up to the ministerial level coordination committee, with identified obstacles and proposed solutions.
vi. If such a process is already being implemented under an existing committee, such as the National Committee on Trade Facilitation, for that committee, too, an issue unresolved for six months should be taken up to the ministerial level committee.

- **The need for steps that help quicker establishment of export hubs through GVCs**: Three overlapping policy areas are particularly relevant for establishing export hubs through GVCs, namely, discussion with lead firms in GVCs for new investment (or increasing scale of investment), encouraging contract suppliers of lead firms in other markets to locate in India, and encouraging a larger scale of operation.

  Lead firms managing GVCs and their establishment within the country together with their contract suppliers enables both a quicker establishment of the domestic ecosystem and increase in the scale of operation. Discussions with lead firms would help identify the relevant policy steps, an exercise which has been the hallmark of strategies of countries such as China and Vietnam.[16] Discussions with the lead firms are important because the nature of GVCs and the lead firms are not the same across industries, and sometimes differ even with the same industry, e.g., laptops and mobile phones.[17] Further, the lead firms are not necessarily foreign. They may be foreign in one industry, Indian in another and a mix of both in yet another.[18] Discussions can help identify the precise policy steps required and the manner in which they fit into existing policy initiatives or whether new ones need to be implemented. Most of the policy requirements would be in terms of financial incentives, reducing time and costs involved in the GVC, and predictability and stability of policies. Several of the requisite policies are already being implemented by the government. Thus, efficient implementation of the policies becomes a crucial factor. This would require dovetailing these initiatives into the consultation and monitoring mechanism discussed above.

Three areas where new policy-related thought processes would be needed to develop relevant policy initiatives are:

i. Establishing the domestic ecosystem;
ii. Facilitating higher scale of operations; and
iii. Platforms/mechanisms required for linking up the production of lead firms and contract suppliers with the domestic industry to help incrementally increase the domestic industry's participation in GVCs. These initiatives are likely to differ across industries.

These will require a joint effort by different parts of the government and industry associations.

STEPS TO A MORE EFFECTIVE POLICY

Other than the points discussed above, there are various other mechanisms that can be used to make policy more efficient. These have been discussed below:

- **Industry associations and export-promotion organizations**: Industry associations and export-promotion organizations are focussed more towards domestic industry to create a larger access to the domestic market for them. Thus, they miss out on an approach which takes into account the requirements of GVCs and exports. To encourage and monitor their contribution to exports, one of the reporting requirements of these organizations should be what they have done for export promotion/augmentation.

  Industry associations play constructive roles in several policy areas mentioned in Table 8 above. They are part of solution-oriented discussions for all policy areas. In addition, they have programmes that can help improve the monitoring exercise discussed above, and to establish training programmes for enhancing skills and providing information. Table 11 shows the main policy areas in which industry associations play a more active role. These initiatives should be dovetailed together with the national objectives, and similar to the monitoring and improvement suggested for the government, the industry association should also monitor and improve performance on its own.

Table 11. Important Areas for Contribution and Coordination by Industry Associations in National Policies

Policy Improves →	Collect Information	Training	Create Opportunities
Reduce regulatory/ operational time	Yes	Yes	
Reduce regulatory/ operational cost	Yes	Yes	
Improve consistency of standards/quality with global markets	Yes	Yes	Yes
Discussion/coordination with lead firms		Yes	Yes
Encourage establishment of contract suppliers to lead firms		Yes	Yes
Encourage establishment of design ecosystem	Yes	Yes	Yes
Bilateral/plurilateral trade agreements	Yes	Yes	Yes

- **Appropriate indices for comparison and guidance of policy focus**: At present, India compares its rank in terms of global indices such as for ease of doing business, logistics index, trading across borders index, competitiveness index, etc. A much more targeted exercise would be to compare India with its main competing economies. This will give more specific and relevant guidance on the issues to be addressed and identify specific practices of competing economies that India needs to give particular attention to. An example of this is provided in Table 7.

  There is a need to develop a new index for the specific areas emphasized by the government, for example, an index which helps track and reduce costs of exports.

An example of the issues to cover is shown in Table 12. Similarly, to get better indication of areas to improve in priority sectors, ease of doing business indices could be developed for individual priority industries, for instance, by export promotion organizations.

Table 12. India's Ranking for Selected Indices/ Performance Levels

Selected Components of Trading Across Border Index (2020):	**Rank among 193 economies**
A. Time to Export - Border Compliance (hours)	111
B. Time to Export - Documentary Compliance (hours)	75
C. Cost to Export - Border Compliance (USD)	64
D. Cost to Export - Documentary Compliance (USD)	65
Selected Components of Logistics Performance Index (2018):	**Rank as indicated below**
A. Lead Time for Export - Port/Airport Supply Chain	52nd out of 95 economies*
B. Lead Time for Export - Land Supply Chain	52nd out of 76 economies*

Source: 'Business Enabling Environment (BEE)*', The World Bank, https://bit.ly/3xog4C6. Accessed on 14 September 2022; Arvis, Jean-François, et al., 'Connecting to Compete: Trade Logistics in the Global Economy', The World Bank, 2018, https://bit.ly/2LLgQiW. Accessed on 14 September 2022.

Note: * = The total number of economies differs because of variation in the number of economies for which data is available on the issue covered by the index.

- **Bilateral agreements**: FTAs are a form of bilateral agreements that normally take considerable time to conclude. Also, they cover many sectors that create more work than an alternative, limited focussed discussion on specific areas where exports face difficulties in markets abroad. Such an alternative is the trade policy forum or regulatory arrangements between India and another nation, where bilateral trade concerns can be discussed and solutions found for the concerns of each country involved. Most of these concerns are likely to involve NTMs that need focussed attention and targeted meaningful solutions that are more easily identified through bilateral discussions.

- **Implement solutions suggested by the reports of expert committees established by the government:** There are several expert committees established by the government that have looked in detail at specific sectors and recommended policy steps for improving capabilities and exports. A number of these suggestions are yet to be considered for implementation; for example, some suggestions discussed in the Report of High Level Advisory Group (HLAG)[19] and a number of those mentioned in the EXIM Bank Report on Domestic Policy Constraints for Exports in Select Sectors.[20]

POSSIBLE SCENARIOS AND THE WAY FORWARD

Out of multiple possible scenarios, consider three likely situations. The country prioritizes trade as an area where coordination of policies and their implementation is monitored to identify areas of concern, which are then addressed through specific time-bound actions. This approach will increase India's world market share to reflect its large economy, and its trade performance will add further momentum to its economic growth. Another scenario could be where such coordination and focus are not provided, and India's trade share would stay nearer 2 per cent of global markets. In this situation, the trade deficit of India would remain a major concern, and many new competing economies will emerge to compress the operational space for India in global markets. Yet another likely situation is where some sectors and states follow the first option while others do not pay much attention to it. The third option is more likely in actual practice. In this background, the efforts of the Centre and states should be to ensure moving towards the first option in as coordinated a manner as possible for the Centre and states, with complementary steps taken by industry associations and export promotion organizations. This will lead to improvement in value addition and trade shares of India, and develop the potential that India has to go beyond the present situation where India's global merchandise exports have remained between 1.6 and 1.8 per cent for the past 11 years.

The discussion in this chapter has charted out a recommended pathway for success, including identifying impacts of various policies and criteria for priority ordering of policies and sectors.

In addition, one of the most important steps would be to examine and learn from the policy initiatives of those countries that have successfully taken away global market share from India. Comparative indices of the kind discussed above should be created to identify specific areas of improvement, i.e., areas in which India's performance lags behind competitors. In addition, a comparison should be made of the key cost items for industries in India and those in its competing economies, such as port charges, power costs, quality of power and time taken for different parts of the GVC. Disadvantages created in India due to policy-determined costs should be addressed within a short period of time.

India has been implementing reform and improvement in several policy areas for some years now. Discussions with lead firms will help identify priority policy steps that are still missing or policy initiatives not properly implemented. For both these groups of policies, it is important to establish a structured and effective monitoring mechanism to identify areas where implementation is tardy. Time-bound programmes should be implemented to improve the situation. In this context, the coordination mechanism discussed in this chapter, including high-level political oversight, is essential for progress.

A necessary complementary approach is to simplify regulations and regulatory systems, rule out introduction of policy changes with a retrospective effect, and not make changes in policy without a consultation process so that policy stability could become a part of the process of policymaking itself.

To the extent the policy initiatives impact multiple sectors, the effectiveness of such policies must be monitored and improved, particularly for the priority sectors. A very important current policy initiative of the government is the PLI scheme available for several sectors. These are obviously priority areas for the government. Special attention must be given to ensuring that operations in these sectors are not slowed down or face obstacles due to policy measures (e.g., tariffs on inputs or domestic standards delaying or adding cost to their operations).

In summary, lessons from an extensive review of industrial policy across several nations provide some key insights, namely that the 'disparate experiences [of different countries] reinforce the need for a strategic approach to trade policy and a close link between trade and competitiveness policies...[and] a structured system for monitoring and assessing programmes is a key ingredient for good policy in general.'[21]

7

WOMEN'S PARTICIPATION IN FUTURE GROWTH

Uma Ganesh and Shilpa Phadke

If India has to take advantage of the demographic dividend it enjoys, it is imperative that women's participation in the economy is enhanced dramatically. Therefore, the narrative has to be centred around not just the social dimension but how to propel the economy with the untapped potential of women at various strata of society.

UN Women defines women's economic empowerment as their ability to participate equally in existing markets; their access to and control over productive resources, access to decent work, control over their own time, lives and bodies; and increased voice, agency and meaningful participation in economic decision-making at all levels, from the household to international institutions.[1] Studies[2] have shown that the financial performance of firms improves with more gender-equal corporate boards. International Monetary Fund (IMF) evidence—from macroeconomic, sectoral and firm-level data—shows that women and men *complement* each other in the production process, creating an additional benefit from increasing women's employment on growth, such as a boost in wages for everyone.[3] In other words, adding more women to the labour force should bring larger economic gains than an equal increase in male workers (reflecting the fact that, in economists' jargon, the elasticity of substitution between women and men in production is low).

The World Bank reports that India's GDP growth rate would climb above 9 per cent if women had an equitable share of jobs, and that India could boost its growth by 1.5 percentage points per year if 50 per cent of women joined the workforce.[4] When more women participate in the labour force, men also benefit. A report of MGI suggests that if women participated in the Indian economy at the level men do, annual GDP could be increased by 60 per cent above its projected GDP by 2025, with underlying assumptions.[5] This brings to the fore the tremendous untapped potential of half of the population. The same analysis also suggested that India's potential GDP gains through achieving economic gender parity were larger than gains in any of the other regions they studied. In recognition of this potential, government and industry have initiated several steps resulting in positive changes to the status and contribution of women. Despite this, there are several areas that require urgent attention.

THE STORY SO FAR: SUCCESSES AND SHORTCOMINGS

The key indicators of progress are literacy and education amongst the female population. According to the All India Survey of Higher Education Report-2016 (AISHE), Indian higher education has maintained a steady female enrolment rate of around 45 per cent.[6] Although the gender gap in enrolment has decreased significantly post Independence, there still exists a disparity amongst different departments. Technology, medicine and commerce are some of the areas of study that are heavily male-dominated, while humanities departments show the opposite trend.[7] According to the report of AISHE 2019–20,[8] with the gross enrolment ratio (GER) in higher education in India crossing the 27 per cent mark, GER for females (27.3) for the second consecutive year recorded a higher percentage compared to males (26.9). In the five-year period from 2014–15 to 2019–20, female enrolment recorded an

18.2 per cent increase, as overall enrolment in higher education grew by 11.4 per cent in the same period.

However, school education for girl children continues to be a matter of concern. According to the report by Right to Education Forum,[9] even after 10 years after the Right to Education (RTE) Act came into being, 40 per cent of adolescent girls in the 15–18 years age group are not attending school, while 30 per cent of girls from the poorest families have never set foot in a classroom. Female literacy rate is still a long way to go. From a literacy rate of mere 18.3 per cent in 1951 to 74.4 per cent in 2018, three-fourth of India's population is considered literate after 75 years of independence. India's male literacy rate stood at 82.4 per cent and female literacy at 65 per cent in 2018.[10]

Historically, female labour force participation rates (FLFPR) in the formal, organized sectors of the Indian economy have been low. Decision-making to enter and remain in the labour force is based on a complex set of factors at both the household and the macro levels. At present, women workers in India constitute significant proportions of domestic workers, construction workers, street vendors, waste-pickers, home-based workers and day labourers. While work in the informal economy with its uncertain income streams and lack of safety nets can take various forms, women tend to be employed in or occupy the most vulnerable and the lowest-paid jobs, leading to a lack of adequate savings. Over 90 per cent of India's workers continue to be employed in this informal economy, without realizing their full potential or being able to contribute in a meaningful manner towards the growth story in the absence of a sustainable savings and investment model.

Just prior to the start of the pandemic, in January/February 2020, The Economic Survey,[11] released alongside the Annual Budget presentation of the Government of India, acknowledged and highlighted that the state should design policies that better involve women in the economy. It quoted the World

Bank, noting that 'no country can develop and achieve its full potential if half of its population is locked in non-remunerative, less productive and non-economic activities.'[12] Unfortunately, when it came to allocating funds, the 2022–23 Budget relegated women's economic participation to secondary importance, as the budget for the Ministry of Women and Child Development as a portion of the expenditure has declined from 0.57 to 0.51 per cent. The Economic Survey 2022,[13] released at the beginning of this year, nearly two years after the pandemic began, reiterated the importance of creating social safety nets for the masses whilst increasing spending to strengthen the infrastructure in the county. However, it did not include a detailed discussion on women-centric strategies to be adopted, especially against the backdrop of large numbers of women dropping out of the formal labour force during the lockdowns.

Worryingly, India's rapid urbanization has not yet encouraged more women to join the labour force. Rural jobs have been decreasing, and not enough rural women have been able to make the transition to working in urban areas. By any measure, the gap is particularly large and has been widening. NSSO data (2011–12)[14] shows that a majority of women take on employment in the primary sector, within the realm of agriculture and farm work. Within the manufacturing sector, they are found to be employed in low-paying, casual, home-based work or in unpaid work within family-run enterprises. In the tertiary sector, women are seen more in number in retail trade, education-related work and paid domestic household work. In the absence of support from male members of the household, women tend to gravitate towards these sectors to avail the flexibility to manage their unpaid and care responsibilities along with paid work. As per a report, women and girls in India contribute 3.26 billion hours of unpaid care work every day, representing the equivalent of at least $271 billion in unpaid income in India per year.[15] This burden of unpaid work negatively impacts women's economic gains and traps them at the bottom of the economy. On average, women tend to spend a disproportionately greater amount of time, often twice as much, than men on household work and almost five times more than men on childcare.[16]

The WEF reports that women's global average annual income stands at only $11,000 in purchasing power parity (PPP), compared to nearly twice that, $21,000, for men.[17] The Government of India revised the Companies Act in August 2013, making it mandatory for listed companies to have at least one women director on the board, a move that improved the representation from 5 per cent in 2012 to 55 per cent as of 2019, in the top 1,000 listed companies. However, women continue to occupy less than one-fifth of managerial positions[18] across corporate India. In firms with women in top leadership positions, the percentage is under 10 per cent.

Sattva Consulting, in collaboration with United Nations Development Programme,[19] found with respect to women's employment that:

1. There is a lack of jobs that match the skills and ambitions of educated women.
2. After 2000, as household incomes rose, competing outcomes of the household and the labour market have resulted in women forgoing their employment. Married women substituted their own economic participation to contribute to the household economy (deep-rooted social norms, lack of agency and gendering of occupations lead women to have little choice in this).
3. Women also might not be able to move and migrate as freely as men, and face several barriers to migration when it comes to work.
4. While many women might not possess the social support they require in order to work, many are made to work under compulsion. In India, the socio-economic

> disaggregation of participation rates also suggests that more disenfranchised social groups have higher rates of labour participation. So, participation rates themselves do not signal work by choice.

Addressing each of these constraints with long-term policy implementation will go a long way in fixing the declining FLFPR in India.

Several restrictive factors, such as higher education lag compared to male counterparts, motherhood penalty, societal and peer pressure to take on reduced-function professional roles, are all responsible for the low and downward trend of women's formal labour force participation. Other barriers to women entering the formal labour force include tax distortions, systemic discrimination and unequal share of childcare, senior/elderly/sick care, household chores and other errands.[20] Far too many women simply have had no choice but to undertake this work. It's the expectation—women will provide most of the childcare and other unpaid household labour, often at the expense of their own basic needs—which creates the disparity and inequality.

WEF's 2022 Global Gender Gap Report[21] figures indicate that 70.1 per cent of the participants in the labour force are men, while the percentage of women is significantly lower and accounts for only 19.2 per cent. This is one of the lowest workforce participation rates in the world for women, ranking India 135th out of 146 countries. The FLFPR in the country has fallen from 30.27 per cent in 1990 to 20.8 per cent in 2019, as per data from the World Bank. It's hard to develop in an inclusive and sustainable way when half of the population is not fully participating in the economy. At 17 per cent of GDP, the economic contribution of Indian women is less than half the global average, and compares unfavourably to the 40 per cent in China, for instance.

In India, much of the discussion on the falling trends has focussed on four key explanations: (i) rising educational enrolment of young women; (ii) lack of employment opportunities; (iii) effect of household income on participation; and (iv) measurement.[22] Over the last decade or so, India has made considerable progress in increasing access to education for girls, as increasing numbers of women of working age are enrolling in secondary schools. Nonetheless, the nature of economic growth in the country has meant that jobs were not created in large numbers in sectors that could readily absorb women, especially for those in rural areas. Despite inadequate job creation, household incomes did rise, which potentially reduced women's participation, especially in subsidiary activities ('income effect') due to change in preferences. Finally, though most women in India work and contribute to the economy in one form or another, much of their work is not documented or accounted for in official statistics, and thus, women's work tends to be under-reported. In India, a substantially high proportion of females report their activity status as attending to domestic duties.[23]

In order to address some of the key issues highlighted and create an environment for transformation and lasting change for the women in our nation, this chapter proposes some key imperatives and pathways that would lead to economic prosperity for women and their families as well as lead to incremental contribution to the nation's GDP.

PATHWAY OPTIONS AND IMPERATIVES

- **Agency building**

In order to facilitate more women entering the workforce, women and their potential have to be brought into the national consciousness in a planned and systematic manner, utilizing multiple avenues as a focussed agenda—there is an urgent need to move women's agenda from a 'good to have' status to 'must have' status in policies and implementation processes. It has to be brought centre stage, giving it a substantially enhanced focus as compared to the current status afforded by political parties and civil society, and make women's empowerment the core theme of their mandate, aligned with the transformation agenda of the nation. It has to occupy significant mind space of society by detailing the requirements to enhance the status and rights of women, just as the Right to Information Act (RTI) or Right to Education (RTE) had created few years ago. Career counselling and exposure to career pathways aimed at women should be instituted in high schools as a nationwide compulsory initiative, which could be supported by CSR programmes. Bold initiatives such as reservation of jobs for women within the existing framework or fresh framework could be considered for a limited period of time until equality in numbers is established, just as other marginalized segments of society have fought and won the opportunity to elevate themselves in the society.

As per an Oxfam India report, Indian women's unpaid work plays a crucial role in sustaining economic activity, equivalent to 3.1 per cent of GDP.[24] However, much of the contribution goes unrecognized or is incorrectly measured, amounting to a systemic transfer of hidden subsidies to the economy. Accounting for unrecognized work to bring more players into the care and household work sectors and informal sector work along with establishing social nets should be actively considered.

- **Workforce reforms**

The only possible equalizers across our vast, complex and unequal nation in this scenario are long-term education, quality skills training and 'good jobs' leading to a meaningful addition to the domestic income/savings/investments model and thereby contributing positively to the growth story over the long term.

A UNICEF study[25] highlighted the difficulties faced by young girls and women, especially in rural India, when not in school—lack of access to clean washrooms, sanitary products and regular nutritious meals; risk of exposure to violence at home, and a further increase in burden of household chores during the pandemic-induced lockdowns. Additionally, anecdotal evidence points towards girls, especially those in the urban poor communities or in rural areas, dropping out of formal schooling in high school (after standard 7 or 8) for numerous reasons—primarily, the onset of puberty, poor connectivity from their homes to the place of learning, looking after younger siblings/completing chores at home. However, more recent survey findings[26] report that there is a decline in dropout numbers for children aged between six and 14, and a shift from private to government schooling in rural areas. Three International Graduate Centre studies[27] assessed the Government of Bihar's bicycle programme from 2006, which provides girls in standard 9 with money to buy bicycles. It was found that the programme reduced the gender gap in age-appropriate secondary school enrolment by 40 per cent and led to a 32 per cent increase in the enrolment of girls in secondary school, and school dropouts for girls falling below 5 per cent.

Transitioning from traditional low-paying, informal sector jobs to more productive, better-paid work is the key to retaining women in the formal workforce. In emerging economies, there is a visible trend of jobs being displaced in agriculture-related occupations. For instance, agricultural work is one of the three top occupational groups driving job displacements for men (21 per cent of losses) in Mexico but is not in the top three for women.[28] However, in India, where so many women work in subsistence agriculture, losses in this occupational category could account for 28 per cent of jobs lost by women, compared with 16 per cent of jobs lost by men.

The Skill India Mission not only provides women with relevant skills sought by employers, it also ensures that training programmes are sensitive to their needs by helping provide safe transport, flexible schedules and childcare support. Women must monetize their skills to create unconventional job opportunities through compulsory vocational training programmes designed to address the needs of women from different segments based on the dynamic opportunities at different locations. Skilling will, therefore, be a mix of employment in corporates as well as sustainable livelihoods. Just as in the 1960s and the 1970s there was an impetus to job creation through public sector enterprises, to create an impetus for job creation on a massive scale for many and livelihood opportunities for others, SEZs could be set up. Incentives could be given to encourage investment in large-scale ventures, which would result in exclusive or maximum jobs for women. The digital platform announced recently by the Ministry of Rural Development in partnership with Amazon for enabling women artisans to reach out to customers is a welcome initiative.[29] In order to make this initiative a success, a cooperative movement to support women's livelihood initiatives should be encouraged, with finances and market access.

Using multiple communication channels such as social media, targeted emails, surveys, firms may highlight viable re-entry opportunities for women who may have stepped away from the formal sector or for women who may be starting off at a later stage in life. Mentoring of such newly recruited professionals by senior colleagues will help build confidence and enhance teamwork and productivity.

- **Reimagining MGNREGA**

The MNREGA programme has attracted more than 50 per cent women participation, although it was originally conceived as a scheme with priority to women participation being a minimum of one-third. Although this scheme has been beneficial to creating economic independence for women, it has to be noted that most men in the villages migrate to towns in search of jobs, leaving women to be part of MNREGA-led earning opportunities. The implementation of the scheme in most places is by men and, even with the introduction of women as counsellors or supervisors, the specific needs of women are not being fully addressed in many states. In time, many of the jobs performed by women that are pure physical labour will be replaced with automation. Therefore, it is time women from rural areas are trained for specific skills and are enabled to shift from sheer physical labour towards higher income opportunities in value-added agriculture or services or manufacturing sectors.

The government has announced an ambitious plan to provide healthcare support through Ayushman Bharat to every Indian citizen. In order to make this plan a success, the healthcare system in India will require last-mile touch points to provide timely and customized affordable medical care. The success of this plan will rest, to a great extent, on data collection of health status of citizens in every village and by deriving insights to enable deployment of resources and expertise to provide quality attention. Rural women could be encouraged to acquire skills in technology and data collection, and should be offered higher earnings through MNREGA or a similar new scheme aimed at technology adoption amongst rural women and aiding in healthcare transformation in rural areas.

- **Policy for women's welfare**

Policy changes that result in more women entering the workforce, such as removal of barriers to access secondary education, alternatives for quality and safe childcare, flexible work arrangements, increased access to health, access to legal counsel, sanitation and personal safety measures, opportunities to work for women, should be encouraged.

The government has taken certain steps in this direction; it has enacted the Maternity Benefit (Amendment) Act, 2017, which provides paid maternity leave from 12 weeks to 26 weeks. Implementation of this amended Act has not had the intended effect, as smaller firms are discouraged from hiring more women due to rising costs. In order to ensure women do not take advantage of the 26 weeks paid maternity leave on one hand and exit the organization after 26 weeks of leave, laws should be suitably amended to provide safeguards for organizations to encourage them to hire and retain more women.

Additionally, it has issued an advisory to the states under the Factories Act, 1948, to permit women workers to work in night shifts with safety measures and has provided training to women through a network of women industrial training institutes, and national and regional vocational training institutes. It has also enacted the Equal Remuneration Act, 1976, which provides payment of remuneration to men and women on a uniform basis without discrimination.

The current provisions for childcare for working women require attention, as the number of childcare centres and their standards are woefully inadequate in the country. In addition to encouraging firms to set up childcare centres for their employees to expand the network of quality and affordable childcare centres, there is also a need for well-qualified childcare providers with multiple skill sets, and a registration and certification system for childcare providers in order to build the required support system that instils confidence for working women.

Research from the ILO and UN[30] indicates that climate change-related impacts increase women's workload, as water scarcity in rural areas forces women to walk long distances in search of water. The provision of basic services and infrastructure enhances their power and agency, reduces their workload and increases the amount of time they can spend on productive activities. Additionally, promoting the equal sharing of unpaid care and domestic work between men and women can also help change social norms and transform labour markets.

- **Building networks in the workplace**

Training to network effectively will serve as a useful tool for women building their base as well as for career advancement.

A recent paper[31] documents that large gender gaps in research output persist across 50 years despite a significant increase in the fraction of women in the field of economics over that time. The paper demonstrates that output differences are closely related to differences in co-authorship networks of men and women: in that, women have fewer collaborators, they collaborate more often with the same co-authors and a higher fraction of their co-authors collaborate with each other. At the grassroot levels, there have been significant efforts to form self-help groups (SHGs) on the strength of collaboration in the community for the common good, and currently, there are 6 million SHGs covering 67 million members.[32] However, the ability to utilize the capital for generating income and market access continues to remain a challenge. Policies would be required to form clusters of specialization amongst the SHGs to provide training, upgrade finish and quality of their produce, and facilitate collective bargaining. It would also help to introduce guidelines that ensure minimum mandatory procurements from SHGs by large retailers.

- **Workplace health and safety**

An often-cited reason for women not being permitted to work outside the home is safety—the commute, mostly via public transport, including last-mile connectivity and concerns of bullying and harassment in the workplace. Gender-based planning is vital to eliminate these challenges and achieve a more equal ratio of female to male workers in the formal sectors.

In order to boost female participation in the mainstream economy, the first milestone that needs to be accomplished is providing egalitarian healthcare to all. Clean, sanitized washrooms, with access to feminine hygiene products, and break areas, including safe spaces for nursing mothers, will go a long way in retaining female employees and increasing diversity and experience for the organization. Large organizations have started creating women-friendly work environments, while smaller organizations and offices functioning from shared spaces are not equipped to address these requirements. It would be prudent to make these specifications mandatory for every commercial complex being sanctioned where common facilities for nursing mothers as well as crèche for childcare is provided.

- **Changes at the household and society levels**
    1. Reduce excess female child mortality (increase birth registration; improve family incentives to value girls).
    2. Reduce malnutrition (increase attention to gender dynamics of feeding practices).
    3. Improve adolescent sexual and reproductive health outcomes (increase targeting of adolescent boys and girls in health and nutrition projects).

Using a Gender Parity Score, or GPS, calculated using these indicators, MGI[33] has established a strong link between gender equality in society and gender equality at work—and shown that the latter is not achievable without the former. Women regularly sacrifice wages, career progression and education opportunities to meet family responsibilities, safety considerations and other restrictions.

A two-fold mindset change is required at the family level: firstly, that household jobs or chores are the responsibility of all members of the household and, secondly, ensuring equal access to opportunity and education to all. The importance attached to an earning member of the family needs to be re-articulated and re-emphasized for all adults—this will, in turn, start the conversations of shared duties in household chores and care work, both of which are often automatically delegated to female members of the family. Sensitization programmes should be planned at schools so that society's respect for women is enhanced and children learn to treat women as true equals.

Another worrying and continued trend is that of 'missing

women'[34]—Amartya Sen argued that 'In South Asia, West Asia and China, the ratio of women to men can be as low as 0.94 or even lower'; this is due to a direct result of discrimination derived from cultural and economic reasons. When women are seen as economic agents and not burdens, societies prosper. Women's economic empowerment is highly connected with poverty reduction, as women also tend to invest more of their earnings in their children and communities. The top five reasons for females making an investment include future security, child's education, saving tax, retirement and family emergencies. The other reasons for making an investment were higher returns, regular income, improving lifestyle, accumulating wealth, buying a home, child's marriage and liquidity.[35]

At the same time, availability of work at the place of residence has proven beneficial to both women and households. Flexitime and less restrictive work arrangements favour women workers while also reducing time and resources spent on commuting. In order to enhance such opportunities for women, interventions to create awareness and build commercial linkages amongst the key stakeholders in each district would be necessary.

- **Covid-19 and the Aftermath**

The impact of Covid-19 on the workplace has presented new challenges for women. Trends that existed long before the pandemic, from disproportionate home care responsibilities to greater representation in low-wage employment, to long-standing gender inequalities in corporate leadership, have been exacerbated and have contributed to this unprecedented regression. The pandemic and its related economic shock resulted in massive job losses for women, especially informal workers, and slower recovery of women-led microbusinesses. A report released by UN Women[36] projects that the pandemic will push 96 million people around the world to extreme poverty by 2021. This will constitute approximately 47 million women and girls. Job volatility has hit the population as a whole, but the female workforce, in particular, has been disproportionately impacted by pandemic-related economic distress.

As per the study conducted by Dalberg in India, women comprised only 24 per cent of the workforce prior to the pandemic yet accounted 28 per cent of all job losses as the pandemic took hold.[37] Women, on an average, lost over two-thirds of their incomes during the lockdown, and as their unpaid workload increased, they were far more likely than men to report a loss of rest time. It also increased domestic work, deepened gender digital divides, disrupted girls' schooling and placed millions of female health workers at increased risk of loss of life and livelihood. India has experienced lowering of participation rate in labour by women since 2005, which stood at 24 per cent prior to the pandemic, whereas in our neighbouring countries Bangladesh and Sri Lanka, it stood favourably at 30 per cent. Although the argument has been around the increase in income leading to women dropping out from the labour force, this may be applicable to women from middle-income groups, but in the lower-income strata, more women have been forced to take up work in the informal sector. While the nation-rebuilding exercise is underway, women from the marginalized sections of society would require special attention to overcome gender-based income gaps further perpetuated by the pandemic. In recognition of a large percentage of women being part of the informal sector, policy interventions and economic frameworks are necessary to provide safeguards for their minimum earnings, work conditions, safety and health. Simultaneously, as work from home becomes the new normal, technology access is a crucial asset for India's labour force. In the post-Covid-19 recovery phase, the 'Make in India' dream can become a reality only if women are promoted as key drivers of technology-enabled growth. Expanding digital literacy amongst women and upskilling those to take advantage of the possibility of working from home with the help of digital access needs to be facilitated through a well-orchestrated strategy.

The corporate world should try and keep women in the workforce and ensure the pandemic doesn't erase years of progress. This requires a commitment from the top to drive measurable results. For starters, as women return to the workplace, a top-down approach of clear signalling of support towards all female employees, including zero tolerance of harassment, will foster a more conducive environment for all workers, irrespective of gender. Employers, community organizations, media and social influencers can play a vital role in spreading the message of making men equal care-work partners.

- **Access to Nutrition and Healthcare**

Starting with providing adequate nutrition to the girl child to ensuring antenatal care and the well-being of expectant mothers, the health sector must focus on customizing care and treatment at every stage and across geographical and socio-economic constraints. For example, a vast majority of Indian women are anaemic, a serious but easily corrected condition yet often-neglected. The World Bank[38] reports that the absence of a comprehensive gender lens in nutrition policies and programmes is contributing to the continuation of pervasive undernutrition across the region. Undernutrition compromises the overall health and well-being of a large share of South Asia's adult and child population. Gender disparities in nutrition are the most pronounced for women in the reproductive age group. The impact of a malnourished mother giving birth is well known—India has the dubious distinction of having a record number of underweight babies and severely stunted infants and children. Investment in human capital health must, therefore, become a vital national priority, ably supported and implemented by governments and decision-making bodies at the sub-national levels.

- **Promoting women-led start-ups**

An International Growth Centre[39] project in India found that greater access to microfinance loans led to a significant increase in female labour force participation, with the effect driven by self-employment and not by salaried jobs. However, on a cautionary note, while participating women were more likely to have the last word regarding household spending, it was not associated with an increase in their empowerment (which suggests that greater work to change mindsets of the other decision-making adults in the family was required). Results also suggested that as a consequence of increasing participation in the labour force, greater access to microfinance reduces fertility in the long run.

The start-up ecosystem in India has started picking up momentum. However, the Government of India estimates that currently only 10 per cent of start-up founders are women, and women fill just 22 per cent of positions in the field of AI despite India having the second-largest AI workforce in the world.[40] The lack of tech adoption and high expansion cost remains a major issue for 'femtech' start-ups looking to expand beyond urban boundaries.

Aggressive campaigns to encourage women to consider becoming entrepreneurs and attractive schemes to provide capital and mentoring would be necessary to create a flourishing women-led start-up ecosystem in the country. Low-cost loans, simpler turnaround processes for loan approvals and financial inclusion should receive more focus in the next decade. The government needs to facilitate wider public–private partnerships to enable the value creation for femtech start-ups in non-urban areas of India.

CONCLUSION

Harnessing the fullest potential of women is no longer a social imperative but an economic necessity. The dawn of the new era of innovation for India would have to be envisioned on the twin engines of women and technology. Hence, policies and programmes aimed at the well-being of women should no longer be drawn up with the view to just reduce the inequities, and therefore provide concessions to them, but should be seen with the lenses of economic potential and outcomes that can catapult India to new spheres of growth and sustainability.

8

SUSTAINABLE LIVELIHOODS AND SOCIAL COMMITMENT

Ejaz Ghani, Ganesh Natarajan and Abhay Vaidya

India has one of the youngest populations in a rapidly ageing world. While China's spectacular growth has already benefited from its demographic dividend, India is yet to do so. However, the growth benefit of a demographic dividend is not automatic. There is mounting concern that future economic growth in India and other developing countries could render a part of the population jobless due to the rise of the fourth industrial revolution and accelerated use of AI.

Digital and artificial intelligence are becoming integrated into many aspects of our life, powering everything from voice and facial recognition systems to automatic language translation services to customer support and virtual assistants. Their applications are now supporting the development of smart city infrastructure, automation of manufacturing processes, healthcare, drug discovery and cyber security. This rapid integration of digital economy into everyday life has generated widespread attention from industry, academics and policymakers alike that the benefits of the digital revolution and demographic dividend may not be automatic.

As the adoption of digital technology is likely to accelerate in the coming years, and a small number of countries are driving the development of AI, it has raised questions about job creation, fairness and transparency. A new global digital divide is emerging that may potentially adversely impact India and other developing countries that have played only a limited role in the global AI value chain that is taking shape.

Policymakers need a better understanding of where India is in the global digital and AI value chain, and how this will impact jobs and trade. Automation and robotics will be accelerated by AI, and there is already evidence that increased automation in high-income countries has created wage inequality and employment polarization. Many types of jobs—particularly those that comprise routine and predictable tasks—are already susceptible to automation using existing technologies. This shift has big implications for future job growth in India. Even if India does not adopt AI technologies, it will still be exposed to competition from higher-wage economies that have automated or high-income countries that decide to re-shore manufacturing by leveraging the efficiencies created by AI.

Policymakers also want to understand how demographic dividend will impact labour markets and job creation in the future. India will continue to add 10 million new workers every year during this coming decade. How will new jobs be created? While digital technologies may enable the creation of new products and more productive jobs, they may also substitute existing jobs. Lack of jobs with demographic dividend may increase the share of the population that is dependent on the working population. This will increase thc economic insecurity of the elderly, as there will be fewer people generating wealth.

DIGITAL REVOLUTION AND JOBS

Policy choices will affect how AI is deployed in India, which will, in turn, determine the extent and effect of the digital revolution and AI on jobs. These choices are related to whether to develop digital infrastructure, R&D capabilities, investment into high-capacity data infrastructure, the regulatory frameworks that are applied to data and technology. The scale of investments made in education and skills will also determine the impact of AI on job creation. India also has a role to play in global forums on how AI approaches are being developed at the global level.

If policymakers can scale up investments in human and physical infrastructure in India, AI technologies can augment labour productivity and increase capital accumulation, enabling new products, services and business models. The AI value chain depends on both 'soft' and 'hard' infrastructure. Hard infrastructure refers to the physical networks such as data networks, compute capacity and data storage capabilities that support the successful delivery of services and applications. Soft infrastructure is the set of institutions and AI ecosystem that are crucial for countries to develop and sustain a thriving AI sector. There remains a big gap in India between the current state of hard infrastructure and the development needed to participate in segments of the AI value chain. Since, in India, hard infrastructure is inadequate, policy actions should focus on creating and scaling up hard infrastructure.

Soft infrastructure allows the introduction and continuity of digital and AI-enabled services and applications. This includes institutions and an enabling digital and AI ecosystem. Institutions reflect policy, law and regulation, ethical principles and effectiveness of regulatory models (co-regulation, self-regulation, industry standards), and data access, use and sharing policy. The digital and AI ecosystem includes human capital for AI development and user adoption, and creating a network of stakeholders (for example, in research and industry programmes) that allow knowledge spillover, knowledge transfer and co-production of knowledge and know-how to develop AI applications from ideation to application.

There is a huge potential for applying digital and AI technology in the public and private sectors, based on capabilities and functions—enhancing human labour, reducing market frictions, optimizing resource allocation, governance, health, social protection, gender, climate change, disaster risk management, transport, energy, agriculture and finance. India needs both the hard and soft infrastructures to enable stakeholders to develop the applications.

A rising concern for policymakers is the impact of the digital economy and AI on the labour market and the extent to which AI will augment or replace labour. Experience with automation and AI worldwide has shown that computers and robotics can be a substitute for workers performing cognitive and manual tasks while it may complement workers who perform non-routine problem-solving tasks. The extent to which tasks can be replaced by machine learning depends on several factors such as the relative cost of capital over the cost of labour, the returns to productivity of capital versus that of labour, elasticity of substitution between tasks and the creation of new types of tasks or more complex tasks in the production process. The empirical evidence on which AI-enabled automation can displace workers at the task level is still scanty and at an early stage in India. With more adoption and diffusion of AI, there is a possibility that job polarization can become more accentuated. In the context of developed countries, the displacement of labour by automation is prevalent in middle-skill jobs, thus hollowing out the middle. The impact of AI on labour market polarization in developing countries remains largely unexamined. The empirical evidence on estimates of differences between demographic characteristics at the worker level and at the job level (e.g., informal/formal, job quality such as unemployment insurance fund, paid sick leave, full/part-time, contractual) in the tasks and occupations that are affected is still missing in India.

DEMOGRAPHIC DIVIDEND AND JOBS

India will continue to add 10 million new workers to the labour market every year during this coming decade. Whether the demographic dividend will promote growth or transform into a curse will depend on how prepared are the states that will benefit from a young population. Bihar and Uttar Pradesh, along with other lagging states, will experience a much bigger bulge in working population than more developed states like Tamil Nadu. Unfortunately, the less developed states are also the least prepared to take advantage of the demographic change they will undergo.

Investing more and more efficiently in people will enable India to tap into its demographic dividend and prepare India for the future. There is a powerful link between these investments and economic growth, stability and security. Investing in people through healthcare, quality education, jobs and skills helps build human capital, which is key to supporting economic growth, ending extreme poverty and creating more inclusive societies. Human capital is now the fastest-growing component of India's wealth. However, if the correct quality and quantity of investments are not made in our human capital, the demographic dividend may well turn out to be a demographic disaster.

India's human capital base may not be adequate for the future to benefit from demographic dividend. India is home to the world's largest concentration of illiterate people in the world. India has made gains in human development, but challenges remain, including big barriers to secondary schooling, low-quality public services and gender discrimination. New technology could be exploited to accelerate the pace of building human capital, including massive open online courses (MOOCs) and virtual classrooms.

Pursuing a more aggressive education agenda fits very well not just with countries that will benefit from demographic dividend but also with what many governments in rich countries are trying to do, even in the absence of demographic dividend. Demographic dividend is a time-limited opportunity, and policymakers should have a greater incentive to redouble their efforts to promote human capital so that demographic dividend can contribute to economic growth and job creation.

No country can achieve its potential and meet the challenges of the twenty-first century without the full participation of the working population, both women and men. A high-quality education is one of the strongest ways for countries to reduce poverty, achieve gender equality and create more jobs. Building human capital translates into higher rates of economic growth and job creation. Demographic dividend without investments in human capital will be a wasted development opportunity, and it will further widen economic and social gaps instead of narrowing them.

LIVELIHOOD OPPORTUNITIES OF THE FUTURE

Traditionally, jobs in India were created in agriculture and then in manufacturing, particularly in the small and medium sectors. Services, including the government as large employers, added significantly to the working population and, in recent times, more jobs have been created in services than manufacturing. In 2020, while the service sector contributed a major share to GDP, and agriculture the lowest, the employment figures were reversed with agriculture employing the most people. Since 1990–91, the construction sector added a large number of non-farm jobs and has emerged as one of the top job-generating sectors along with trade, transport, storage, education and miscellaneous services.

The challenge for India is to generate jobs or sustainable livelihoods for the tens of millions more youth who will be entrants into the work force and also ensure that job losses are minimized in any sector. There are many looming threats. Digital technology has changed globalization, as goods and services can now be unbundled, splintered in a value chain and transported anywhere in the world. While the emphasis on creating wealth is well-placed, the time has also come to examine its implications for jobs in developing countries. Although India is ranked third in the world in terms of attracting investments for technology transaction, and its outsourcing industry is huge with more than half a billion internet users, the digital divide remains huge in India, with adverse implications for job growth.

India needs to promote women entrepreneurship. This growth in the role of women entrepreneurs will come in many forms: better education and health that will increase female labour force participation, reduced discrimination and wage differentials that encourage greater effort and improved advancement practices that promote talented women into leadership and managerial roles. Simply put, empowering half of the potential workforce has significant economic benefits beyond promoting gender equality.

Key drivers of women entrepreneurship remain investments in infrastructure and education, which predict higher female entry shares in India. Women entrepreneurs benefit from agglomeration economies in both manufacturing and services, where higher female ownership among incumbent businesses within a district-industry predicts that a greater share of subsequent entrepreneurs is women entrepreneurs. Moreover, higher female ownership of local businesses in related industries (e.g., similar labour needs, input-output markets) predict greater relative female entry rates. Gender networks clearly matter for entry into entrepreneurship. Likewise, interactions between the informal and formal sectors may not be as strong as interactions within each sector.

For India to become a $5 trillion economy, entrepreneurship, including women entrepreneurship, will need to play a bigger role in economic growth and development. Despite its recent economic advances, India's gender balance for entrepreneurship remains among the lowest in the world. Improving this balance is an important step for India's development and its achievement of greater economic growth and gender equality. While achieving economic equality sometimes requires tough choices (e.g., progressive taxation that may discourage effort), the opposite is true here.

There are many who have chosen it as a mission to make the millions of youth who seek their place in the sun employable and placed in successful livelihoods through employment or entrepreneurship. Lighthouse Communities Foundation in Delhi, Maharashtra and Odisha has committed to enabling a million successful livelihoods. Global Talent Track, which has already brought nearly 2 million college students to full-paying jobs, is now embarking on large-scale women's entrepreneurship in urban and rural India, and many non-profit and for-profit social enterprises have committed to contribute to this nation-building endeavour. More such efforts are required for greater effect.

STRENGTHENING SOCIAL HARMONY

The significance of social harmony for a large, complex, multi-religious, multiethnic and multicultural nation like India cannot be underestimated in any measure. Social harmony—the peaceful coexistence of people in society in the pursuit of collective well-being—is the essential lubrication that facilitates a society in motion. Higher the social harmony index of a nation, greater will be its ability to achieve its objectives. The lower the social harmony index, the higher will be the disharmony in society, and consequently, discord and disruption, which cause impediments in the path to progress. By and large, this has been the story of India in the last 75 years.

None can deny the multifaceted progress achieved by India in various sectors—be it space, IT, horticulture and dairy development, to mention a few. This has been achieved in spite of the numerous inter-caste and inter-religious upheavals, small and big, that the country has witnessed from time to time. Seventy-five years after Independence, India still needs to come to terms with its identity as a liberal, secular, inclusive democratic republic and pave the way for the harmonious coexistence of all communities that constitute the Indian identity.

The upliftment of the Scheduled Castes, resolution of inter-caste conflicts and the harmonious coexistence of Hindus and Muslims are the three big challenges of social harmony in India. A vibrant, throbbing and populous nation like India will necessarily be argumentative in its character and suffer from some amount of disharmony as it advances to realize its destiny. However, as long as the fundamentals are sound, the free flow of debate and opposing viewpoints will remain constructive and not destructive.

These challenges are an opportunity to, once again, reinforce the 'Idea of India', and one definitive pathway towards this is that of broad political consensus as was practised by the late PM Atal Bihari Vajpayee. This spirit stands reflected in the '*Sabka Saath, Sabka Vikas* (Collective Efforts, Inclusive Growth)' slogan of the Modi government, although there is a strong need for the government and the Bharatiya Janata Party to demonstrate its commitment to the letter and spirit of this promise.

Rapid economic progress, the creation of jobs and the intermingling of people from all sections of society will lead to greater social cohesion, social harmony and '*Sab Ka Vikas, Sab ke Saath*'.

On 29 July 2014, the then US Secretary of State John Kerry said: 'The new Indian government's plan, "Sabka Saath, Sabka Vikas", together with all, development for all that's a concept, a vision that we want to support. We believe it's a great vision, and our private sector is eager to be a catalyst in India's economic revitalisation.'[1] Kerry was delivering an address at the Center for American Progress, a US think tank in Washington, on the eve of his departure to India.

The Chinese aggression in Galwan in May 2020 and the

escalation of border disputes leading to new geopolitical alignments came with the realization that if India is to rise to the China challenge, the pathway is through aggressive economic growth. The nation will be able to focus on economic growth, attract investments and undertake key reforms only if there is a certain degree of social harmony on the domestic front.

CASTE AND SOCIAL DISHARMONY

The divisive caste system continues to wield its iron grip on the Indian society even though the nation has come a long way from the time when untouchability was practised, inter-caste dining was non-existent and inter-caste marriages were taboo.

The politics of the caste system fundamentally revolves around two main causes of social tension and disharmony:

- Demand for jobs; and
- Demand for reservations in professional educational courses.

The poorest of the poor in India from all sections of society, and irrefutably those who have suffered for centuries on account of the caste system, deserve affirmative action policies in education and employment. At the same time, these deficiencies will be addressed on their own through economic progress and a gradual dissipation in the demand for reservations in jobs and education.

The caste system will not die or disappear altogether from the Indian society. However, as India progresses economically in all spheres, the country is bound to witness a greater degree of inter-regional migration for education and employment, rising numbers of inter-caste and inter-religious marriages, and greater tolerance and embracing of liberal values. A lot of this has already happened across India, in the various states and cities like New Delhi, Mumbai, Pune, Bengaluru and Chennai, which have witnessed rapid economic growth since liberalization.

The fastest way to make the caste system irrelevant is through economic growth, and we are already a witness to that over the decades since Independence.

The challenges before India are manifold, be it in the realms of national security with specific attention to China, achieving economic growth of 8 per cent, employment generation, reduction of rural distress and better healthcare, to list a few. How can a nation become cohesive and achieve progress on the economic and other fronts if the very air it breathes becomes increasingly toxic with social disharmony? Every aspect of life and governance then suffers, and like cancer, spreads and weakens the very innards of the body politic.

In its extreme form, disharmony can lead to rising levels of disillusionment and distress, as was seen in the build-up to Partition in the 1930s–40s. There is a stark difference between what happened then and what is being witnessed now. Then, the two-nation theory and the politics of separatism was promoted aggressively by a section of the leadership of the Muslim minority and fed into by a section of the non-Muslim leadership too. Today, however, it is the pro-Hindutva and anti-Muslim rhetoric that is fast gaining traction in the majoritarian, mainstream sections of society, right down to influencing children, who are found parroting the divisive opinions of their parents.

On the eve of India's 75th Independence Day, the eminent social commentator Pratap Bhanu Mehta recalled the social disharmony witnessed in pre-Partition India. He noted: 'The moral of the 1930s was clear. Once unleashed, communalism always breaks nations. It took the sheen off India's renaissance in the 1930s; it will again corrode new India's energies.'[2]

It is not just politics and elections that have been poisoned by this disharmony, but the polarization is seen even in other arms of society, notably the media. Such an observation was made by the Chief Justice of India, Justice N.V. Ramana, when he noted: 'The problem is, everything in this country is shown with a communal angle by a section of media...The country is going to get a bad name ultimately.'[3]

Hindu–Muslim disharmony is triggered in parts of India mostly by politically driven agenda. Barring this Hindu–Muslim equation, which is influenced by factors both internal and external, there is comparative harmony amongst all other communities and religious groups of India. This in itself is evidence of the secularism, tolerance and liberalism that is germane to the Indian subcontinent, not since Independence but over millennia.

In today's India, issues relating to Hindu–Muslim disharmony, social inequality and inter-caste tensions need to be addressed on priority if India is to achieve all-round progress and welfare for its people.

POLICE REFORMS AS A WAY TO SOCIAL HARMONY

Social harmony can be effectively maintained if a nation has a professional law enforcement machinery as is seen in many developed western nations. India has been deprived of this for far too long. One of the most critical reforms, police reforms, are yet to be initiated by the central and state governments. Fifteen years have passed since the landmark 22 September 2006 order of the three-judge bench comprising Justices Y.K. Sabharwal, C.K. Thakker and P.K. Balasubramanyan, in the Prakash Singh and Ors v. Union of India case of 1996. The Supreme Court had upheld the petition and directed the central and state governments to undertake structural changes in the police force to free it from political and other influences, and make it accountable to the people.

'If implemented, they will be game-changers for the citizens of India and the police,' observed Meeran Chadha Borwankar, a retired IPS officer who was director general of Maharashtra's Bureau of Police Research and Development. Borwankar made some critical observations in her opinion piece titled 'Creating a Citizen-Centric Police,'[4] published on the fifteenth anniversary of the Supreme Court verdict. She blamed politicians and corrupt police officers for obstructing the implementation of the reforms. The reforms would empower honest police officers to concentrate on their professional work of crime prevention, investigation and maintenance of public order instead of being used and abused by those in power, said Borwankar. According to her, one major cause for the tardy progress of police reforms was the lack of public awareness and sustained interest in law enforcement.

Borwankar noted that as directed by the Supreme Court, the reforms would bring in citizen-centric policing, and merit-based postings, transfers and promotions of police officers instead of political appointments and would ensure protection from unwarranted political pressures.

Thus, the need for a firm, fair and professional law enforcement machinery cannot be emphasized enough if India is to be counted among modern democracies with strong institutions.

The country is immensely fortunate to have professionalized armed forces. This level of professionalism needs to be achieved in other institutions, notably, law enforcement.

INDIA'S INTRINSIC STRENGTH

The inherent and intrinsic strength of the Idea of India as a multi-religious, multiethnic and multicultural society lies deeply embedded in the ethos of the Indian nation. This idea has been shaped by the forces of history over the millennia in the vast region of the Indian subcontinent. It lies so deeply entrenched in the psyche of the Indian people that it has become an integral part of their identity over the centuries. In ancient times, the land across the Himalayas was fabled as 'the land of milk and honey,' endowed with plenty of water, fertile soil and a salubrious climate compared to the harsh terrain of west and central Asia.

The idea of India as a nation state emerged only after the British consolidated their power pan-India after 1857. And yet, large parts of the subcontinent were united in thought and spirit, and by geography, even as empires rose and fell since the first pan-Indian empire of the Mauryas. Established around 321 BCE, this empire covered most of central and northern India and stretched right up to Iran. This empire ended in 185 BCE and saw legendary emperors such as Chandragupta Maurya, Bindusara and Ashoka rule over large parts of the subcontinent.

Hinduism, in its most ancient form, brought in the idea of the oneness of the soul in all living beings and the concept of the entire world as one family. As the author Pavan Varma has noted in his book *The Great Hindu Civilisation: Achievement, Neglect, Bias and the Way Forward*, 'If hatred of the other was Hinduism's dominant emotion, why would the Upanishads say—Anno bhadra kritavo yantu visvatatha: Let good thoughts flow to us from all directions? If religious exclusion was the defining belief of Hinduism, why would our ancient seers stress—*Udar charitanam vasudhaiva kutumbukam*: For the big-hearted, the entire world is a family?'[5] (The extraordinary relevance of the concept of *vasudhaiva kutumbukam* in these times of climate change stands emphasized by the government in global assemblies such as COP26 and the UN.)

As noted by Varma, while resentment against some of the injustices done to Hinduism in the past may have its reasons, hatred and violence 'cannot become the defining features of a religion which rejects both. Moreover, these sentiments are completely counterproductive in a modern republic whose stated goal is respect towards all faiths, and which aspires for progress and prosperity, whose sine qua non is social peace and harmony.' [6] It is, therefore, not surprising why N.R. Narayana Murthy, the legendary IT entrepreneur states: 'The founding fathers of independent India wanted a nation where every religion would flourish and every voice would be heard. Thus, India very rightly adopted secularism as its credo.'[7]

Adi Shankaracharya, one of the greatest proponents of Hinduism, was born in Kerala in the eighth century CE. He traversed the length and breadth of India and established four mathas (monasteries) in Odisha, Karnataka, Gujarat and Uttarakhand. Sant Namdev (c. 1270–1350) is not only revered as a saint in Maharashtra but also in Punjab, and 61 of his hymns are included in the holiest of Sikh scriptures, the Guru Granth Sahib. People like the Shankaracharya and Sant Namdev epitomize the true multiethnic multi-community culture that is our ethos and should define our future.

Empires in the South had their own identity and culture distinct from the North, and were yet united with the rest of the subcontinent by a common religion, trade and geography. Repeated invasions from the north brought in the Mughals and led to the spread of Islam in large swathes of India over the 800 years that the Mughals ruled over India. But even that powerful influence driven by the sharpness of the sword under some regimes had to give way to harmony, coexistence and cultural amalgamation of a people even as they practised their individual faiths over the centuries.

The purpose of religion is meant to be constructive, not destructive, and it is meant to spread harmony and not disharmony in society. Delivering a lecture at the 22nd Foundation Day Celebration of Vivekananda Institute of Human Excellence, Hyderabad, Chief Justice N.V. Ramana said, 'There is greater need today, in contemporary India, to pay heed to the words spoken by Swami Vivekananda as early as in 1893.' The Chief Justice of India said that Swami Vivekananda 'was prophetic' in that he 'advocated secularism as if he foresaw the events to unfold' much before the freedom struggle and the churning it entailed and an egalitarian Constitution was framed. 'He firmly believed that the true essence of religion was the common good and tolerance.'[8]

Swami Vivekananda and his historic speech delivered in

Chicago at the World Parliament of Religions in September 1893 was also cited by the well-known economist and columnist Dr Ajit Ranade while reacting to the phenomenally vitriolic hate speeches delivered at the three-day Haridwar Dharma Sansad in December 2021. He made the point that Vivekananda was inclusive instead of being divisive: 'He said: "I am proud to belong to a religion which has taught the world both tolerance and universal acceptance. We believe not only in universal toleration, but we accept all religions as true." Not tolerance, but acceptance, and all religions as equally true and valid.'[9]

Dr Ranade noted that Vivekananda quoted a popular hymn in that speech that emphasized the Hindu belief in the oneness of all religions: '...As the different streams having their sources in different paths which men take through different tendencies, various though they appear, crooked or straight, all lead to Thee.'[10]

Thus, in spite of the two-nation theory and the horrors of partition in 1947, it was only natural for India to adopt a secular, liberal constitution that guaranteed the right to the freedom of religion. The deep polarization on Hindu–Muslim lines in the Indian society today is undeniable, and yet, the liberal and secular ethos of India stands reiterated by the government at international assemblies like the UN.

Exercising India's right of reply to Pakistan prime minister's references to Kashmir in his United Nations General Assembly (UNGA) virtual speech, one of the things that Sneha Dubey, first secretary at the UNGA said was: 'India is a pluralistic democracy with a substantial population of minorities who have gone on to hold the highest offices in the country including as President, Prime Minister, Chief Justices and Chiefs of the Army Staff.'[11]

The social fabric of India created by the multitudinous threads of a thousand faiths, thoughts, ideas and philosophies has weathered enormous wear and tear over the centuries, and under the 'Divide and Rule' politics of the British Raj. It has come under enormous stress and strain, and yet, by and large, it has remained intact. To go against this is to go against the grain of the Idea of India that lies embedded in its soul, right down to the last of the more than 650,000 villages, where people of various faiths have been living in harmony over the centuries.

ECONOMIC REFORMS, JOBS AND SOCIAL STABILITY

In October 2017, Viraj Mehta, Head of Regional Agenda – India and South Asia, and Member of the Executive Committee, WEF, Geneva, made some cryptic observations in his analysis titled 'India can bring prosperity and social justice to a fifth of the world.'[12]

He drew a contrast between the India of the 1980s and the post-liberalized India of 2017, showing the stark benefits of economic liberalization and reforms. In the 1980s, the country had one black-and-white television channel, inferior quality goods and services offered by domestic companies protected by the 'licence raj' and a country that progressed at a sluggish pace of growth, 'affectionately known by economists as the 'Hindu rate of growth.'

People marvelled and envied their NRI friends and relatives who brought with them out-of-this-world products—be it electronic gadgets, kitchen equipment, cosmetics or simple stationery. Almost every middle-class family aspired to become a part of the American Dream by doing well in studies, getting a scholarship to study abroad and flying out of India, by and large, for good. Contrast this with the situation in India in 2017, 25 years later.

'The India many of us grew up with has disappeared completely. Self-assured, dynamic, assertive, armed with ubiquitous cell phones, numerous TV channels, nuclear weapons and a world-class IT industry, India is today one of the fastest-growing economies of the world,' said Mehta.

The new economic environment saw Indian companies

embark on ambitious growth plans and trajectories within and outside India, especially in sectors like IT and telecommunications. There were new highways, airports and digital pathways coming up in India, and the country had emerged as one of the fastest-growing economies of the world with a forecast for GDP growth in 2017 at 7.2 per cent.

Indeed, India's economy grew at 8.26 per cent in 2016, 6.8 per cent in 2017 and 6.53 per cent in 2018.[13]

CONFLICT AND DEVELOPMENT

Research shows a strong correlation between conflict and poor economic growth, although there are other factors too that are causative of conflict. By and large, countries with low per capita income have a higher conflict rate, although this relationship is not very tight, say Ejaz Ghani and Lakshmi Iyer in their paper 'Conflict and Development—Lessons from South Asia'.[14] India, for example, is among the countries that have higher conflict rates than expected for their state of development. The paper notes that conflict is higher in lagging regions, with a close relationship between higher poverty rates and greater conflict. Some parts of eastern India have both high levels of poverty and high levels of conflict. Social divisions constitute another driver of conflict, and this can be seen in India's northeastern states, which are socially and ethnically different from the majority of the Indian states and have seen long-running separatist movements.

The consequences of conflict on development are most severe in lagging regions due to weak institutions, poor geography and weak integration with global markets. In contrast, leading regions are able to better contain and manage conflicts, although they too suffer on account of conflict.

While insurgencies can be dealt with through negotiations and signing of peace agreements, the expansion of welfare programmes in economically backward areas aimed at reducing poverty is also an economic solution to conflict resolution. Cross-border cooperation between countries should also be an integral part of the strategy to reduce conflict as many of the internal conflicts in South Asia have cross-border dimensions, researchers have noted. This is particularly relevant in the India–Pakistan and Hindu–Muslim context.

The pathways to achieving social harmony are as clear as daylight, as are also the consequences of social disharmony for a nation the size of India. The future of India depends on the pathways that we chose for ourselves, individually and collectively. If we can inspire our youth to eschew all divisions based on class, caste or community, and develop the 'agency' or aspiration to be successful wage-earners and job-givers in society, India will truly progress towards its tryst with a global destiny and happiness for all its people.

9

STRENGTHENING SOCIAL CAPITAL TO LAY THE FOUNDATIONS FOR GROWTH

Vijay Kelkar and Ajay Shah

India had a powerful growth episode between 1991 and 2011. The question that is now faced is about rekindling that high growth, of creating an environment of high private sector confidence and private investment. The diagnosis of this growth episode and the difficulties thereafter showed the chain of reasoning from the evolution of the Indian state to the changed behaviour of the Indian private sector. A sophisticated market economy requires a state that acts in predictable, rational and fair ways. The Indian state has faltered in two respects: central planning (i.e., intervention into the economy that is unconnected with market failure) and the rule of law (i.e., arbitrary and unchecked power in the administrative state).

A great deal of policy thinking in India starts at the level of the working of the state. The bulk of the ideas of this book are centred on the working of the state. While recognizing the importance of those problems, a key facet of India that needs to also be emphasized is social capital. In this essay, we shift our gaze to think about social capital, about trust. The reasoning here starts from the people, and the ability of the people to enter into complex contracts with each other. The analysis of social capital is richly interlinked with the problems of the state and of the public policy strategies to achieve high growth.

Social harmony has been a major factor in strategic thinking about the Indian state through the decades of the freedom movement, and particularly, after the large-scale violence of Partition. In this book, it is the subject of the chapter 'Sustainable Livelihoods and Social Harmony', by Ghani, Natarajan and Vaidya. Social harmony lies at the foundation of a civilized society, where peace is maintained every day, where mobs do not gather, where the criminal justice system works effectively and even-handedly.

Social capital is allied to social harmony and yet distinct. It goes beyond the simple question of physical safety to a deeper examination of the bonds of trust between individuals. When there is greater trust, people are able to collaborate more. Oral contracts are negotiated in good faith; people are oriented towards living up to oral promises and, in turn, expect others to generally live up to oral promises.

High trust is valuable in and of itself as an enabler of a prosperous and sophisticated society. Alongside this, social capital connects into the question of economic policy when we see that market failure—the fundamental justification for all state intervention—is itself about difficulties of negotiation between people. Pareto-superior outcomes can be obtained by wielding the coercive power of the state correctly. All the four classes of market failure (public goods, externalities, market power, asymmetric information), where when social capital is high, a larger class of market failures can be solved by voluntary action by the people, through 'Coasean bargains' and other kinds of community-level solutions, without requiring state coercion.

WRONG OBJECTIVES AND WRONG EXECUTION

As Max Weber defined it, the state is *a community* that achieves and maintains a monopoly of physical force in a given territory.

In this, politicians and officials are fused together and viewed as a coherent community. In an ideal liberal democracy, the state is the *agent* of the people, but when the political system works poorly, the state becomes a *ruler*.

Two foundational problems afflict the Indian state. The difficulties of the political system have led the state and the people to have conflicting incentives. As a consequence, the state often pursues objectives that run counter to the interests of the citizenry.

Alongside this is weak execution—what is generally termed 'the problem of state capacity'. Across a wide range of situations, the Indian state fares poorly in achieving the objectives that it establishes for itself. Here also, the foundation of the problem is the misalignment in the political system. The fact that the state is not accountable creates conditions of state failure, where state personnel favour personal gains over effective delivery of certain functions.[1]

These two problems have been extensively discussed, from scholars like Arun Shourie in the 1970s, leading up to the present.[2] The development of institutional capacity in the political system and in state structures only takes place slowly. Hence, it is likely that for some decades, the difficulties of the Indian state are likely to persist. Chronic state failure, hence, needs to be internalized by thinkers of development strategy for India. By now, simple optimism about the objectives and the capabilities of the Indian state has subsided, and there is considerable interest in the questions: *Why is state capacity poor, and what can be done to change this?* Alongside this, it is equally important to ask: *when state capacity is low, how does this change our thinking about development strategy?*

The main rhythm of modern public economics is crafted around market failure and state interventions that address market failure. In the standard first-world public economics and public administration setting, this discussion is undertaken assuming a benevolent and capable state. This is partly because of the rule of law and liberal democratic environment that is found in the first world. The early literature on the problem of low state capacity in developing countries was written by scholars in the western world. This literature often tends to treat the *objectives* chosen by the state as inherently legitimate, and only concerns itself with failures of *execution*.

In India, however, understanding the difficulties of the political system, of the low accountability of the state are essential to understanding state failure. When the political system works poorly, the *objectives* of the state diverge from the objectives of the citizenry. This induces many a state intervention on problems that are unconnected with market failure. Even when the state embarks on the right projects, the results are likely to disappoint, owing to the low accountability of the state and the associated low state capacity. The Indian landscape is replete with state projects on core public goods that have worked out poorly. Public choice theory guides us that when the state embarks on some projects that benefit itself as opposed to the people, the problem of accountability is reduced, and higher competence and higher state capacity are displayed. As an example, the Indian state has been relatively more effective in building surveillance mechanisms that increase the power of state personnel upon the people. This has involved a combination of coercive powers that forces individuals to live in ways that are visible to the state, combined by mechanisms to harvest this data and put it to work for surveillance.

NEGOTIATIONS BETWEEN THE PEOPLE

Under these conditions, it is worth rethinking the role of society and state when faced with market failure, at a more fundamental level. At the core, all market failures relate to complexities of negotiation between private persons. As an example, if private people could manage to negotiate with each other, the traffic rule of 'Keep Left' would evolve out of this difficult negotiation. Similarly, if property rights were properly allocated, the archetypal steel mill and the fishery would find mutually beneficial Coasean bargains, and the state would not be required in solving the negative externality of pollution that the steel mill imposes upon the fishery.

Private negotiations can be an attractive pathway for discovering negotiated solutions that address market failure, without resorting to state intervention and inflicting state violence. Ordinarily, such pathways are of great interest. In this chapter, we argue that there is a feedback loop that induces a low capability trap.

A healthy society is one in which large groups of people are able to talk *to each other*, thrash out their problems and arrive at satisfactory compromises instead of requiring state intervention. The essential feature of the state is the monopoly of violence. State-led solutions involve coercion, and this is intrinsically problematic, at a moral level, when compared with voluntary solutions where individuals negotiate with each other and find the right middle road. We find it useful to think about a capability called 'negotiation muscle' in a society: the ability of people to talk with each other in good faith, negotiate solutions and abide by agreements. Negotiation muscle is a finite resource in every society. Negotiations and give-and-take between large numbers of private persons are not easy. They require social capital and skills in good-faith negotiation. Years of successful negotiation on small problems creates the presumption of good faith under which negotiation can take place for more complex problems.

Conversely, an environment of state violence degrades social capital because violence harms human relationships. Even under the best political system, where state action is fully legitimate, the use of violence tends to harm social capital. Under a weak political system, where the state is often not behaving as the agent of the people and state violence is imprecisely directed, these dangers are even greater. For example, consider an environment like

Afghanistan that is suffused with guns. In such an environment, social conflict tends to often spill over into gunfire, which will, in turn, inevitably induce collateral damage. Once violence is deployed, it creates bitterness and reduces the space for good-faith negotiation. It creates a greater temptation to renege upon agreements. In similar fashion, when individuals and social groups in India call down state violence into their world, they create bitterness and damage negotiation muscle, particularly because the violence of the Indian state is often imprecise and there is greater collateral damage.

THE LOW-TRUST TRAP IN INDIA

In India today, conflicts between individuals and social groups tend to readily bubble into summoning state violence, whether it is filing cases, calling the police or lobbying for state coercion that assists one faction at the expense of another. This is a reflection of low social capital. In a healthier environment, neighbours are able to talk things out and find a middle ground without coercion in the picture. When social capital is high, negotiations take place within communities and middle roads are found without calling upon the coercive power of the state.

Survey-based measurement of social capital is done using the question: generally speaking, would you say that most people can be trusted or that you need to be very careful in dealing with people? Cross-country evidence on this is available from the World Values Survey for the 2010–14 period.[3] India fares poorly in this regard, with only 16.7 per cent of the population feeling that most people can be trusted. As an example, in Germany, the comparable value is 44.6 per cent. In China it is 60.3 per cent.

The oldest values for the 'people can be trusted' question in the World Values Survey for India pertain to 1990–94. The value seen there is 33.5 per cent, about two times higher than the value seen for 2010–14. This evidence suggests that social capital in India has declined over the years.

The question then remains: why is social capital in India low? Traditional scholarship on India has emphasized the remarkable extent of ethnic, linguistic and religious fractionalization present in India when compared with many countries. Commonality of caste and of the *jati* tend to induce better behaviour, e.g., with the higher extent of business dealings within the *jati*. Alongside this, we suggest that the long history of state coercion, of rival groups inflicting violence upon each other through a state that has misaligned incentives and lacks the rule of law, has exacerbated mistrust.

There is, then, the possibility of being trapped in a bad equilibrium. Low social capital is an inability of the people to negotiate with each other and solve situations with market failure. This leads to low trigger points for the people to rush to state-led solutions.

But the state is, at heart, a violent creature. Liberal democracies limit state violence to a controlled, predictable and just form. In an ideal democracy, we consent to an ethical regime of coercion. When the checks and balances surrounding the state are imperfect, state violence is applied in unjust ways. The state has misaligned incentives when compared with the welfare of the people.

In India today, state coercion is regularly unleashed by interest groups when faced with problems that are not market failure. Rival groups in society inflict violence upon each other by firing from the shoulders of the state. All uses of state power involve collateral damage and create fresh cycles of hatred.

In the low-trust trap, weak negotiation muscle induces excessive state intervention, which, in turn, induces weak negotiation muscle. Along this path, every outrage harms social capital. Unjust and illegitimate state violence chips away at the foundations of trust, of the presumption of good faith. It damages the ability of the people to solve problems of negotiation on their own.

India has always had high levels of ethnic, linguistic and religious fractionalization. The great thinkers of the previous century, such as Mahatma Gandhi, Jawaharlal Nehru and Rabindranath Tagore, brought out the best within each person and helped create a new level of social capital, of conversations between individuals that took place in good faith. We suggest there is a causal connection from large-scale intervention by the colonial state, which set out to do development policy, to the decline in social capital that has been experienced in the following decades.

ISOLATED POOLS OF TRUST CAPITAL

We can think of the social capital problem from two points of view. On one hand, there is the traditional economics reasoning about contract enforcement and Coasean bargains. When there is negotiation in good faith, an orientation towards living up to promises, clarity on property rights and enforcement by the judiciary, there is a greater ability to enter into formal or informal private agreements. This is welfare-enhancing.

In the reasoning of traditional economics, when contract enforcement is weak, when property rights are not clearly allocated, these pathways are more limited. It is important to see contract enforcement as being not just about the state but largely about norms and social contracts. The role of state violence is significant in damaging trust, in weakening norms, in disrupting the conversations through which negotiations take place in good faith and agreements are adhered to.

When placed in such a low-trust environment, we see the Indian populace as 'broken up into fragments by narrow domestic walls.' There are small circles of trust within which negotiation, and norms of contract performance function well. Value is indeed created through these discussions and contracts—whether for economic purposes or otherwise—but the range of persons that can be involved within each feasible contracting network is limited.

Each of these limited networks of people, within which collaborating is feasible, is characterized by a certain aggregate capability. Some of these networks are closed systems (e.g., those shaped by religion or caste) and others are open systems. These open-access systems are particularly important according to Daron Acemoglu and James A. Robinson, who have argued that closed systems are important in inducing national failure.[4]

It is interesting to reflect that while the importance of English in Indian politics has declined sharply, the most important open-access network in India remains the world of business, science, education and culture, where a pan-India community is able to engage with each other and with the outside world using English as the *lingua franca*. This is an open-access system. There is an interesting connection between this reasoning and the larger view of caste as seen in M.N. Srinivas's work titled 'An Obituary on Caste as a System.'[5]

THE WAY FORWARD

We find useful analogies with the problems of an insurgency. When faced with an insurgency, state violence is deployed with a high error rate. This induces collateral damage and creates fresh cycles of hatred. Wisdom in counterinsurgency (COIN) lies in reducing the levels of violence so as to close down the pathway for collateral damage.

In similar fashion, strategic thinking in Indian development policy would do well to reduce the levels of state violence and the probability of this violence being misdirected. This involves four elements:

1. It would help if it was less feasible for the people to call down an unpredictable violent agent into their lives. This calls for removing pathways to state intervention in the form of laws and agencies.

2. Establishing mechanisms for the rule of law, where due process is sacrosanct and there are elaborate checks and balances that constrain state actors, will help reduce the imprecision of state violence and thus the collateral damage.
3. Greater effort and resourcing into building the Indian judiciary is well-advised, as the judiciary can play a role in reducing the amount of harm that is inflicted by the state.
4. Formal law needs to be modified so as to reduce the authorization for state violence in the form of powers of investigation, ability to inflict harm outside of the rule of law and the magnitude of punishments. This will reduce the extent of collateral damage that takes place when state violence is applied imprecisely.

These four pathways represent an approach of reducing state interference, the imprecision of state violence and of the levels of violence.

The reasoning presented here is also connected to the concepts that Mahatma Gandhi espoused, of self-governing villages where faraway authorities do not interfere. It is consistent with a greater emphasis upon decentralization. Negotiation-based solutions at the level of a village or a city are closer to the political system working at the level of a village or a city. Game theory teaches us that when strangers interact with each other occasionally, there is a greater risk of 'fink-fink' strategies, where each is bad to the other. But when there is a repeated game played between people who know each other, the optimal strategy goes closer to 'tit for tat' where misdeed is punished by misdeed, but after that, there is a greater willingness to revert to cooperation. In contrast, when state power is wielded from afar, avoiding excesses is harder.

This suggests a fresh emphasis upon the federal character of the Constitution, on living up to the 73rd and 74th amendments, and on building sound checks and balances for politics at the state and city level, and on the full devolution of funds, functions and functionaries to sub-national governments. The third tier of government requires a sound fiscal base, e.g., by getting a slice of the GST which as a consumption tax generates the correct incentives for the city government.[6]

CONCLUSION

A great deal of public policy reasoning in India is conducted within one domain at a time. As an example, thinkers on climate change worry about how best to obtain lower Indian emissions and how best to prepare India for the coming climate change. Similarly, thinkers on health worry about how to do better on vaccination when faced with the next pandemic. The considerations of this chapter are cross-cutting: all across the Indian state, we need a greater concern about social capital, bottom-up community solutions and the dangers that flow from state action.

State failure in India is present across most domains. Occam's razor suggests that there are features of the Indian state that are inimical to high capability and that these features are not specific to the domain. By this reasoning, it was not the political economy of health or analytical failures in health or health-specific problems that inhibited Covid-19 vaccination. There were deeper problems that generated the difficulties. This perspective encourages going to the root cause, understanding the foundational sources of failure and addressing them. This is an optimistic view because it shows the path to a deeper set of reform pathways that can improve performance across a large number of domains.

The question of social capital is one which requires greater attention from the intellectual community. It is a cross-cutting problem that influences the ability of society to arrive at complex working arrangements and a bottom-up evolution of rational mechanisms that address market failure.

EPILOGUE
A Once-in-a-Lifetime Opportunity

We have traversed a long distance through the chapters of this book, visualizing the dream of a successful and inclusive India, and looking at the past and the present, and considering possible pathways to the future. For the dozen of us who collaborated in thinking through the various facets of this development that have been elucidated in this book, cautious optimism is the sentiment we collectively feel. Here, we will share with you our vision of the India of 2030, call out what could go wrong and end with a set of factors that we must get right as a country to march forward with conviction and meet our tryst with an inspiring destiny for our country.

A GLORIOUS VISION—THE POSSIBLE DESTINATION

Instead of articulating a vision of India in cold prose, let us see the new successful India from the eyes of Bharat, a young man who was born at the turn of the millennium in 2000, grew up in a village of the country in Jharkhand, moved to the city of Mumbai for his graduation and then to Nagpur for employment. Bharat's parents, who are farmers with a small land holding of less than two acres, have moved from traditional farming methods to more productive means and doubled their household income in real terms. Bharat had himself started his career in IT services, but after five years of experiencing technology and location changes, returned to the field he was trained in and works in a very advanced electric car manufacturing facility, where he has brought his training in smart manufacturing and technology skills to bear in designing new production systems.

Bharat enjoys his life in a tier 2 city and marvels at the excellent education his children are receiving, and the harmony and sense of inclusion that prevails in his neighbourhood. Home automation has made his home and office smart and connected like the factory he works in, and the erstwhile traffic issues in the city have been eased by smart traffic control and adequate safety and surveillance equipment. He is delighted that all suppliers to the company, in spite of having manufacturing bases in semi-urban and rural locations, have full telecommunications and connectivity, and the supply and demand chains that take his company's products to domestic and global markets have been optimized.

Healthcare and entertainment are now available at the fingertips of Bharat and his family, and the local university has been enriched by collaborations with industry and international sources of skills and research, which makes it redundant for his children to seek education outside the country. Bharat exults in the physical, digital and social infrastructure that prevails in his city, and is convinced that India is the best place to live his life and bring up his family.

What has happened to transport Bharat and indeed two hundred million of his countrymen from a place of despondency and underachievement across most key sectors to the promised land where opportunities abound for the motivated and hard-working, and the quality of life and work has changed substantially for the better? In this book, we have outlined the opportunities and the pathways in a manner which is not only credible but achievable. This is the India that is within reach, not fully immediately but certainly in a very substantial manner by December 2030.

WHAT COULD GO WRONG

There is a well-worn phrase that goes, 'If we do what we have always done, we will get what we have always got.' In the context of this book, we have mentioned the many lacunae, the inadequacy of vision and very often the absence of concerted and focussed action that have thwarted our ambitions in many fields and many points in our history of 75 years as an independent nation.

For a start, the many points we have listed above on 'what must go right' can easily be missed and we could slip back into our somewhat sloppy ways in many sectors. What concerns our group of contributors and well-meaning India lovers at the Pune International Centre is the presence of many divisive forces that seek to place their communal or caste or class agenda above the needs of the nation. If we do not address these negative forces and take strict action when they raise their head or voices, we may get distracted into highly unproductive activities, and our youth could dissipate their energies in discordant actions rather than focussing on success for themselves, their families and their countries.

On a macro level, we are all well aware that growth cannot be taken for granted. India will face many structural and transformational hurdles, and we must remember that no more than a dozen countries that have managed to sustain an average growth rate of 10 per cent a year. A number of developing countries have experienced rapid growth and reached middle-income status, but very few have gone beyond. Recent economic history has shown that only five countries—Japan, South Korea, Taiwan, Hong Kong and Singapore—have successfully transitioned the middle-income phase and moved into the high-income category. The structural constraints to growth are many: dilapidated infrastructure, low levels of entrepreneurship and job growth, urban gridlocks, climate change, gender inequality, social tensions and conflict. If not managed well, structural constraints could choke off growth; well-managed, they can open new doors.

What can be done? There is no magic formula for development. There is a great deal of diversity within India. The problems they face are different across leading and lagging regions. Pluralism in development will have great value. The challenge is to find out what works best, in what context and in what setting. All Indians share a common culture, geography and history, and a common set of development challenges will shape the future.

WHAT MUST GO RIGHT

Through the chapters of this book, we have articulated multiple pathways towards the India envisioned above and categorically set out what must go right for us to succeed. To recap just a few of the many points, we must:

- Continue to be a liberal democracy with equal opportunities for all citizens, regardless of class, caste, community and gender.
- Grow our spirit of free enterprise and a vibrant stock market, and grow demands as well as encourage investments from all over the world.
- Implement agriculture market reforms and avoidance of trade-distorting policies to open up export markets for our farmer produce.
- Develop infrastructure and services in rural India so that no segment is left behind in the growth process.
- Reorient Indian manufacturing to become 'Aatmanirbhar' in all key industries and focus on global market leadership in some sectors like ICT, automobile components and pharmaceuticals.
- Take a leadership position in smart manufacturing and digital supply chains, with a conscious focus on physical and digital manufacturing to make India a natural leader

or the preferred 'China plus One' destination for global manufacturing.

- Consolidate and expand our gains in services and expand our service delivery to include tier 2 and tier 3 locations and markets to include all major destinations.
- Focus on innovation, research, education, skills and opportunity creation to ensure that the next 400 million see opportunities for employment and entrepreneurship.
- Achieve the trillion-dollar digital India milestone expeditiously by a strong focus on expansion of services to include platforms, products and AI applications, invest in digital infrastructure and data protection policies and exploit the core ICT layer to build robust companies in semiconductors and hardware.
- Develop new models of urbanization that will enable hundreds of smaller towns beyond the metros and the hundred-odd smart cities to create new high-quality jobs and relieve the pressure off the urban infrastructure in chosen cities. Make the compulsions created by Covid-19 the model of jobs distribution for the future.
- Have a strong focus on mobility for people and goods, and develop new transportation modes as well as alternative ways of getting work done. Develop new models like the hydrogen economy to enable India to catch up and then take the lead in autonomous, connected, electric and shared motion.
- Optimize the ecological footprint and ensure that natural capital is optimally used and the transition to a circular economy is accelerated to build a sustainable environment for growth in the country.
- Promote India as a global leader in inclusive innovation and accelerate real investments in education, research and innovation in the country. The 10 tenets we have suggested for strengthening India's position in STI would

greatly help us in this regard.

- Consider a massive exports thrust as the best way to meet our accelerated GDP growth targets for the next decade and more. Create an enabling environment and ecosystem partnerships to ensure that policies to provide this export thrust can be announced and supported through robust actions by all concerned.
- Create policies, encouragement, platforms and market access networks for women from urban and rural India to seek and sustain well-paid jobs and also embark on entrepreneurship.
- Open up opportunities for sustainable livelihoods across the country by ensuring distribution of jobs, enhance readiness and access for all, and create start-up hubs for entrepreneurship to be supported and blossom.
- Work with the Indian diaspora to create more outsourced jobs to India and encourage more and more Indians to seek global opportunities for jobs and entrepreneurship.
- Stem the increasing trend towards the creation of disharmony amongst communities and ensure that the role of social media in propagating discord is effectively controlled.
- Invest in the creation of social capital to build and strengthen the bonds of trust and true collaboration between individuals and within society.

In India, we have a big opportunity to leverage our demographic dividend to build a position of eminence in all chosen sectors. It will need assiduous planning; enabling policies with a strong focus on community development, education, skills, innovation; and industry and agriculture capability transformation to enable this dividend to pay off in the future. By 2030, the median age in India will be around 30 years, compared to around 45 in Europe and more than 40 in China and the US. This demographic dividend creates both the potential and an imperative for faster economic growth, and policymakers must address the opportunity and the challenge to ensure we capitalize on this dividend.

Another reality of the country is the further rise of the middle class, which can increase dramatically if rapid economic growth is created and sustained. Our middle class has the potential to be the largest in the world by 2030, and will expect a reasonable quality of home ownership, formal-sector jobs and economic security. The base exists in India, which, unlike China, has relied on both exports and domestic consumption as twin engines of growth and, as already mentioned, it will be progressive trade policies that enable both the youth and middle class to flourish in the country.

To create opportunities of a highly aspirational citizenry, the government must also take steps to keep global relationships active to enable increased human mobility and migration to various parts of the world. Labour shortages are already being felt in ageing countries of Japan and Western Europe, and open up possibilities for profound and far-reaching changes in business practices and government policies in these countries to enable Indian talent to seek opportunities in these parts of the world. Very similar to the progressive immigration policies that built America, the Organisation of Economic Cooperation and Development (OECD) governments will also search for alternative mechanisms that respond to their labour market pressures without triggering strong public and political opposition. India must ensure our citizens benefit from these changes.

STOP NOT TILL THE GOAL IS REACHED

Policymakers are aware of what needs to be done. However, the pace of reform to harness the favourable trends in growth and remove structural constraints has been slow. India's demographic dividend is a time-bound opportunity. Dividend could morph into disaster unless education levels improve substantially and continuously in the foreseeable future. Human capital is a prerequisite for higher labour productivity, which is necessary for sustained higher per capita income growth. If labour quality does not improve adequately, there is likely to be an increase in inequality, since capital will substitute for labour, as we observe in parts of India.

A lot is at stake. India still has the largest concentration of people living in poverty and human misery. More people can be lifted out of poverty in India than in any other part of the world if high growth can be sustained and is made more inclusive. Economic growth and social policy should not be thought of separately. Inequalities and social exclusions cannot be viewed as a price to pay for high growth or a residual outcome of necessary market-led growth. A development response that aims to get markets right first and then deal with any remaining pockets of the poor, may no longer be appropriate, given the high concentration of poverty and gender disparities in India. Rising inequalities in different dimensions are a real and present danger to India's political stability and thus medium-term growth. Success that is inequitably shared is difficult to sustain. The bridge to the future, therefore, needs a framework that ensures both fast and inclusive growth, i.e., policies to raise growth wherever it happens and policies to redistribute the gains of growth efficiently.

Globalization, too, does not automatically engender growth. Increased trade and financial global integration need to be complemented by appropriate structural reforms to take advantage of globalization, i.e., to enable resources to be allocated from the low-productivity and non-tradable sectors into high-productivity and tradable sectors. We need a deeper understanding of the process of how an economy's structure evolves. This is not just about the shift from agriculture to industry and services over time. We need to know much more about the process of moving into higher quality goods and services, what determines economic dynamism and what contributes to the flexible adjustments in the structure of an economy. India has a huge room to expand its tradable sector. While this integration carries some risks, with the right mix of policies, India can benefit from the inexorable trend of globalization.

The changing dynamics of the global economy has started to shift economic and political power towards emerging economies. A number of developing countries have become centres of strong growth, raising their shares of global income significantly. This has the potential to change the landscape for the global middle class in the developing world. India could become a predominantly middle-class region, with more than 1 billion people in this category. The middle class has played a special role in economic thought for centuries. It can be a powerful source of entrepreneurship, innovation, education, hard work and thrift—the small businesses that make a modern economy thrive.

While the long-term growth drivers are favourable, India will face many transformational hurdles in how it modernizes, remains inclusive and manages risks. We need to avoid lopsided and fragmented urbanization that benefits a few and leaves millions in the countryside. Perhaps a unifying theme is human development and demographic dividend, and how the two can generate growth that is more conducive to reducing inequality. While the movement of labour from low-productivity agriculture to high-productivity manufacturing and service sector would be key for such growth, we need to better understand how access to economic opportunities can be broadened to ensure inclusive and sustainable development. A large segment of the population in India remains especially vulnerable to shocks—natural disasters, civil strife, oil and food price shocks, etc. Climate change adds to the risks. The list of challenges and risks are long, and not all of them have been discussed in this book.

Where India@2030 ends up will ultimately depend on whether the policymakers, entrepreneurs and civil society can take timely action today to reshape tomorrow—harness the potential growth drivers and minimize transformational risks. India needs to bridge its future now. The great sage Swami Vivekananda exhorted his countrymen, 'Arise, awake and stop not till the goal is reached.' India may have faltered at various points in the 75 years we have been an independent country, but we have remained a proud democracy and succeeded in various aspects of our growth while faltering and lagging behind in many others. The good news is that the slow years of Covid-19 have enabled deep introspection, and many intelligent brains in the country have a clear view of what could and should be done to redress the internal and external imbalances, and set the country on a path to significant growth and unprecedented success.

As philosopher Joel Barker has said, 'Vision without action is merely a dream. Action without vision just passes the time. Vision with action can change the world.' As we complete the third year of a decade, we are committed to the road ahead. It needs a collective resolve to step forward with steadfastness and vigour on a path of success. We believe that this can be done, and an entire nation of over a billion people deserves no less—we must act and succeed!

NOTES

INTRODUCTION

1 Maddison, Angus, *Development Centre Studies The World Economy: Historical statistics*, OECD Publishing, 2003, p. 261.

2 Nagaraj, R., 'Growth Rate of India's GDP, 1950-51 to 1987-88: Examination of Alternative Hypotheses', *Economic & Political Weekly*, Vol. 25, No. 26, June 1990, pp. 1396–1403, https://bit.ly/3oT8URP. Accessed on 4 August 2022; Jones, Geoffrey, 'Restoring a Global Economy, 1950–1980', Harvard Business School, Working Knowledge, 22 August 2005, https://bit.ly/3OZMPvE. Accessed on 5 August 2022.

3 'Roti, Kapda, Makan and Bandwidth', *The Telegraph Online*, 26 September 2000, https://bit.ly/3OZv4ws. Accessed on 5 August 2022.

4 'India: Distribution of gross domestic product (GDP) across economic sectors from 2011 to 2021', Statista, https://bit.ly/3Rk7wmU. Accessed on 28 September 2022. This resource also gives the values for 2021.

5 Lal, Neeta, 'India's Population Surge: Dividend or Disaster?', Centre for Governance Studies, 30 July 2022, https://bit.ly/3JE0kQr. Accessed on 5 August 2022.

6 Chidambaram, P., 'Precious Resource in Peril', *The Indian Express*, 6 December 2021, https://bit.ly/3brMF2t. Accessed on 5 August 2022.

7 Sharma, Samrat, 'Will Budget 2022 Heal India's Sagging Education System?', *India Today*, 30 January 2022, https://bit.ly/3p1DN6s. Accessed on 5 August 2022.

8 'Number of India's Elderly to Triple by 2050', *The Hindu*, 7 January 2021, https://bit.ly/3A14yi4. Accessed on 5 August 2022.

9 Bambawale, Gautam, et al., *Rising to the China Challenge: Winning Through Strategic Patience and Economic Growth,* Rupa Publications, 2021.

10 'Indian Equities: Digital Transformation as Private goes Public', Goldman Sachs Global Strategy Paper, 19 September 2021, https://bit.ly/3zBm0YK. Accessed on 5 August 2022.

11 'Why NUDM?', National Institute of Urban Affairs, https://bit.ly/3LOw32i. Accessed on 28 September 2022.

12 Hamel, Kristofer, 'Look East Instead of West for the Future Global Middle Class', OECD, 7 May 2019, https://bit.ly/2WQmXqY. Accessed on 5 August 2022.

13 Baron, Ethan, 'H-1B: Foreign Citizens Make Up Nearly Three-quarters of Silicon Valley Tech Workforce, Report Says', *The Mercury News*,

8 May 2018, https://bayareane.ws/3vKZlrV. Accessed on 5 August 2022.

14 Kerr, Sari Pekkala et al., 'High-Skilled Migration and Agglomeration,' *Annual Review of Economics*, Vol. 9, 5 May 2017, pp. 201–234, https://bit.ly/3zYSJZD. Accessed on 5 August 2022.

15 'Final Consumption Expenditure (% of GDP) - India,' The World Bank, https://bit.ly/3Ssh3dx. Accessed on 5 August 2022; 'India Investment: % of GDP,' CEIC, https://bit.ly/3BIQue4. Accessed on 5 August 2022.

CHAPTER 1: GROWTH PILLARS OF THE ECONOMY—AGRICULTURE, INDUSTRY AND SERVICES

1 Bambawale, Gautam, et al., *Rising to the China Challenge: Winning Through Strategic Patience and Economic Growth,* Rupa Publications, 2021.

2 Ibid., p. xxxvii, p. 15.

3 Gulati, Ashok, and Sudha Narayanan, *The Subsidy Syndrome in Indian Agriculture,* Oxford University Press, 2003.

4 *Report of Task Force on Agricultural Marketing Reforms,* Ministry of Agriculture and Farmers Welfare, Government of India, https://bit.ly/3zE7SOo. Accessed on 19 October 2022.

5 *Economic Survey, 2021-22,* Ministry of Finance, Government of India, p. 236, https://bit.ly/3pb45nc. Accessed on 10 August 2022.

6 Census report on workers adjusted with data from NSSO rounds.

7 'Critical Evaluation of MGNREGA,' PRS Legislative Research, 2 February 2022, https://bit.ly/3AbFWDa. Accessed on 10 August 2022.

8 Census report on workers adjusted with data from NSSO rounds.

9 'Decrease in Agricultural Holdings,' Ministry of Agriculture & farmers Welfare, Government of India, 3 March 2020, https://bit.ly/3d8t9bt. Accessed on 10 August 2022.

10 Reddy, A. Amarender, 'Here's why 40% of India's Farmers Want to Quit,' *DownToEarth,* 24 July 2018, https://bit.ly/2NJ0zf1. Accessed on 10 August 2022.

11 This is indicated in various studies.

12 Draft of the public report submitted to Supreme Court of India by the committee appointed to repeal the three farm laws.

13 Though the Supreme Court did not publish the document for public discussion, it has surfaced on many platforms.

14 Kumar, Vinod, 'Depleting Water Table in Punjab & Haryana Big Concern,' 25 March 2022, https://bit.ly/3Pfnzlc. Accessed on 11 August 2022.

15 *Report of Task Force on Agricultural Marketing Reforms,* Ministry of Agriculture and Farmers Welfare, Government of India, https://bit.ly/3zE7SOo. Accessed on 19 October 2022

16 See, for example, Kumar, Rajiv, 'Manufacturing in India: Have we Missed

the Bus?', *Indian Journal of Labour Economics*, Vol. 58, No. 2, May 2016, https://bit.ly/3Aoy3dy. Accessed on 16 August 2022; Jagannathan, R., 'No Jobs Nirvana: India May Have Missed the Manufacturing Bus Altogether', *Swarajya*, 28 April 2016, https://bit.ly/3PlxCVK. Accessed on 16 August 2022.

17 *Telecom Global Market Report 2022*, The Business Research Company, https://bit.ly/3Cu6Iq7. Accessed on 12 October 2022.

18 *Telecommunications*, Indian Brand Equity Foundation, https://bit.ly/3CSnNMa. Accessed on 12 October 2022.

19 Tomás, Juan Pedro, 'China's Telecom Sector Revenues Reach Almost $100bn in Jan-May', *RCR Wireless News*, 5 July 2022, https://bit.ly/3yyZqAh. Accessed on 12 October 2022.

20 'China Telecom Operators Country Intelligence Report', GlobalData, https://bit.ly/3g119rS. Accessed on 12 October 2022.

21 'After a $20 Billion Jio Frenzy, India's Richest Man Is Now Seeking Money For Retail', *The Economic Times*, 16 July 2020, https://bit.ly/3QJFySh. Accessed on 23 August 2022.

22 'Jio Investment First, Biggest of India Investment Plans: Google CEO Sundar Pichai', *The Economic Times*, 15 July 2020, https://bit.ly/3wjexwP. Accessed on 23 August 2022.

23 'Total Revenue of the Chemical Industry Worldwide from 2005 to 2021', Statista, https://bit.ly/3dIdjEJ. Accessed on 23 August 2022.

24 'Chemicals Industry India', IBEF, https://bit.ly/3wnLR5M. Accessed on 23 August 2022.

25 'Chemicals', Confederation of Indian Industry, https://bit.ly/3fVhwpP. Accessed on 12 October 2022.

26 Mukherjee, Swarnabha, 'Chemical Sector - Catalytic Substitution in Play', Edelweiss Professional Investor Research, 18 June 2020, https://bit.ly/3T2mC2y. Accessed on 23 August 2022; 'Selected figures About the Economic Impact of the Chemical Industry in China as of 2017', Statista, https://bit.ly/3CnSAjQ. Accessed on 23 August 2022; Ramanujalu, Janardhanan, 'Chemical Industry Poised to Bring Indian Economy Back on Growth Track', *Business World*, 17 October 2020, https://bit.ly/3KhCRoG. Accessed on 23 August 2022.

27 'Health care – India', Statista, https://bit.ly/3Exj2Zp. Accessed on 12 October 2022.

28 'Global Pharmaceutical Industry - Statistics & Facts', Statista, https://bit.ly/3VpjfUO. Accessed on 12 October 2022; 'Indian Pharmaceutical Industry', IBEF, https://bit.ly/3Ct3mUm. Accessed on 12 October 2022.

29 'China's Pharmaceutical Industry Posts Revenue, Profit Growth in 2021', China.org.cn, 11 May 2022, https://on.china.cn/3CSbT4X. Accessed on 12 October 2022.

30 'Global Manufacturing Risk Index: 2021,' Cushman & Wakefield, https://cushwk.co/3Cn1Tkf. Accessed on 23 August 2022.
31 Kalra, Puneet, Shama Gupta and Vijuraj Eranazath, 'Transforming Manufacturing in the Era of Industry 4.0: A Perspective from India,' Russell Reynolds Associates, https://bit.ly/3S9AzKE. Accessed on 14 October 2022.
32 'Press Release: World Bank Approves $500 Million Program to Strengthen Performance of Micro, Small, and Medium Enterprises in India,' The World Bank, 4 June 2021, https://bit.ly/3dJ6h2B. Accessed on 23 August 2022.
33 'PLI Schemes Worth US$ 26 Billion Covering 13 Sectors Will be Operationalized in the Next 5 Years: Mr. Piyush Goyal,' IBEF, 27 July 2021, https://bit.ly/3pBtne7. Accessed on 23 August 2022.
34 Kharas, Homi, Ejaz Ghani, and Arti Grover, 'Can the Service Industry Be the Next Growth Escalator?,' Brookings, 12 December 2011, https://brook.gs/3MovlsS. Accessed on 12 October 2022.
35 Enache, Maria, Ejaz Ghani, and Stephen O'Connell, 'Structural Transformation in Africa: A Historical View,' Policy Research Working Paper Series 7743, The World Bank, 2016, https://bit.ly/3R7OyjK. Accessed on 24 August 2022.
36 'Services Contributed Over 50% To GDP,' Ministry of Finance, Government of India, 31 January 2022, https://bit.ly/3TayWOl. Accessed on 24 August 2022; 'Sector-wise GDP of India,' Ministry of Statistics and Implementation, https://bit.ly/3wt3H7n. Accessed on 24 August 2022.
37 Mitra, Arup, 'Productivity Growth in India: Determinants and Policy Initiatives Based on the Existing Literature,' Working Paper Series, Economic and Social Commission for Asia and the Pacific, June 2016.
38 Ibid.
39 G., Sangeetha, 'Jobs Grew by Average 4 per cent in Last 7 Years: Labour Ministry Survey,' *Deccan Chronicle*, 28 September 2021, https://bit.ly/3R5ziE1. Accessed on 24 August 2022; Desmet, Klaus, Ejaz Ghani, and Esteban Hansberg, 'India's Spatial Disparities: Have Big Cities Become Too Congested?,' Ideas for India, 17 January 2014, https://bit.ly/3TCKl9e. Accessed on 20 October 2022.
40 Ghani, Ejaz, and Homi Kharas, 'The Service Revolution,' Poverty Management and Economic Management Network, The World Bank, May 2010, https://bit.ly/3Fd9Aen. Accessed on 20 October 2022.
41 Ibid.
42 Ghani, Ejaz, 'Opinion | India's Spatial Development Challenge Needs Attention,' *mint*, https://bit.ly/3eq8516. Accessed on 12 October 2022.
43 Misra, Neeta, 'Is India's Spatial Development lopsided?,' *Business World*, 22 August 2022, https://bit.ly/3CQ72AY. Accessed on 12 October 2022.

CHAPTER 2: THE TRILLION-DOLLAR DIGITAL ECONOMY

1 'Programme Pillars,' Digital India, Government of India, https://bit.ly/3AqIn3w. Accessed on 26 August 2022.
2 NASSCOM, *The Technology Sector in India: Strategic Review*, 2022, https://bit.ly/3fHcb5p. Accessed on 4 October 2022.
3 Dossani, Rafiq, 'Remembering Y2K: The Impact Today,' Walter H. Shorenstein Asia-Pacific Research Center, Stanford, 3 March 2005, https://stanford.io/3ALzXVZ. Accessed on 26 August 2022.
4 Majumdar, Romita, and Sai Ishwarbharath, 'TCS Beats Street Estimates With 8.4% Growth in Profit,' *The Economic Times*, 11 October 2022, https://bit.ly/3g2hwEo. Accessed on 12 October 2022.
5 McKinsey Global Institute, *Digital India: Technology to Transform a Connected Nation*, 27 March 2019, https://mck.co/3Kp67K1. Accessed on 26 August 2022. The figures in the following sections are drawn from this report.
6 'NASSCOM Launched FutureSkills PRIME Beta Platform to Make India a Digital Talent Nation,' NASSCOM, https://bit.ly/3e50cya. Accessed on 4 October 2022.
7 Paneerselvan, A.S., 'Is Artificial Intelligence Fuelling Natural Stupidity?,' *The Hindu*, 10 July 2017, https://bit.ly/3yce1Bu. Accessed on 4 October 2022.
8 Patel, Neel V., 'A.I. Poised to Add Almost $16 Trillion to World Economy by 2030,' Inverse, 30 June 2017, https://bit.ly/3pRpx0F. Accessed on 29 August 2022.
9 'Amazon Wants to Join Cyber Valley,' Max-Planck-Gesellschaft, 23 October 2017, https://bit.ly/3dXyx1z. Accessed on 29 August 2022.
10 'India Outlines $10-Billion Plan To Woo Global Chip Makers,' *Business World*, 17 December 2021, https://bit.ly/3Q1XNB8. Accessed on 29 August 2022.
11 'Digital Infra Calls for $23bn Investment by 2025: Report,' *The Economic Times*, 24 January 2022, https://bit.ly/3V1xPBC. Accessed on 4 October 2022.
12 *Readying India for a USD 1 Trillion Opportunity Through Digital, Newsline*, NASSCOM, Vol. 8, No. 9, December 2017, https://bit.ly/3V2RtNF. Accessed on 4 October 2022.
13 Poojary, Thimmaya, 'Indian SaaS Industry Can Create $1T in Value and 5 Lakh Jobs by 2030, Says Report,' YourStory, 7 July 2021, https://bit.ly/3ToLwtp. Accessed on 29 August 2022.
14 Gupta, Sanjay, 'India's Quest to Take the Lead in Semiconductor Manufacturing,' *The Times of India*, 26 February 2022, https://bit.ly/3cnunjn. Accessed on 29 August 2022.
15 Prof. A. Paulraj lecture at IESA Vision Summit 2020.

16 Ahaskar, Abhijit, and Prasid Banerjee, 'India, US Semiconductor Industry Bodies Sign MoUs to Bring Chip Firms into Country,' *mint*, 12 April 2022, https://bit.ly/3Tp8n8o. Accessed on 29 August 2022.

17 'Cabinet Clears Rs 76,000-cr Incentive Scheme for Semiconductors,' *The Economic Times*, 16 December 2021, https://bit.ly/3Tpcgu0. Accessed on 29 August 2022.

18 '3 of World's Largest Public Digital Platforms Are From India,' Asianet Newsable, 24 August 2021, https://bit.ly/3e8WBik. Accessed on 29 August 2022.

CHAPTER 3: NEW MODEL FOR URBAN DEVELOPMENT IN INDIA

1 Ghani, Ejaz, 'India's Urban Awakening,' Project Syndicate, 19 January 2018, https://bit.ly/3fHgvBF. Accessed on 4 October 2022.

2 Ibid.; Ghani, Ejaz, 'The Smart Cities Project Must Promote Diversity,' *mint*, 21 May 2018, https://bit.ly/3cx3BoG. Accessed on 30 August 2022.

3 See Ghani, Ejaz, Arti Grover Goswami, and William R. Kerr, 'Is India's Manufacturing Sector Moving Away From Cities ?,' Policy Research Working Paper Series 6271, The World Bank, https://bit.ly/3TmlreJ. Accessed on 30 August 2022.

4 Ghani, Ejaz, William R. Kerr, and Stephen O'Connell, 'Promoting Entrepreneurship, Growth, and Job Creation,' *Reshaping Tomorrow: Is South Asia Ready for the Big Leap?* Ejaz Ghani (ed.), pp. 168–201, Oxford University Press, 2011.

5 Ghani, Ejaz, William R. Kerr, and Stephen O'Connell, 'Spatial Determinants of Entrepreneurship in India,' *Regional Studies*, Vol. 48, No. 6, 2014, pp. 1071–89, https://bit.ly/3CvPMAY. Accessed on 4 October 2022.

6 Ghani, Ejaz, 'The Smart Cities Project Must Promote Diversity,' *mint*, 21 May 2018, https://bit.ly/3RVb6nR. Accessed on 12 October 2022.

7 Desmet, Klaus, et al., 'The Spatial Development of India,' *Journal of Regional Science*, Vol. 55, No. 1, 2015, pp. 10–30, https://bit.ly/3rLL6AK. Accessed on 12 October 2022.

8 Kahn, Matthew E, 'The Silver Lining of Rust Belt Manufacturing Decline,' *Journal of Urban Economics*, Vol. 46, No. 3, 1999, pp. 360–76; Kahn, Matthew E, 'New Evidence on Eastern Europe's Pollution Progress,' *Topics in Economic Analysis & Policy*, Vol. 3, No. 1, 2003.

9 Greenstone, M., and R. Hanna, 'Environmental Regulations, Air and Water Pollution, and Infant Mortality in India,' *American Economic Review*, Vol. 104, No. 10, 2014, pp. 3038–72.

10 Kahn, Matthew E., 'The silver lining of rust belt manufacturing decline,' *Journal of Urban Economics*, Vol. 46, No. 3, 1999, 360–76.

11 'About NAMP', Central Pollution Control Board, https://bit.ly/3pTaMub. Accessed on 30 August 2022.

12 'Census Tables', Office of the Registrar General and Census Commissioner, Government of India, https://bit.ly/3Upl5nD. Accessed on 10 November 2022.

13 Chay, Kenneth Y., and Michael Greenstone, 'The Impact of Air Pollution on Infant Mortality', Working Paper 7442, National Bureau of Economic Research, December 1999; Greenstone, M., and R. Hanna, 'Environmental Regulations, Air and Water Pollution, and Infant Mortality in India', *American Economic Review*, Vol. 104, No. 10, 2014, pp. 3038–72.

14 Costa, D.L., and M.E. Kahn, 'Changes in the Value of Life, 1940–1980', *Journal of Risk and Uncertainty*, Vol. 29, pp. 159–80, 2004.

15 Zhang, Yan, et al., "Foreign direct investment and cleaner production choice: Evidence from Chinese coal-fired power generating enterprises." *Journal of Cleaner Production*, Vol. 212, 2019, 766–78.

16 Ghani, Ejaz, and Arti Grover Goswami, and William R. Kerr, 'Spatial Dynamics of Electricity Usage in India', World Bank Policy Research Working Paper No. 7055, https://ssrn.com/abstract=2506962. Accessed on 4 October 2022.

17 Glaeser, Edward L., and Matthew E. Kahn, 'The Greenness of Cities: Carbon Dioxide Emissions and Urban Devlopment', *Journal of Urban Economics*, Vol. 67, No. 3, 2010, pp. 404–18.

18 Duggan, Wayne, 'Millennials Have $68 Trillion Coming Their Way From "Greatest Wealth Transfer In History"', Yahoo! Finance, 5 October 2020, https://yhoo.it/3EAnir7. Accessed on 12 October 2022.

19 Sridhar, Kala Seetharam, 'Impact of Land Use Regulations: Evidence from India's Cities', *Urban Studies*, Vol. 47, No. 7, 2010, pp. 1541–69.

20 Ejaz Ghani, 'Opinion | Turbocharge India's Youth for a Sustainable Economic Comeback', *mint*, 27 July 2020, https://bit.ly/3M3wdmB. Accessed on 4 October 2022.

CHAPTER 4: THE FUTURE OF MOBILITY AND SUSTAINABILITY

1 'Vehicular Emissions in India', Centre for Energy Finance, 8 December 2021, https://bit.ly/3KxfKq2. Accessed on 31 August 2022.

2 Banerjee, Prasid, 'Microsoft's Enterprise Metaverse Plans Include Avatars on Teams, Connected Factory Floors', TechCircle, 3 November 2021, https://bit.ly/3A3hByY. Accessed on 10 November 2022.

3 'Localization –A Solution-Multiplier', Local Futures, https://bit.ly/3CqiiD1. Accessed on 4 October 2022.

4 'Top 3 Indian Companies in the Space Race', *mint*, 8 September 2021, https://bit.ly/3RySJoG. Accessed on 4 October 2022.

5 'About 60 Startups Registered with ISRO since Unlocking of Indian Space Sector, Says Jitendra Singh', *mint*, 12 July 2022, https://bit.ly/3rvAc26. Accessed on 4 October 2022.

6 'Air Taxi Market Size Expected to Be 1,700 Trillion Won in 2040', *ET Auto*, 7 January 2022, https://bit.ly/3C6ccax. Accessed on 4 October 2022.

7 'In 2021, Delhi Most Polluted Capital in World, No Indian City Met WHO Air Quality Standard: Report', *The Economic Times*, 22 March 2022, https://bit.ly/3yfy2qS. Accessed on 4 October 2022.

8 'India's Oil Import Bill Falls 10 Per Cent to USD 101 Billion in Fiscal Year 2020', *The New Indian Express*, 29 May 2020, https://bit.ly/3e59Oce. Accessed on 4 October 2022.

9 '70% of Diesel, 99.6 % of Petrol Consumed by Transport Sector', Ministry of Petroleum and Natural Gas, Government of India, 28 January 2014, https://bit.ly/3TboGEX. Accessed on 4 October 2022.

10 S., Vasudevan, 'Space Tourism, Flying Taxis and Drones - The Future of Aerial Mobility?', LinkedIn, 29 October 2021, https://bit.ly/3y9IVuf. Accessed on 4 October 2022.

11 Sen, Somit, '30 Per Cent Vehicles in India Will Be Electric By 2030: Study', *The Economic Times*, 17 June 2022, https://bit.ly/3EfhAeg. Accessed on 4 October 2022.

12 'As Work From Home Ends, 73% Indian Firms Plan Hybrid Working Model For Employees: Report', India.com, 6 July 2022, https://bit.ly/3Sy4m0w. Accessed on 4 October 2022.

13 Peek, Sean, 'Communication Technology and Inclusion Will Shape the Future of Remote Work', *Business News Daily*, 13 August 2022, https://bit.ly/2qdhzj9. Accessed on 4 October 2022.

14 Mashelkar, R.A., and Ravi Pandit, *Leap Frogging to Pole-Vaulting: Creating the Magic of Radical yet Sustainable Transformation*, Penguin Viking, 2018.

15 'Status Quo Analysis of Various Segments of Electric Mobility and Low Carbon Passenger Road Transport in India', GIZ in association with NITI Aayog, https://bit.ly/3e81JDp. Accessed on 4 October 2022.

16 'India Lithium-Ion Battery Market - Growth, Trends, COVID-19 Impact, and Forecasts (2021 - 2026)', *GlobalNewsWire*, 22 March 2021, https://bit.ly/3yhR2VN. Accessed on 4 October 2022.

17 'Germany Leads Pack of Countries Pouring Finance into Hydrogen', Decarbonisation Technology, 26 March 2022, https://bit.ly/3EoW7xU. Accessed on 21 November 2022.

18 'About', Hydrogen Mobility Europe, https://h2me.eu/about/. Accessed on 31 August 2022.

19 'FCEV Sales, FCEB, & Hydrogen Station Data', Hydrogen Fuel Cell Partnership, https://bit.ly/3SAMguM. Accessed on 4 October 2022.

20 Calculated based on fuel cost (₹32/liter w/o taxes) and the fuel consumption by long-distance transportation (~40 metric tonne).

21 Calculated based on development of hydrogen infrastructure, FCEV sales and hydrogen consumption.

CHAPTER 5: THE SEAMLESS INTERCONNECT OF SCIENCE, TECHNOLOGY AND INNOVATION

1 Narlikar, Jayant, *The Scientific Edge: The Indian Scientist from Vedic to Modern Times*, Penguin India, 2003.

2 Pulakkat, Hari, *Space. Life. Matter.: The Coming of Age of Indian Science*, Hachette, 2021.

3 'India Tops China, Publishes 135,000 Scientific Articles in 2018: Report', *Business Standard*, 18 December 2019, https://bit.ly/3RtqMz8. Accessed on 1 September 2022.

4 'RT-PCR Test Rate Reduced To ₹350', *The Hindu*, 20 January 2022, https://bit.ly/3UYYWx2. Accessed on 4 October 2022.

5 Mashelkar, R.A., 'Technonationalism to Technoglobalism', R.A. Mashlelkar, https://bit.ly/3CqI8Xs. Accessed on 12 October 2022.

6 Jayakumar, P.B., 'Only 26 Indian Companies in Top 2500 Global R&D Spenders', *Business Today*, 2 November 2020, https://bit.ly/3RpkRe7. Accessed on 1 September 2022.

7 'GDP Per Capita (Current US$)', The World Bank, https://bit.ly/3C3FWVr. Accessed on 4 October 2022; 'Research and Development Expenditure (% of GDP)', The World Bank, https://bit.ly/2HqM9OL. Accessed on 4 October 2022; 'Scientific and Technical Journal Articles', The World Bank, https://bit.ly/3EahynU. Accessed on 4 October 2022.

8 Taylor, Andrea, Erin Escobar, and Krishna Udayakumar, 'Expanding Access to Low-Cost, High-Quality Tertiary Care: Spreading the Narayana Health Model Beyond India', The Commonwealth Fund, 9 November 2017, https://bit.ly/3EfoXlL. Accessed on 4 October 2022.

9 Mashelkar, Raghunath, 'Reinventing Healthcare', Civil Society, 29 July 2022, https://bit.ly/3M5zWAe. Accessed on 4 October 2022.

10 Gupta, Anil K., *Grassroots Innovation: Minds on the Margin Are Not Marginal Minds*, Random House, 2016.

11 Bora, Garima, '1% Inspiration, 99% Perspiration: Budget Should Incentivise Turning Jugaad into Innovation', *The Economic Times*, 20 January 2022, https://bit.ly/3AYbYBZ. Accessed on 1 September 2022.

12 Mehta, Udai S., and Jaideep Mehta, 'How Chinese Brands Left Indian Mobile Brands Gasping', CUTS International, 10 June 2020, https://bit.ly/3fuJCYI. Accessed on 4 October 2022.

13 'Keeping Traditional Knowledge Free', CodeBlue, 20 July 2022, https://bit.ly/3CvIs8r. Accessed on 4 October 2022.

14 Mashelkar, R.A., 'Economics of Knowledge', *Current Science*, Vol. 77, No.

2, 25 July 1999.

15 Mashelkar, R.A., 'What Will It Take For Indian Science and Technology To Be Globally Competitive?,' *Current Science*, Vol. 109, No. 6, 25 September 2015.

16 'Intellectual Property Rights Strongly Benefit The European Economy, EPO-EUIPO Study Finds,' European Patent Office, 25 September 2019, https://bit.ly/3fI3nfp. Accessed on 4 October 2022.

17 Radjou, Navi, 'One Man's Crusade to Overhaul India's Insular R&D Culture,' *Harvard Business Review*, 15 July 2008, https://bit.ly/3fAhZO1. Accessed on 4 October 2022.

18 Aristodemou, Leonidas, and Frank Tietze, 'The State-Of-The-Art on Intellectual Property Analytics (IPA): A Literature Review on Artificial Intelligence, Machine Learning And Deep Learning Methods For Analysing Intellectual Property (IP) Data,' *World Patent Information*, Vol. 55, December 2018, pp. 37–51.

19 Aggarwal, B.S., 'Indian Science Congress 2000 - A Report,' https://bit.ly/3CR60oR. Accessed on 27 October 2022; 'PM's Address at the 98th Indian Science Congress,' PMO, Government of India, 3 January 2011, https://bit.ly/3q2TFGu. Accessed on 27 October 2022; 'PM's Remarks at the 102nd Indian Science Congress,' Narendra Modi, 3 January 2015, https://bit.ly/3ejXvIQ. Accessed on 2 September 2022.

20 Mashelkar, R.A., 'On Realising CSIR's Amazing Potential,' *Science Reporter*, Vol. 59, No. 9, September 2022.

21 Vijay, Nandita, 'Govt Needs to Widen Weighted Tax Rate From 200 to 250% To Drive Innovation: Ajay Shah,' PharmaBiz, 24 January 2018, https://bit.ly/3ydpTU1. Accessed on 4 October 2022.

22 Koshy, Jacob, 'Scientists Criticise GST Hike On Scientific Equipment,' *The Hindu*, 23 July 2022, https://bit.ly/3y9kttd. Accessed on 4 October 2022.

23 'About', SBIR STTR, https://www.sbir.gov/about. Accessed on 4 October 2022.

24 'An Assessment of the SBIR Program,' National Library of Medicine, https://bit.ly/3rtOCzv. Accessed on 4 October 2022.

25 Krishnan, Aarati, 'All You Wanted to Know About...Swiss Challenge,' *BusinessLine*, 7 December 2021, https://bit.ly/3fHXJdv. Accessed on 4 October 2022.

26 '20 Startups Enter the Indian Unicorn Club in 2022: Here's Everything You Need to Know,' *Business Insider*, 27 August 2022, https://bit.ly/3SASlr6. Accessed on 4 October 2022.

27 Chen, James, 'Unicorn: What It Means in Investing, With Examples,' Investopedia, 31 May 2022, https://bit.ly/2NpFj0P. Accessed on 4 October 2022.

28 Mashelkar, R.A., 'Science Led Innovation,' RA Mashelkar, https://bit.ly/3e1Ue11. Accessed on 4 October 2022.

29 Kant, Amitabh, (ed.), *The Path Ahead: Transformative Ideas of India*, Rupa Publications, 2018.

30 'Scientific Social Responsibility (SSR) Policy', Ministry of Science and Technology, Government of India, https://bit.ly/3Rkcn8v. Accessed on 5 September 2022.

CHAPTER 6: INTERNATIONAL TRADE POLICY

1 'Our Endeavour is to Create Demand for High Value-Added Products of India Across the World: PM', Narendra Modi, 6 August 2021, https://bit.ly/3D0Mias. Accessed on 5 September 2022.

2 Ratios calculated based on World Trade Organization and World Bank data.

3 See, for example, UNCTAD, 'Global Value Chains: Investment and Trade for Development', World Investment Report, 2013.

4 See the speeches on the Indian PM in 2013 (https://bit.ly/3UM6hiL) in comparison to the next Indian PM on 6th August 2021 mentioned in footnote 1.

5 For importance of stable policies, see, for instance, Table 2 of Export-Import Bank of India, *Domestic Policy Constraints for Exports in Select Sectors – Report on Export Hubs*, March 2020, https://bit.ly/3RGfqs3. Accessed on 14 September 2022.

6 The erstwhile FTAs have evolved into wider agreements such as Comprehensive Economic Partnership Agreement (CEPA).

7 Data sourced form WTO Stats.

8 Data sourced form WTO Stats.

9 In 2020, the Asian economies with higher merchandise exports than Vietnam and India were China, Japan, Hong Kong (China), South Korea, Singapore and Taiwan.

10 The annual growth rates ranged between 13.6 per cent (2002) to 30 per cent (2004 and 2005). During 2004 to 2008, the annual growth rates were above 20 per cent each year.

11 For comparison, its ranks were 30, 15 and 7, respectively, in 1980, 1990 and 2000.

12 This is now a norm in FTAs, e.g., the African Continental Free Trade Area aims to reduce tariffs to zero on 90 per cent of the tariff lines.

13 An important policy instrument that is often not a primary focus of trade policy discussions is the exchange rate. The exchange rate addresses multiple objectives and there is an independent regulator, the Reserve Bank of India, to assess the appropriate level of the exchange rate taking these various issues into account. However, the relevance of this policy instrument for trade policy should be kept in mind by the appropriate institutions that

manage this policy. For discussion on exchange rate and trade, see pp. xxi, 7, 10, 13, 14 and 120 of *Report of the High-Level Advisory Group*, https://bit.ly/3QDLT0B. Accessed on 14 September 2022. The exchange rate policy was an important part of the efforts to manage the economic impact of trade policy changes introduced in 1991 (see, for example, pp. 9, 23 to 25, 42, 44 and 52 of Singh, Harsha Vardhana, 'Trade Policy Reform in India since 1991', Brookings India Working Paper, March 2017, https://brook.gs/3qAdmFN. Accessed on 14 September 2022.)

14 See, for example, 'Joint Statement from the United States - India Trade Policy Forum', Office of the United States Trade Representative, 23 November 2021, https://bit.ly/3Bh9yhR. Accessed on 14 September 2022.

15 An example of such a list of obstacles is contained in Export-Import Bank of India, *Domestic Policy Constraints for Exports in Select Sectors - Report on Export Hubs*, March 2020, https://bit.ly/3RGfqs3. Accessed on 14 September 2022.

16 For a summary of their practices, see pp. 10-11 of Export-Import Bank of India, *Domestic Policy Constraints for Exports in Select Sectors - Report on Export Hubs*, March 2020, https://bit.ly/3RGfqs3. Accessed on 14 September 2022.

17 See Export-Import Bank of India, *Domestic Policy Constraints for Exports in Select Sectors - Report on Export Hubs*, March 2020, https://bit.ly/3RGfqs3. Accessed on 14 September 2022; and Chapter 2 of ICEA, Increasing India's Electronic Exports and Share in GVCS, https://bit.ly/3C0UdSS. Accessed on 10 November 2022.

18 See pp. 18 to 21 and Table 6 of Export-Import Bank of India, *Domestic Policy Constraints for Exports in Select Sectors - Report on Export Hubs*, March 2020, https://bit.ly/3RGfqs3. Accessed on 14 September 2022.

19 *Report of the High-Level Advisory Group*, https://bit.ly/3QDLT0B. Accessed on 14 September 2022.

20 See pp. 27, 69, 115, 135-136, and page 146 to 151 of Export-Import Bank of India, *Domestic Policy Constraints for Exports in Select Sectors - Report on Export Hubs*, March 2020, https://bit.ly/3RGfqs3. Accessed on 14 September 2022.

21 Salazar-Xirinachs, J.H., I. Nübler and R. Kozul-Wright, 'Industrial Policy, Productive Transformation and Jobs: Theory, History and Practice', *Transforming Economies: Making Industrial Policy Work For Growth, Jobs And Development*, J.H. Salazar-Xirinachs, I. Nübler and R. Kozul-Wright (eds), ILO, 2014.

CHAPTER 7: WOMEN'S PARTICIPATION IN FUTURE GROWTH

1 'Facts and Figures: Economic Empowerment', UN Women, https://bit.ly/2Mae7U8. Accessed on 4 October 2022.

2 Chatterjee, C., and T. Nag, 'Do Women on Boards Enhance Firm Performance? Evidence From Top Indian Companies', *International Journal of Disclosure and Governance,* 2022.

3 Dabla-Norris, Era, and Kalpana Kochhar, 'The Economic Benefits of Bringing More Women Into the Labor Force Are Greater Than Previously Thought', International Monetary Fund, March 2019, https://bit.ly/3BgypDB. Accessed on 6 September 2022.

4 The World Bank, *Global Economic Prospects,* June 2022, https://bit.ly/3zItxWG. Accessed on 28 October 2022.

5 Woetzel, Jonathan, et al., *The Power of Parity: Advancing Women's Equality in India, 2018,* McKinsey & Company, 1 May 2018, https://mck.co/2tyGX4R. Accessed on 6 September 2022.

6 'AISHE Reports', All India Survey on Higher Education, Government of India, https://bit.ly/3SNaiSq. Accessed on 28 October 2022.

7 Roy Chowdhury, Sunandan, *Politics, Policy and Higher Education in India,* Palgrave Macmillan, 2017.

8 '75 Years, 75% Literacy: India's Long Fight Against Illiteracy', The *Times of India,* 14 August 2022, https://bit.ly/3U3rOUb. Accessed on 4 October 2022.

9 Union Budget 2022–23.

10 'Literacy', Know India, https://bit.ly/3qaqRfr. Accessed on 6 September 2022.

11 *Economic Survey, 2019–2020,* Ministry of Finance, Government of India, https://bit.ly/3NbHeTC. Accessed on 28 October 2022.

12 'No Economy Can Reach Its Full Potential Where Women Do Not Have Equal Opportunities', The World Bank, 8 March 2022, https://bit.ly/3V3c18L. Accessed on 4 October 2022.

13 *Economic Survey 20221–22,* https://bit.ly/3U4F8qN. Accessed on 28 October 2022.

14 *National Sample Survey 2011-2012 (68th round) – Schedule 1.0 (Type 1) – Consumer Expenditure,* International Household Survey Network, https://bit.ly/3QkGzPN. Accessed on 6 September 2022.

15 Dhawan, Himanshi, 'Women Put in 3.26 Billion Hours of Unpaid Care Work Globally: Report', *The Times of India,* 20 January 2020, https://bit.ly/3TG5kIu. Accessed on 28 October 2022.

16 Oxfam India, *Time To Care: Wealth Inequality and Unpaid Care Work for Women in India,* 2020, https://bit.ly/3fg4iUG, Accessed on 28 October 2022.

17 World Economic Forum, *Global Gender Gap Report 2020,* https://bit.

ly/3fg4pQ6. Accessed on 28 October 2022.

18 17 per cent, Labour Force Survey, 2020.

19 Female Work and Labour Force Participation in India: meta-analysis of 13 national-level databases, 58 research papers, and 53 national-level policies in order to map the policy and data landscape, and derive policy implications.

20 'Having Kids Sets Back Women's Labour Force Participation More So Than Getting Married,' ILOSTAT, https://bit.ly/3DgC8kl. Accessed on 28 October 2022.

21 World Economic Forum, *Global Gender Gap Report 2020*, https://bit.ly/3fg4pQ6. Accessed on 28 October 2022.

22 Chaudhary, Ruchika, and Sher Verick, 'Female Labour Force Participation in India and Beyond,' ILO Working Papers, ILO, 2014, https://bit.ly/3f8TBTX. Accessed on 28 October 2022; Kapsos, Steven, Evangelia Bourmpoula, and Andrea Silberman, 'Why Is Female Labour Force Participation Declining So Sharply in India?' ILO Research Paper No. 10, ILO, August 2014, https://bit.ly/3DEuYaY. Accessed on 28 October 2022; Mazumdar, Indrani, and Neetha N., 'Gender Dimensions: Employment Trends in India, 1993-94 to 2009-10,' Working Papers id:4502, eSocialSciences, 2011, https://bit.ly/3sIf0WU. Accessed on 28 October 2022.

23 ILO data; in 2011–12, 35.3 per cent of all rural females and 46.1 per cent of all urban females in India were attending to domestic duties, whereas these rates were 29 per cent and 42 per cent, respectively, in 1993–94.

24 *Oxfam Inequality Report: Public Good or Private Wealth: The India Story*, Oxfam India, 21 January 2019, https://bit.ly/3Qp35H7. Accessed on 7 September 2022.

25 UNICEF, *India Case Study, Situation Analysis on the Effects of and Responses to COVID-19 on the Education Sector in Asia*, 2021.

26 *Annual State of Education (ASER) Report*, November 2021.

27 International Graduate Centre, *Cycling to Shool: Increasing High School Enrollment for Girls in Bihar*, 2013.

28 McKinsey Global Institute, *The Future of Women at Work: Transitions in the Age of Automation*, June 2019.

29 'Collaboration between MoRD and Amazon for Online Marketing of SHG Products through MOU Signing and Exchange,' Ministry of Rural Development, 12 May 2022, https://bit.ly/3NcElC3. Accessed on 28 October 2022.

30 'Global Commission on the Future of Work,' ILO, https://bit.ly/2PaQ9Wk, Accessed on 10 November 2022; 'Explainer: How gender inequality and climate change are interconnected,' UN Women, 28 February 2022, https://bit.ly/3Aw573g. Accessed on 21 November 2022.

31 Ductor, Lorenzo, Sanjeev Goyal, and Anja Prummer, 'Gender and Collaboration,' *Review of Economics and Statistics*, 2021.

32 'In India, Women's Self-Help Groups Combat the COVID-19 (Coronavirus) Pandemic', The World Bank, April 2020.
33 Power of Parity Report, 2015 onwards.
34 Sen, Amartya, 'More Than 100 Million Women Are Missing', *The New York Review*, 20 December 1990, https://bit.ly/2KMaBeU. Accessed on 28 October 2022.
35 Sharma, Manish, and Hima Bindu Kota, The Role of Working Women in Investment Decision Making in the Family in India, *Australian Accounting and Business Journal*, Vol. 13, 2019, https://bit.ly/3SEbYxC. Accessed on 28 October 2022.
36 UN Women, *From Insights to Action: Gender Equality in the Wake of COVID-19*, 2020.
37 'The Disproportionate Impact Of Covid-19 On Women In India — And New Hope For Recovery Efforts', Dalberg, August 2021, https://bit.ly/3Wnv91Z. Accessed on 28 October 2022.
38 South Asia Regional Gender Action Plan (RGAP), 2016–2021.
39 'Access to Credit and Female Labour Supply in India', International Growth Centre, https://bit.ly/3DdBkgd. Accessed on 28 October 2022.
40 Ranz, David J., 'Empowering Half of the Workforce', *The Economic Times*, 14 February 2021, https://bit.ly/3znMPAv. Accessed on 28 October 2022.

CHAPTER 8: SUSTAINABLE LIVELIHOODS AND SOCIAL COMMITMENT

1 'Narendra Modi's "Sabka Saath Sabka Vikas" is Visionary: John Kerry', *Financial Express*, 29 July 2014, https://bit.ly/3qqPCnE. Accessed on 9 September 2022.
2 Mehta, Pratap Bhanu, 'The 1947 We Choose', *The Indian Express*, 14 August 2021, https://bit.ly/3U3IGtj. Accessed on 28 October 2022.
3 Rajgopal, Krishnadas, 'CJI Flags Communal Content in Media', *The Hindu*, 2 September 2021, https://bit.ly/3RD1S0s. Accessed on 9 September 2022.
4 Chadha Borwankar, Meeran, 'Creating Citizen-Centric Police', *The Indian Express*, 23 September 2021, https://bit.ly/3qqvORu. Accessed on 9 September 2022.
5 Varma, Pavan K., *The Great Hindu Civilisation: Achievement, Neglect, Bias and the Way Forward*, Westland, 2021, pp. 350–51.
6 Ibid.
7 Varma, Pavan K., 'Pavan Varma | Abbajaan! The Basest Lingo Taints Our Faith', *Asian Age*, 19 September 2021, https://bit.ly/3ROn96L. Accessed on 9 September 2022.
8 'Swami Vivekananda Advocated Secularism, Religion for Common Good, Says CJI Ramana', *The Indian Express*, 13 September 2021, https://bit.

ly/3BtCCUL. Accessed on 9 September 2022.

9 Ranade, Ajit, 'What Haridwar Can Learn from Vivekananda's Chicago Speech', *The Times of India*, 31 December 2021. https://bit.ly/3L0HuDK. Accessed on 9 September 2022.

10 Ibid.

11 'Watch: IFS Officer Sneha Dubey's Befitting Reply to Pakistan's Imran Khan at UN', *mint*, 25 September 2021, https://bit.ly/3Bp64uW. Accessed on 9 September 2022.

12 Mehta, Vijraj, 'India Can Bring Prosperity and Social Justice to a Fifth of the World', World Economic Forum, 4 October 2017, https://bit.ly/3RuLbUQ. Accessed on 9 September 2022.

13 'India GDP 1960–2022', Macrotrends, https://bit.ly/3qmvFym. Accessed on 9 September 2022.

14 Ghani, Ejaz, and Lakshmi Iyer, 'Conflict and Development—Lessons from South Asia', The World Bank, September 2010, https://bit.ly/3QweoNF. Accessed on 9 September 2022.

CHAPTER 9: STRENGTHENING SOCIAL CAPITAL TO LAY THE FOUNDATIONS FOR GROWTH

1 Acemoglu, D., and J. Robinson, *Why Nations Fail: The Origins of Power, Prosperity and Poverty*, Crown, New York, 2012.

2 Kelkar, V., and A. Shah, *In Service of the Republic: The Art and Science of Economic Policy*, Penguin Allen Lane, New Delhi, 2019; Shourie, A., 'Controls and the Current Situation: Why Not Let The Hounds Run', *Economic & Political Weekly*, Vol. 8, No. 31, 1973, pp. 32–33.

3 'WVS Wave 6 (2010-2014)', World Values Survey, https://bit.ly/2ATDfq8. Accessed on 12 September 2022.

4 Acemoglu, Daron, and James A Robinson., *Why Nations Fail: The Origins of Power, Prosperity and Poverty*, New York: Crown, 2012.

5 Srinivas, M.N., 'An Obituary on Caste as a System', *Economic & Political Weekly*, Vol. 38, No. 5, 2003.

6 Kelkar, V., 'Towards India's New Fiscal Federalism', National Institute of Public Finance and Policy, 2019. https://bit.ly/2IRU3nE. Accessed on 10 November 2022.

ABOUT THE CONTRIBUTORS

Pradeep Apte is a PhD in economics and contributes as visiting faculty at various reputed educational institutions. He has authored five books and more than 25 research papers. He is a senior fellow at Pune International Centre.

Aravind Chinchure is a PhD in Physics, and has an experience spanning 25 years in R&D, innovation, intellectual property, start-up venture investment, policy, social development and teaching. He is a Senior Fellow at the Pune International Centre.

Uma Ganesh is executive chairperson and co-Founder of GTT Foundation, pioneers in skills and women's entrepreneurship in Asia. Uma was CEO of Zee Education and the chief corporate development officer in HSBC Global Resourcing before she founded GTT in 2008. She has co-authored a book titled *Unleashing the Knowledge Force* and is a regular speaker and columnist on technology-enabled skills and entrepreneurship.

Ejaz Ghani is currently senior fellow at the Pune International Centre. He was previously lead economist at the World Bank and has worked on Africa, East Asia, South Asia, corporate strategy and independent evaluation unit. He contributes economic

opinion columns to a number of prominent publications and has edited several books, including *Reshaping Tomorrow: Is South Asia Ready for the Big Leap?* (2011); *The Poor Half Billion in South Asia* (2010); *The Service Revolution in South Asia* (2010). Prior to joining the World Bank, he taught economics at St. Anne's College (Oxford University) and Shri Ram College of Commerce (Delhi University). He is an Inlaks scholar.

Vijay Kelkar is vice president, Pune International Centre. He served as chairman of the Thirteenth Finance Commission and was executive director at the International Monetary Fund, overseeing its operations in South Asia during 2000–02. He has served as petroleum secretary and finance secretary, among other high positions in the Government of India. He was chairman of the Forum of Federations, Ottawa, Canada (2010–13). Dr Kelkar has a PhD from the University of California at Berkeley. He is a recipient of the Padma Vibhushan.

Raghunath Mashelkar is a fellow of the Royal Society, president at Pune International Centre and a former national research professor. He was the former director general of Council of Scientific and Industrial Research (CSIR), New Delhi; president of Indian National Science Academy, New Delhi; chairman of National Innovation Foundation, Gandhinagar; and president of Global Research Alliance, New Delhi. He has more than 60 honours to his name, including the prestigious Lenovo Science Prize of the World

Academy of Science, JRD Tata Corporate Leadership Award and Star of Asia Award. He was a member of the Prime Minister's

Science, Technology and Innovation Advisory Council for almost 30 years. He is a recipient of Padma Shri, Padma Bhushan and Padma Vibhushan.

Ganesh Natarajan is a trustee and founding member of Pune International Centre. He is also the executive chairman and founder of 5F World, a platform for skills, start- ups and social ventures. He is also the board chair of Honeywell Automation India Ltd and Lighthouse Communities Foundation, and board member of Global Talent Track (a pioneer in employability skills training in Asia), State Bank of India, Hinduja Global Solutions, Educate Girls, Asian Venture Philanthropy Network and Kalzoom Advisors. He led APTECH, a global training major, for 10 years and Zensar Technologies as vice chairman and CEO till early 2016. He is a former chairman of NASSCOM and SVP India, and was president of the HBS Club of India. He has authored and co-authored eleven books on business, technology and inspired leadership.

Ravi Pandit is a founder trustee of Pune International Centre. He is the co-founder and chairman of KPIT Technologies Ltd. He also serves on the board of Finolex Cables Ltd. Pandit was a member of the Government of India's Core-Group on Automotive Research Program Committee (CAR) and was on the Department of Technology's Technology Development Board.

Kaustubh Pathak works in the field of clean and sustainable mobility. Currently, he is working on development of technologies for generation of Hydrogen from biomass. Kaustubh also has expertise in technology assessment. He has worked on evaluation of technologies from diverse fields to assess their commercial viability.

Shilpa Phadke is a development sector and public policy professional. She has extensive experience working with international organizations, including the United Nations and the World Bank on assignments based in Eastern Europe, Latin America, South and East Asia, Africa and the Middle East. She began her career as a market research analyst at the International Trade Centre in Geneva, a specialized agency of WTO/UNCTAD, and was staff of the World Bank group at its headquarters in Washington, DC in the Office of the Chief Economist and later in New Delhi as part of the Agriculture and Rural Development team.

Ajay Shah has a BTech in aeronautical engineering from Indian Institute of Technology, Bombay, and earned his PhD in economics from the University of Southern California, Los Angeles. He has held positions at the Centre for Monitoring Indian Economy (CMIE), Indira Gandhi Institute for Development Research (IGIDR), Department of Economic Affairs at the Ministry of Finance and National Institute for Public Finance and Policy (NIPFP). Prof. Shah has co-authored *In Service of the Republic: The Art and Science of Economic Policy* (2019) with Dr Vijay Kelkar.

Harsha Vardhana Singh is a senior fellow at Pune International Centre. He is also a senior fellow of the Council on Emerging Market Enterprises (Fletcher School). Singh was deputy director-general at World Trade

Organization for eight years till 30

September 2013.In India, Singh was economic advisor and then secretary of the

Telecom Regulatory Authority of India.

Manoj Soman is an analog, RF, mixed-signal VLSI and DSP architect and designer and has led numerous full-chip IC design projects. He has worked with both multinational chip design companies as well as high-tech start-upsCurrently, he serves as technology advisor with Aaroh Labs Pvt. Ltd and also a member on the research council of Council of Scientific and Industrial Research (CSIR)-Central Electronics Engineering Research Institute (CEERI).

Abhay Vaidya is director, Pune International Centre. He was previously resident editor at *The Hindustan Times* and *DNA* newspapers, and Washington correspondent for *The Times of India*. He is a fellow of the international network Leadership for Environment and Development (LEAD) and has undertaken field studies in Nagaland, Thailand, Mexico and the United Kingdom to study sustainable development under this fellowship.

INDEX